The Sartre Dictionary

Also available from Continuum

Sartre: A Guide for the Perplexed, Gary Cox
The New Sartre, Nik Farrell Fox
Sartre's Ethics of Engagement, T. Storm Heter
Sartre's Phenomenology, David Reisman

The Sartre Dictionary

Gary Cox

continuum

Continuum International Publishing Group
The Tower Building, 11 York Road, London SE1 7NX
80 Maiden Lane, Suite 704, New York NY 10038

www.continuumbooks.com

© Gary Cox 2008

First published 2008

British Library Cataloguing-in-Publication Data
A catalogue record for this book is available from the British Library.

ISBN: HB: 0-8264-9891-4
        978-0-8264-9891-5
        PB: 0-8264-9892-2
        978-0-8264-9892-2

Library of Congress Cataloging-in-Publication Data
Cox, Gary, 1964-
    The Sartre dictionary / Gary Cox.
        p. cm.
    ISBN-13: 978-0-8264-9891-5 (hb)
    ISBN-10: 0-8264-9891-4 (hb)
    ISBN-13: 978-0-8264-9892-2 (pbk.)
    ISBN-10: 0-8264-9892-2 (pbk.)
    1. Sartre, Jean-Paul, 1905-1980--Dictionaries. I. Title.

    B2430.S33Z84 2007
    194--dc22

Typeset by Kenneth Burnley, Wirral, Cheshire
Printed and bound in Great Britain by Athenaeum Press Ltd, Gateshead,
Tyne and Wear

Contents

For my father, Thomas

Acknowledgements

I am indebted to the many Sartre scholars mentioned in the Bibliography whose knowledge of various regions of the Sartre galaxy made this project possible. Many thanks to philosophers I have known personally at the universities of Southampton, Birmingham and Bristol. Thanks also to friends and family, particularly Sharon, for their encouragement and support.

Introduction

Do you want to know what Sartre means by 'being-for-itself', 'transcendence', 'facticity', 'bad faith', 'useless passion' or 'existence precedes essence'? What his novels and plays are all about, or why *Being and Nothingness* is his most important work? If so then this is the book for you. *The Sartre Dictionary* is the only comprehensive round-up of Sartre's terms, titles, influences and intimates currently available in English. It has hundreds of extensively cross-referenced entries providing clear definitions and explanations of all things Sartrean. It defines and evaluates key terms used by Sartre, terms often used by Sartre scholars when writing about Sartre and terms used by philosophers that relate closely to Sartre's own ideas or shed light on Sartre's own ideas. It also includes a wealth of information about Sartre's major philosophical works, biographies, novels, short stories and plays, as well as information on his major influences and intellectual contemporaries.

As a small, precocious and very serious child, Jean-Paul Sartre started writing furiously. He never stopped and as an old man his pen still moved briskly over reams of paper. He wrote almost every day of his life, for at least six hours a day if he could. 'If I go a day without writing, the scar burns me' (*Words*). During one eight-month period 1939–40 he is reputed to have written a million words: his *War Diaries*, notes for what became *Being and Nothingness*, a draft of his novel *The Age of Reason* and a myriad letters to his mother and his lovers. Sartre wrote to make something of himself, not simply his great fame, but his very identity. The child saw himself travelling on life's train without a ticket, a superfluous creature without meaning or purpose. According to his own philosophy, every person must attempt to justify their superfluous existence by giving it a purpose, so he chose writing as his ticket to life and his reason to be. Confronted by a choice between philosophy and literature, this man of letters *par excellence* could not bring himself to abandon either, so he decided to excel at both and to amalgamate them whenever possible. He wrote philosophical works rich in descriptions of real life that read like literature. He wrote novels, plays and biographies that are truly philosophical. A vast outpouring of both completed and uncompleted texts, ideas branching in all directions but always carrying the same philosophical vision, the same comprehensive, compelling, uncompromising existentialist theory of the human condition.

It is all too easy for the newcomer to Sartre to become entangled and disorientated in the vast and intricate web of his thought, or to fail even to penetrate its mysteries in the first place for lack of time and opportunity; all too easy for a wealth of inspiring profundity and insight to be missed then dismissed as so much verbose nonsense. Perhaps, at times, Sartre is verbose. Most often, he is brilliantly concise. Undoubtedly, there is great value in his philosophy and almost all of it is far from nonsense, a quality this dictionary endeavours to reveal in an undiluted yet easily digestible manner.

This dictionary, with its extensive cross references, allows easy movement around the wide Sartre territory in whatever direction the reader chooses or needs to go. The major features of Sartre's world – consciousness, transcendence, temporality, freedom, responsibility, bad faith, authenticity and being-for-others – are all detailed and the all-important relations between them indicated. A host of allied ideas are also pinpointed and explored – absurdity, mortality, nihilism, love, hate, sexual desire and so on – as are the many published works of philosophy, literature, drama and biography in which Sartre evolves his various concepts and technical terms. Sartre did not think and write in a vacuum and can only be properly understood in context. To that end this dictionary explores Sartre's major philosophical influences and contemporaries and the main aspects of his intellectual relationship with each of them.

What this dictionary is depends to some extent on how the reader wants or needs to use it. On one level, it is a handy ready-reference tool that explains and contextualizes the key technical terms of Sartre's existentialism as well as offering summaries and evaluations of all his major works. Hence, it is the ideal companion to any of the many books by or about Sartre available today. Simultaneously, on another level, it is a comprehensive guide to Sartre that will reveal a host of interesting and often surprising connections, not only between areas within his philosophy, but also between his philosophy and that of many associated philosophers from Camus, Kant and Kierkegaard to Hegel, Husserl and Heidegger. If a broad general knowledge of Sartre's philosophy is what is needed – and surely every thinking person wants to know something about Sartre – then this book may be all that is required.

Chronology: Sartre's Life and Works

1905 Born in Paris on June 21, the only child of Jean-Baptiste Sartre and Anne-Marie Schweitzer.

1906 Death of father, Jean-Baptiste.

1915 Attends the Lycée Henri IV in Paris.

1917 Mother, Anne-Marie, marries Joseph Mancy, much to the distaste of her doting son.

1922 Attends the Lycée Louis-le-Grand in Paris and studies philosophy under Colonna d'Istria who introduces him to the ideas of Bergson. Progresses to the prestigious École Normale Supérieure to study philosophy.

1929 Starts lifelong friendship with Simone de Beauvoir who is in the year below him at the École Normale. Graduates from the École Normale at his second attempt, first among 76 finalists.

1931 Begins teaching in the Lycée François Ier in Le Havre, a post he will hold for five years. Continues drafting what will eventually become his first novel, *Nausea*.

1933 Introduced to the phenomenology of Husserl by Raymond Aron at a now legendary meeting in a Parisian café. Begins studying Husserl and Heidegger during a nine month sabbatical at the French Institute in Berlin after exchanging places with Aron.

1935 Experiments with the psychoactive drug mescaline under experimental conditions in order to research the phenomenon of hallucinations and has a bad trip.

1936 First published work, *Imagination: A Psychological Critique*.

1937 *The Transcendence of the Ego*, a critique of Husserl's philosophy of mind. Drafting of *The Imaginary*.

1938 *Nausea*, a philosophical novel exploring the themes of contingency, absurdity and nihilism. A seminal work of existentialism, *Nausea* establishes his reputation and celebrity.

1939 *Sketch for a Theory of the Emotions* and *The Wall*, an acclaimed collection of short stories. Conscripted into the meteorological section of the French military he begins his extensive *War Diaries* (published posthumously, 1983).

1940 Captured by the Germans and detained in various prison camps. Spends his time in captivity writing plays and teaching the philosophy of Heidegger. *The Imaginary*, a phenomenological investigation of the imagination.

1941 Released by the Germans with the aid of a fake medical certificate declaring him unfit for military service, he returns to German occupied Paris and founds the resistance group, Socialism and Freedom.

1943 *Being and Nothingness*, a detailed exposition of his existential phenomenology and his major philosophical work. *The Flies*, his play based on the Greek legend of Orestes and an implicit commentary on the political situation, is performed in occupied Paris. Start of friendship with Albert Camus.

1944 *In Camera*, a play exploring the idea that 'hell is other people'.

1945 Founds the literary and political review, *Les Temps modernes*, with de Beauvoir and Merleau-Ponty. *The Age of Reason* and *The Reprieve*, the first two volumes of a trilogy of novels, *Roads to Freedom*, set before and during World War II.

1946 *Existentialism and Humanism*, a book originally delivered as a popular and controversial lecture the previous year; *Men Without Shadows,* a play about a group of resistance fighters facing torture; *The Respectable Prostitute*, a play about racism in the USA; the essay *Anti-Semite and Jew* and a psychoanalytical biography of the poet Baudelaire.

1948 His atheism and anti-authoritarianism leads the Catholic Church to place his entire works on the Vatican index of prohibited books. *What is Literature?*, a work of literary theory with political overtones, and *Dirty Hands*, a play about an assassin and his questionable motives.

1949 *Iron in the Soul*, the third volume of a trilogy of novels, *Roads to Freedom*, set before and during World War II.

1951 *Lucifer and the Lord,* a play set in Medieval Germany considering various philosophical, theological and political issues.

1952 End of his friendship with Camus following a very public row on the pages of *Les Temps modernes*. *Saint Genet*, an extensive psychoanalytical biography of his friend and contemporary, the writer Jean Genet.

1954 First of many trips to the Soviet Union. Publication of *Kean*, a play about the actor Edmund Kean that explores questions of personal identity.

1956 *Nekrassov*, a darkly comical play satirising the French right-wing press.

1959 *The Condemned of Altona*, a play about Nazi collaborators and German post-war collective guilt.

1960 Signs the treasonable 'Manifesto of the 121' calling for insubordination by French troops in Algeria. Visits Castro in Cuba with de Beauvoir. *Critique of Dialectical Reason, Volume One* (*Volume Two* published posthumously, 1985), an ambitious attempt to amalgamate existentialism and Marxism and the most important philosophical work of his later years.

1961 Paris apartment bombed by the O.A.S., a terrorist organization opposed to Algerian independence (bombed again the following year).

1964 *Words*, the acclaimed autobiography of his childhood. Declines the Nobel Prize for Literature on the grounds that writers must refuse to be transformed by institutions.

1965 Adopts Arlette Elkaïm, his close female friend of several years. *The Trojan Women*, a play commenting on the Algerian War and imperialism generally, adapted from the tragedy by Euripides.

1967 Heads a tribunal set up by Bertrand Russell to investigate US war crimes in Indochina.

1968 Lends support to the student riots and French General Strike whilst continuing to work on *The Family Idiot*, a vast, psychoanalytical and sociological biography of the writer Flaubert.

1971 The first and second volumes of *The Family Idiot*.

1972 The third volume of *The Family Idiot*.

1973 The health of his long abused body deteriorates rapidly. Hypertension causes his eyesight to fail, destroying his ability to write.

1974 Visits the terrorist Andreas Baader in Stammheim Prison, Germany.

1977 Claims he is no longer a Marxist but continues to support left-wing political causes actively.

1980 Dies in Paris on April 15 of oedema of the lungs. Buried in Montparnasse Cemetery. Over fifty thousand people line the streets at his funeral.

abandonment Following **Heidegger**, **Sartre** argues that humankind is abandoned in the world. This is not to say humankind has been abandoned in the sense of 'left behind' or 'neglected' by something or someone – for Sartre, there is nothing 'out there' that could have abandoned us in this way. Rather, for Sartre, humankind is abandoned because there is no **God** to give human life purpose or moral direction. Humankind has always been and will always be alone in an ultimately meaningless universe. Sartre does not go into the question of intelligent life on other planets, but if there is intelligent life elsewhere in the universe it is equally abandoned and alone in Sartre's sense of inhabiting a Godless, meaningless universe. Sartre's adoption of the notion of abandonment is the clearest possible expression of his profound **atheism**, his view that humankind is a cosmic accident and not the product of some higher design on the part of God or gods. As humankind is uncreated (the process of reproduction that works through parents is not *creation* on their part) the idea or essence of each person does not precede his existence. This is what Sartre means when he says, **'existence precedes essence'**. People exist first – accidentally, unnecessarily, superfluously – and must invent their meaning and purpose thereafter. For this reason, Sartre argues that each person's life has only the meaning they choose to give it. Ultimately, like **Nietzsche**, Sartre does not see humankind's abandonment as grounds for pessimism. In their abandonment people are free to create themselves and to become masters of their own destiny. To be free of the will and design of a creator, as one of the inescapable **existential truths** of human existence, is or should be a source of inspiration rather than **despair**. See also **absurdity, authenticity, contingency, existential freedom,** *Existentialism and Humanism* and **nihilism**.

aboutness **Consciousness** exists only in so far as it *intends* something or is *about* something. The **intentionality** of consciousness is sometimes referred to as the aboutness of consciousness. 'Aboutness' is a modern, post-Sartrean term having the same meaning as 'intentionality'. See also **'consciousness is consciousness of __'.**

absence   See **existential absence, formal absence** and **lack**.

abstract absence   A less common term for **formal absence**.

absurdity   For **Sartre**, life is absurd in that it has no meaning or purpose in itself. Human existence has no meaning or purpose other than the meaning and purpose each person chooses to give his own existence. Sartre's philosophy, particularly his novel **Nausea** (1938), explores **contingency**, absurdity and meaninglessness and the **despair** that may result from dwelling upon them, but his interest in absurdity and his opinion that viewed in the widest context human existence is absurd, does not make him a nihilist. See **nihilism**.

action   The state or process of doing or not doing something intentionally. For **Sartre**, intention is the defining characteristic of action. He distinguishes an action from a mere accidental act in that the latter does not involve intention. Action often involves purposeful bodily actions such as words, gestures or the manipulation of tools. These bodily actions aim at rearranging the world in such a way that a perceived **lack** is overcome, but doing nothing is also action if doing nothing is the result of a **choice**. Sartre's **existentialism** is a philosophy in which choice and action are more or less inseparable. Choice gives meaning to action and action gives reality to choice. An intention, a chosen end to be realized in the **future**, gives meaning to the actions that aim at it and are a means to it. When intentions are realized and ends achieved, however, they themselves immediately become means to further ends, with no achieved end ever able to fully and finally satisfy, define and determine the **for-itself**. The for-itself, as a being that must perpetually choose its future and act to achieve it, must always surpass whatever chosen ends its actions achieve towards further chosen ends to be achieved by further action. In his **Critique of Dialectical Reason** (1960) Sartre uses the term *praxis* (Greek for 'action') to refer to any purposeful human activity. See also **existential freedom**.

affirmation of freedom   See **freedom, affirmation of**.

affirmation of mortality   See **mortality, affirmation of**.

The Age of Reason (1945)   The first volume of Sartre's trilogy of novels,
Roads to Freedom. As **Sartre** notes in his **War Diaries**, *The Age of Reason*
was first drafted during the 'phoney war' of 1939–40. Set in Paris in the
summer of 1938, it tells the story of two days in the life of Mathieu Delarue,
an unmarried philosophy professor in his mid-thirties. With few demands
placed on him by his teaching job, Mathieu pursues a life free from serious
commitment or **responsibility**, frequenting bars and cafés with his friends
and students. Politics and the gathering clouds of war are peripheral concerns.
Mathieu and his friends are primarily interested in each other and their
personal anxieties. Mathieu's profligate lifestyle, free from bourgeois expectations and constraints, is threatened when his long-time mistress, Marcelle,
becomes pregnant. Mathieu will no longer be able to maintain his liberty
through a project of non-commitment and avoidance of serious choices. If he
does not act decisively to preserve his independence, his avoidance of serious
choices will see him conform to bourgeois norms as he drifts into parenthood
and marriage with Marcelle. He sets about raising 4,000 francs for a safe
abortion. His wealthy elder brother, Jacques, tells him that now he is in his
mid-thirties he has reached the age of reason, the age when it is morally right
to conform, marry, settle down, sell out. Mathieu is literally invited to sell out
by Jacques who refuses him 4,000 francs for an abortion but offers him
10,000 francs to marry Marcelle and keep the baby. Mathieu intends to define
the age of reason differently, as the age when he asserts his **freedom** and
refuses to conform. He rejects Jacques' offer. Mathieu is also refused the
money by Daniel, a homosexual friend of Marcelle's who dislikes Mathieu for
his smug selfishness and wants to end Mathieu's relationship with Marcelle.
Repeatedly frustrated by his efforts to borrow the money Mathieu eventually
steals it from Lola, a club singer and the mistress of Boris, one of his students.
Lola is relatively wealthy and careless with her cash and Mathieu knows she
will not notice the loss of a few bank notes. He gives the money to Marcelle to
pay for the abortion he has arranged, an act that spells the end of their relationship. Marcelle flings the money in his face and at her insistence he leaves
her for the last time. The novel concludes with Daniel informing Mathieu that
despite being homosexual he plans to marry Marcelle. His reasons are
complex: He cares for Marcelle and wants to help her fulfil her wish of
keeping her baby, he wants to emphasize Mathieu's disgraceful behaviour
towards Marcelle and he wants to conceal his homosexuality, which he is
ashamed of, behind the respectable façade of marriage.

Though Mathieu questions Daniel's motives for marrying Marcelle he nonetheless admires his ability to act decisively, to do something irrevocable. Mathieu realizes that he has always acted on the false understanding that the consequences of his actions are revocable. In coming to realize that they are not always revocable and in no longer wanting them to be so, Mathieu finishes with his youth and obtains his own personal age of reason. He has irrevocably lost Marcelle and Boris' sister Ivich, a petulant and self-obsessed female student he loved and pursued without success. He is alone with nothing but his freedom. Though he has achieved his goal of maintaining his independence and escaping bourgeois conformity he recognizes that he is no freer without Marcelle than he was with her. He has, however, come to view freedom differently. Freedom, he has learnt, is not about avoiding responsibility but about choosing to commit oneself to a course of **action**, to a cause, without **regret**.

Altona   See *The Condemned of Altona*.

ambiguity   A term favoured by Simone **de Beauvoir**, particularly in her book, *The Ethics of Ambiguity* (1947), referring to the ambiguity of **being-for-itself** as an indeterminate being lacking in and unable to achieve coincidence with itself. See also **indeterminacy**.

anguish   See **anxiety**.

annihilation   The utter destruction of **being-for-itself** in the event of it ceasing to be the **negation** of **being-in-itself**. Annihilation would immediately result if being-for-itself coincided with itself as a **being-for-itself-in-itself**. Being-for-itself can never coincide with itself, it can never be what it is by being its own foundation, as it must always be founded upon what it is not.

anti-determinism   A term sometimes used by **Sartre** scholars referring to the position of arguing against **determinism** without offering any explanation of free will. The traditional debate has been between determinists and anti-determinists. Anti-determinism offers various refutations of determinism thereby seeking to make room for free will but it does not say how free will is possible or what it really involves. Sartre goes beyond anti-determinism in offering a positive account of free will. See **existential freedom**.

Anti-Semite and Jew (1946)   A work of social philosophy by **Sartre** that was excerpted in an early issue of *Les Temps modernes* and first published as *Reflections on the Jewish Question*. The work was partly inspired by Sartre's desire to address the taboo subject of French complicity in the Nazi project at the time of the widely unwelcome return to France of French Jews deported by the Nazis. *Anti-Semite and Jew*, like Sartre's play of the same year, **The Respectable Prostitute**, confronts the issue that the defeat of German Nazism was not the defeat of prejudice and hatred in those Western democracies that defeated Nazism.

Sartre explores the nature and causes of the deep-rooted anti-Semitism in his own country, but in his description of the French anti-Semite we are meant to see the essential traits of anti-Semites, racists, nationalist and all other kinds of intolerant bigot everywhere. He identifies the typical French anti-Semite as a nostalgic, lower-middle-class provincial afraid and resentful of social change. The anti-Semite defines himself as a true Frenchman in contrast to the Jewish outsider he hates, believing that birth, language and history give *him* the right to belong. He has nothing to prove, least of all his worth. His worth is intrinsic, assured by the accident of birth that allows him to claim as his own the real and imagined achievements of his nation. In contrast, he views Jews as aliens who lack value because they lack his pedigree. He feels threatened by anyone different from him, but by Jews more so because Jewish intellectuals, lawyers, politicians, financiers and so on, as organizers of society at a level beyond his comprehension, are identified by him as agents of the social change he fears. As communists, capitalists, intellectuals or atheists, Jews, he believes, are scheming against his property, his traditions and his nation and must, therefore, be destroyed.

People, Sartre argues, exist in relation to others (see **being-for-others**). The anti-Semite exists in relation to the Jew he hates and the Jew exists in relation to the anti-Semite who hates him. Anti-Semitism is an undeniable feature of the Jew's situation and requires a response from him. According to Sartre, the Jew's response to anti-Semitism can be either authentic or inauthentic (see **authenticity** and **inauthenticity**). The inauthentic Jew seeks to escape anti-Semitism by escaping his own Jewishness. He assimi- lates himself into the culture around him through religious conversion, intermarriage and so on. He often adopts, like the assimilated Jews Sartre knew personally, a rationalist, cosmopolitan stance. Sartre has been criticized for failing to recognise that for some Jews the project of assimilation may not be so much driven by a desire to hide from anti-Semitism as a desire to escape the traditions, duties and expectations of Jewish culture and religion.

The authentic Jew, on the other hand, is committed to affirming his Jewish identity in defiance of anti-Semitism. He may well be an active defender of Jewish causes such as Zionism. Sartre compares the authentic Jew to the authentic worker who defends the interests of the working class. The authentic worker accepts that social conflict is inevitable until social revolution creates a classless, harmonious society. Until there is a social revolution Jews must assert their *difference*. During the revolution, however, Jews will give up their difference, their Jewishness, in order to enter a classless society free of the pluralism that is the root of all social conflict and oppression.

Sartre has been criticized for implying that Jewishness is nothing more than a reaction to anti-Semitism. Jewish intellectuals in particular argue that this negative definition of Jewishness is symptomatic of the lack of real understanding of Jewish history and culture that is manifest in *Anti-Semite and Jew*. Many Jews who are not Marxist revolutionaries or in pursuit of complete assimilation object to Sartre's claim that Jewish culture, history and religion will end when social revolution makes being Jewish irrelevant.

anxiety   According to **Sartre**, a person's awareness of his **unlimited freedom** and his **responsibility** for it is a source of anxiety or anguish. A person is made anxious by the thought that he could choose to perform a dangerous or embarrassing act at any moment and that there is nothing to stop him from doing so other than his free **choice** not to do so. A man walking along a precipice will fear falling, but he will also be anxious that he can choose to jump. His anxiety expresses itself as a feeling of vertigo. Sartre calls the anxiety that people experience whenever they consider a dangerous experiment in **freedom** 'the vertigo of possibility'. **Bad faith**, as an attempt to deny freedom and responsibility, offers a means of avoiding this anxiety, this vertigo of possibility. Acting in bad faith, a person will fool himself that jumping off the precipice is not a possibility that is open to him. In supposing in bad faith that he cannot choose to jump he will avoid the anxiety involved in the contemplation of this possibility. In this sense, bad faith can be seen as a coping strategy that reduces anxiety and preserves a person's well-being in various ways. See also **Kierkegaard**.

appearances   Those aspects of an object that appear at any one time from a particular perspective. For **phenomenology** there is nothing beyond appearances. Those appearances that appear at any one time do not indicate an object in itself underlying the appearances, but rather the infinite series of **transphenomenal** appearances that could appear or have appeared but which are not currently appearing. See also **horizons, Husserl, intentional object** and **phenomena**.

ascetic ideal   For **Nietzsche**, a person who has adopted the ascetic ideal values self-repression and self-denial above all else and for their own sake. **Freedom** is exercised negatively in order to deny and check itself. To adopt the ascetic ideal is to exercise a **negative will to power** that is opposed to the positive **affirmation of freedom**. To adopt the ascetic ideal is to act in what **Sartre** calls **bad faith**. The ascetic ideal is opposed to Nietzsche's notion of the **noble ideal**. See also **negative choice, negative freedom** and **slave ethic.**

atheism   The doctrine or belief that there is no **God**. A view held by many **existentialist** philosophers including **Sartre**. See also **abandonment, existentialism, Nietzsche** and **nihilism.**

authentic action   **Action** in any situation undertaken in full recognition of the demands of the situation. Action that a person takes full **responsibility** for without **regret** or complaint. See also **affirmation of freedom, authenticity, being-in-situation, positive choice, positive freedom, positive will to power, noble ideal** and *Saint Genet*.

authenticity   The antithesis of **bad faith**. The overcoming of bad faith. A deliberate and sustained project in which a person affirms his **freedom** and takes full **responsibility** without **regret** for his **past**, for his **present** situation and for his actions within that situation. That is, he assumes full responsibility for his **being-in-situation**. Authenticity involves a person recognizing and valuing the fact that he must continually choose what he is without ever being able to become what he is once and for all. An authentic person accepts freedom, responsibility, **indeterminacy** and **mortality** as the inescapable **existential truths** of the **human condition**. He strives to live his life affirming these truths rather than denying them through various projects of bad faith.

In so far as the freedom of other people is one of the existential truths of the human condition, it is authentic to affirm the freedom of other people. This view is at least suggested in Sartre's **Notebooks for an Ethics** (1947–48, published posthumously 1983). In that work, **Sartre** indicates a possible link between authenticity and ethics, implying that ethics is other-related authenticity.

Authenticity is a central notion for **Sartre**, **Heidegger** and **Nietzsche**. Each philosopher emphasizes a different feature of the phenomenon but their views on authenticity are nonetheless remarkably similar. See also **affirmation of freedom, affirmation of mortality, authentic action, being-towards-death, noble ideal, positive choice, positive freedom, positive will to power, radical conversion, Saint Genet** and **sustained authenticity**.

authenticity, sustained   The indeterminacy of **being-for-itself** means that it is impossible for a person simply to *be* such and such. A person, therefore, cannot simply achieve **authenticity** and *be* authentic once and for all. A person who believes he has become authentic once and for all is actually in **bad faith** for believing that there is something that he is in the mode of being it. Authentic existence is a project that has to be continually reassumed with each **choice**. Each choice must be a **positive choice**, an affirmation of **positive freedom** made without **regret**. A person is only as authentic as his present **action**. Even if he has been consistently authentic for a week, if he is not authentic right now then he is not authentic. Given the endless temptations to bad faith that surround a person, the difficulties of always resisting regret and the strong possibility that habit and others' expectations will shape a person's being as much as his capacity to choose, it is unrealistic to suppose that anyone can sustain authenticity for a significant period of time. At best, it appears a person can be authentic occasionally, which does not amount to achieving authentic existence as a sustained project. Sustained authenticity appears to be an unobtainable **existentialist ideal**, though, arguably, an ideal worth aiming at. In *Saint Genet* (1952) Sartre portrays the writer Jean Genet as a hero who manages through sustained effort to come very close to achieving this existentialist ideal.

— B —

bad faith   A central concept of Sartre's **existentialism**. The antithesis of **authenticity**. Inauthenticity. The **choice** not to choose misrepresented as an inability to choose. A project in which a person refuses to take **responsibility** for his actions and the situation in which he finds himself – his **being-in-situation**. Bad faith can manifest itself in many different ways but at heart all projects of bad faith involve a person attempting to invert or separate his **facticity** and his **transcendence**. Transcendence is always transcendence of facticity but bad faith seeks to evade this fact in various ways. For example, a person is in bad faith if he denies that he is the free transcendence of his facticity and instead treats himself as a pure facticity lacking transcendence; as a mere object. Similarly, a person is in bad faith if he seeks to relinquish responsibility for the facticity of his **past** by denying that he is the transcendence of his past. In bad faith he asserts that he is a pure transcendence rather than the transcendence of his facticity. In *Being and Nothingness* (1943) **Sartre** explores the various attempts to manipulate facticity and transcendence that comprise bad faith through a series of concrete examples of people in bad faith: **the flirt**, **the waiter**, **the homosexual**, **the champion of sincerity** and so on. An understanding of these concrete examples is essential to an understanding of the several interrelated forms of bad faith as they are played out in everyday human life.

Sartre also explores bad faith extensively in his novels *Nausea* (1938) and *Roads to Freedom* (1945–49), in his short stories, particularly *Childhood of a Leader* (1939) and *Intimacy* (1939), and in his plays, particularly *The Respectable Prostitute* (1946) and *The Condemned of Altona* (1959). Given the difficulty if not impossibility of **sustained authenticity**, it seems everyone is always in bad faith to some extent. Sartre's fictional works, which always have at their heart a detailed and penetrating examination of the complexities of human behaviour, inevitably reflect this.

Bad faith is often wrongly equated with **self-deception** because it appears to involve a person deceiving himself about his past, his present situation, his motives and so on. Sartre argues that self-deception is not possible within the unity of a single consciousness. Therefore, although bad faith appears to be self-deception it must in fact be something else. Bad faith is far better described as a project of evasion. It is **self-distraction** rather than self-deception.

Despite the generally negative way in which Sartre and other **existentialist** philosophers talk about bad faith, it can be argued that it often has positive consequences. For example, in serving to create the illusion that a person is not free, or more specifically that he does not have a choice in a given situation, it helps to stave off the **anxiety**, the vertigo of possibility, that he may feel in face of his **unlimited freedom**. In this respect it serves as a coping strategy that helps to preserve physical and mental well-being. Arguably, bad faith provides the self with a degree of coherence that it would otherwise lack. Arguably, it allows people to make-believe they have a fixed and determined nature and are something in the mode of being it as opposed to recognizing that they are never anything in the mode of being it. Even authenticity, the antithesis of bad faith, appears to require bad faith at the level of what Sartre calls the **faith of bad faith** or the primitive project of bad faith – what some Sartre scholars refer to as 'weak bad faith'. As a primitive attitude whereby a person ignores the fact that all beliefs by their very nature are doubtable, as a failure to disbelieve or doubt belief, the faith of bad faith is vital to a person's capacity for self-belief. Without the faith of bad faith he would be unable to achieve the suspension of disbelief in the performance through which he creates himself. See also **ascetic ideal**, **buffeted consciousness**, **false consciousness**, **negative choice**, **negative freedom**, **slave ethic**, **sincerity** and *Truth and Existence*.

bad faith, faith of   Also called the primitive project of bad faith. The faith of bad faith is primitive because it emerges at any early stage in personal development and involves a basic and naive faith in the nature of belief that influences all subsequent believing. If a person recognized that he was in **bad faith** his particular projects of bad faith would be undermined; his beliefs would be exposed as mere beliefs by his contemplation of them. The faith of bad faith is a **fundamental project** of bad faith that always underpins particular projects of bad faith and prevents a person from recognizing that he is in bad faith. The faith of bad faith is a fundamental belief about the nature of belief. It is the belief that beliefs should not be examined and questioned too closely; it is the belief that beliefs are not by their very nature open to doubt; it is the belief that beliefs are not *mere* beliefs. The belief that beliefs are not mere beliefs is self-serving, applying first and foremost to itself as a belief. A person is able to hold questionable beliefs because he does not question his primitive faith that beliefs are unquestionable. A person does not choose to adopt the faith of bad faith but falls into it, like falling asleep, at an early age when his **self-consciousness** first emerges.

Arguably, the faith of bad faith serves to maintain the coherence of the personality in that it allows a person to believe in himself as a certain kind of person with a given character. That is, it allows him to maintain his belief in his performance of himself, the performance through which he creates himself. As there is nothing that a person is or can be in the mode of being it, he must play at being what he is. Sartre's play **Kean** (1954) explores the character of the Shakespearian actor, Edmund Kean, who suspects that both on and off stage he is nothing more than the parts he plays. Sartre's **waiter** is an example of a character who 'plays with his condition in order to realize it'. The faith of bad faith, as Kean and the waiter illustrate, involves a person suspending his disbelief in his performance of himself.

The faith of bad faith has been described as 'weak bad faith', as opposed to the 'strong bad faith' exhibited in the examples of the **flirt** and the **homosexual**. People in strong bad faith avoid taking **responsibility** for themselves and their **being-in-situation**. Where strong bad faith occurs weak bad faith always underpins it. As noted above, particular projects of bad faith are always underpinned by the primitive project of bad faith. Weak bad faith, however, does not necessarily imply strong bad faith and can, as in the case of Sartre's waiter, enable a person to take responsibility for himself and his being-in-situation and thus achieve a degree of **authenticity**.

Baudelaire (1946)   A book by **Sartre** about the French poet Charles Pierre Baudelaire (1821–67), author of *Flowers of Evil* (1857) and other works. As with Sartre's other books about writers – **Saint Genet** (1952) and **The Family Idiot** (1971–72) – *Baudelaire* is not so much a biography of Baudelaire, detailing the main events of his life in chronological order, as an exhaustive psychological study of a man that at times reads like a character assassination. Sartre is fascinated by Baudelaire and clearly admires his poetry, but as always in his analysis of character he is merciless in his detailing of faults and foibles. This, of course, is no less than an honest and comprehensive character study demands, and Sartre's intention is not to assassinate Baudelaire but to account for his all-too-human peculiarities and frailties. The book is above all an exercise in **existential psychoanalysis** that takes Baudelaire as its subject, one subject among countless human subjects that Sartre might have taken. Through an analysis of Baudelaire's poems and correspondence, Sartre systematically deconstructs Baudelaire's personality to reveal his **fundamental choice**; his childhood choice of himself as 'the sort of person he would be'. Sartre thereby provides the key to an explanation of the motives, attitudes, evasions, reactions, anxieties and neuroses that are or were Charles Baudelaire.

Sartre identifies the critical event that precipitated Baudelaire's fundamental choice of himself, the event that established his fundamental attitude to life, as his mother's second marriage in 1828 to General Aupick. Baudelaire was extremely close to his mother. She represented an absolute reality in which he had lost himself. He did not have to justify his existence because his existence was justified by its total immersion in hers. In later life he wrote to her saying: 'I was always living in you; you belonged to me alone. You were at once an idol and a friend.' When she remarried, Baudelaire felt that he had fallen from grace, that he had been cast out of her all-consuming love. He no longer felt necessary, but vague and superfluous (see **contingency**). Unable to exist through her any longer he was forced to exist for himself, to confront himself and to realize that he was just another person. This realization was a further humiliation. In having to be himself he became just like everyone else, just another **Other**. Though abandoned to himself, he could not discover in himself any 'special virtue which would at once have placed him beyond comparison with other people'. He could seek only to distance himself from others, to become the special being he had been for his mother, through a fundamental choice of himself that was an act of pure self-assertion. He deliberately chose solitude so that others could never again inflict it upon him. Though solitude was an immense burden that terrified him, he nonetheless embraced it and placed great value on it as his chosen means of asserting his uniqueness. Sartre refers to Baudelaire's 'stoic pride'. Before all else, Baudelaire chose to be proud and aloof as a way of being himself, as a way of existing independently from the mother who had rejected him and as a way of being special.

Sartre conducts a case study of Baudelaire not least because he sees Baudelaire as similar to himself, the brother he never had, whereas he sees Flaubert, the subject of his longest case study, *The Family Idiot*, as his opposite. There are certainly comparisons to be drawn between Baudelaire's early years and those of Sartre himself as recounted in his autobiography, **Words** (1964). Sartre's family, and particularly his doting mother, treated him as though his existence were necessary and absolute. Though he was extremely close to his mother he was never quite fooled into thinking he was the little god his adults made of him. For a time, as most children do, he saw the adults around him as necessary and absolute, but until he chose to define himself as a writer he felt himself to be vague and superfluous, lacking any real identity. He projects this feeling onto many of his characters: Antoine Roquentin in **Nausea** (1938), Lucien Fleurier in **Childhood of a Leader** (1939), Hugo Barine in **Dirty Hands** (1948) and Edmund Kean in **Kean** (1954). Like Baudelaire, Sartre was deeply affected by his mother's second marriage (1917), though he did not respond by embracing solitude as Baudelaire did. All his resentment appears to have been directed towards his stepfather, Joseph Mancy, though it was a resentment tempered by his view that Mancy was merely a convenient means for his mother to escape the financial difficulties and oppressions she suffered as a young widow in the house of her father. Sartre's affection for his mother remained untainted and when Mancy died in 1945 mother and son immediately took an apartment together. Certainly, Sartre's affection for his mother was not tainted or complicated by the great fear that Baudelaire had for his. 'I'm very, very frightened of you', he once confessed to her in a letter.

Baudelaire's fundamental choice of himself is unique to Baudelaire in its particulars but is nonetheless a fundamental choice not unlike that made by many people, and every person must make some fundamental choice or other, even if it is a choice not to. This is the universal lesson Sartre wants to draw from his psychoanalysis of Baudelaire. Baudelaire, though he was a unique event at a particular time and place, typifies, as any person typifies, the **human condition** as Sartre sees it. Like all people, Baudelaire was an indeterminate **consciousness** existing only as a relation to the world, a **temporal flight** in search of an ultimately unobtainable self-identity, a **freedom** that resorted to **bad faith** to relieve the **anxiety** and **responsibility** of being free. For Sartre, Baudelaire serves as a vehicle for expounding an **existentialist** theory of personality formation that is superior to the traditional psychoanalysis of **Freud** in that it preserves individual personality intact rather than explaining it away in terms of pseudo-irreducible drives and desires (see **pseudo-irreducibles**). See also **fundamental project** and **Laing**.

becoming   Echoing the pre-Socratic philosopher Heraclitus, **Hegel** argues that there is neither **being** nor **non-being**, but only becoming. For Hegel, being and non-being are mere abstractions of thought, ideas that arise when becoming is analysed. Hegel's **ontology** is fundamentally different from Sartre's. For Hegel there is ultimately becoming. For **Sartre** there is ultimately being, or what Sartre refers to as **being-in-itself**. Sartre argues against Hegel that being is and non-being is not because being is logically prior to non-being and non-being exists only as a **negation** of being, as a **borrowed being**. Sartre refers to the negation of being as **being-for-itself**.

being   By 'being', **Sartre** usually means '**being-in-itself**', that which *is*, that which exists fundamentally. However, he also refers to the being of the **negation** of being, as in the term '**being-for-itself**'. Other philosophers such as **Hegel** and **Heidegger** use the term 'being' in similar ways to Sartre, although it should not necessarily be assumed that when they use 'being', where Sartre would be happy to use 'being-in-itself', they mean what Sartre means by 'being-in-itself'. In Hegel, for example, **becoming** is fundamental, not being. For Hegel, being is an abstraction. To appreciate exactly what a particular philosopher means by 'being' requires an appreciation of the context in which they are using the term and their **ontology** – their particular theory of what *is*. 'Being' can be a slippery term but its use in **ontological** enquiry tends to prove less problematic than the use of more loaded terms such as 'existence', 'reality', 'actuality', 'life' and so on.

Being and Nothingness: An Essay on Phenomenological Ontology (1943)   Sartre's magnum opus, his major philosophical work. Although by no means his longest work, even at a length of over six hundred pages, it is by far his most important and influential. Most of the analysis of Sartre's **existentialism** conducted by philosophers around the world has centred and continues to centre upon this work. No single book, perhaps, can lay claim to being the 'bible' of existentialism, but *Being and Nothingness* is certainly one of the cornerstones of the **existentialist** school of thought. In its grand proportions and ambitions, in its structural and linguistic density and complexity, the work aspires to take its place alongside other epic, challenging, heavyweight texts of Continental philosophy, such as Heidegger's *Being and Time* (1927), Schopenhauer's *World as Will and Representation* (1818) or Hegel's *Phenomenology of Spirit* (1807), works that in their different ways offer a comprehensive, integrated, holistic account of the various essential features of the **human condition**.

Sartre's abiding question or concern in *Being and Nothingness* is more or less the same as that of his three major influences, **Hegel**, **Husserl** and **Heidegger**: What must be the nature of a being that has and is a relationship to the world, that is an awareness of the world and acts upon the world? Employing the dialectical style and method of his philosophical influences as an effective means of revealing the fundamental, **internal relations** existing between apparently distinct **phenomena**, **Sartre** argues that the only kind of being that can exist as a relation to reality or the world is a being that is, in itself, nothing; a being that is a **negation** or a **non-being**. Some Sartre scholars argue that a more accurate English translation of *L'Etre et le Néant*, the French title of the work, would be *Being and Non-Being*, but *Being and Nothingness* is now so well established as the work's enigmatic sounding English title that it is unlikely any publisher would ever dare change it.

It is certainly the complex dynamics of the relationship between **being** and non-being, or more accurately **being-in-itself** and **being-for-itself** as Sartre calls them, that is at the heart of *Being and Nothingness*. The work develops wide-ranging descriptions of both the relationship between being-for-itself and being-in-itself, and the relationship between one being-for-itself and another, descriptions that highlight seemingly endless implications and ramifications that extend to all aspects of a person's being in the world – **consciousness**, **temporality**, **embodiment**, **action**, **desire**, **freedom**, **anxiety**, **responsibility**, **bad faith**, **being-for-others**, **mortality** and so on. It is the sheer saturation of *Being and Nothingness* with examples, illustrations, associations, insights, suggestions and pointers that most strongly reveals Sartre's genius and makes his philosophy so interesting to study, criticize and develop.

Precisely because Sartre strives at every turn to mention the diverse implications of his complex thought, the arguments in *Being and Nothingness* are somewhat convoluted and the progress of the work rather meandering. Sartre intends to leave no stone unturned, and to 'get through' *Being and Nothingness*, or even significant parts of it, the reader must commit time and effort to taking a rambling but fascinating journey with Sartre as he maps out a vast and complex territory. The committed reader will eventually recognize that the book is relentless, even ruthless, in its pursuit of an overall direction and thesis, building up into an exhaustive, unified, brutally honest and largely coherent theory of human reality.

Starting with an exploration of the **ontology** of being and non-being the book moves on to explain that consciousness *is* non-being as it is manifested at the level of phenomena or the **phenomenological level**. Consciousness is variously and painstakingly described as that which exists for itself rather than in itself (hence Sartre's term 'being-for-itself'), as a **lack** of being which strives in vain to achieve identity with itself by overcoming that lack, and as essentially intentional, temporal, embodied and free. Sartre's radical freedom thesis derives directly from his philosophy of mind. Each person is a **temporal flight** from his **present** nothingness towards a **future** coincidence with himself that is never achieved. Each person is a **futurizing intention**, and it is in that open future that defines him and at which he aims that a person is free. As essentially free, people cannot not be free, they have to choose who they are and what they do and every attempt to evade this responsibility by choosing not to choose constitutes bad faith.

A major theme of the book is how the key phenomena of consciousness, freedom and bad faith function in and are conditioned by relations with others. Sartre describes the fundamental **ontological** structures of the phenomenon of being-for-others before placing flesh on ontological bones through his intriguingly penetrating analysis of concrete relations with others. He brilliantly describes **love**, **hate**, **sexual desire**, **masochism**,

sadism and **indifference**, explaining in a manner perfectly consistent with his overall thesis what is essential to them, how they arise out of the very nature of our being in the world and how they are intimately related to one another. Meanwhile, as he proceeds with his main agenda of analysing these concrete relations, he rewards his reader with a wealth of thought-provoking insights into the nature and significance of various other peculiarly Other-related phenomena such as nudity, **obscenity**, **grace** and humiliation.

Though there is a lot in *Being and Nothingness* that demands criticism and clarification, Sartre's piercing insight, his intellectual creativity, the extraordinary ability he demonstrates throughout the work to identify and describe the essential nature and connectedness of all aspects of the human condition, are remarkable and hugely inspiring.

being, borrowed **Being-for-itself** has no **being** of its own. It exists entirely as the **negation** of **being-in-itself**. It's being as a **non-being** is entirely borrowed from being-in-itself and as such **Sartre** described it as a borrowed being or as having a borrowed being.

being, differentiated The world of **phenomena** or **appearances**. The world from the point of view of **consciousness**. Reality as it appears at the **phenomenological level**. Differentiated being contrasts with **undifferentiated being** and is best understood in direct comparison with undifferentiated being.

being, undifferentiated A way of referring to **being-in-itself** that emphasizes its complete lack of determining features. The only characteristic of being-in-itself is that it *is*. Unlike **differentiated being** – the world of **phenomena** or **appearances** – being-in-itself manifests no differences or contrasts – this as distinct from that, this as not that, this as external to that and so on. In Sartre's view, undifferentiated and indeterminate being-in-itself is determined and differentiated as distinct phenomena by the negations or **negativities** that **being-for-itself** places into **being**. Sartre's view that being is completely undifferentiated apart from **consciousness**, and differentiated only from the point of view of consciousness, characterizes him as a transcendental idealist comparable to **Kant**. See also **noumenon** and **realism**.

being-for-itself   Often abbreviated as 'for-itself'. The single most important notion in Sartre's entire philosophy to the extent that his philosophy can be seen as an exhaustive investigation and description of the phenomenon of being-for-itself. 'Being-for-itself' refers to the essential nature or way of being of **consciousness** or personhood. Every consciousness or person is essentially a being-for-itself, so in many contexts the terms 'consciousness', 'person' and 'being-for-itself' can be used interchangeably. For **Sartre**, the term 'being-for-itself' captures the essential nature of a phenomenon that exists only as a relationship to what Sartre calls '**being-in-itself**'. Unlike being-in-itself, being-for-itself does not exist fundamentally, in itself or in its own right, it borrows its being from being-in-itself, existing only as a **negation**, **nihilation**, denial or **lack** of being-in-itself. Being-for-itself is a **borrowed being**. Like a shadow or a reflection its being is entirely dependent on something other than itself.

Sartre describes being-for-itself as a **non-being** or **nothingness**, but it is not a non-being in itself, its own non-being, it is the non-being of being-in-itself. In not being its own non-being, being-for-itself always has to strive to be its own non-being without ever being able to become it. Being-for-itself always has to be both the project of negating being-in-itself in order to realize itself as the negation of being-in-itself, and the project of negating itself in order to avoid a coincidence with itself that would be its own **annihilation**. Being-for-itself is a paradoxical, ambiguous, indeterminate being that always lacks identity both with being-in-itself and with itself (see **ambiguity** and **indeterminacy**). It is perpetually not what it is (being) and what it is not (non-being) and can only exist in this way, as a **flight** from any kind of self-identity.

Perhaps the easiest way to understand the paradoxical, ambiguous, indeterminate nature of being-for-itself is in terms of time or **temporality**, as a temporal view of it evokes ideas everyone is familiar with from their own experience. Being-for-itself exists as a **temporal flight**, **temporal surpassing** or **temporal transcendence** away from its **past** towards its **future**. It is both its past which is no longer, and its future which is not yet. If it could ever be fixed in the **present** it would cease to exist, but the present does not exist anymore than being-for-itself can be fixed in the present. Being-for-itself is always not what it is (past) and what it is not (future). We all know what this means if we think about it because we all live this paradox all the time. I am my past which is no longer, and all my actions in a world that is the result of the past aim at a future which is not yet. As for the present, there is no such moment as the present, for when being-for-itself reaches the future at which it aims that future immediately becomes the past, or what Sartre prefers to call **past-future**. The present, argues Sartre, is actually the **presence** of being-for-itself to being-in-itself as a temporal flight from being-in-itself towards the future.

Being-for-itself is not in the world as objects are. Being-for-itself transcends the world and it does so by escaping it towards the future. Being-for-itself, however, because it is only the negation of being-in-itself, is an escaping that continues to require the being it seeks to escape. It is an escaping that cannot finally escape. It is a **transcendence** that is constantly re-apprehended by the **facticity** of its **embodiment** and its wider situation, precisely because this facticity is the ground of its transcendence (see **situatedness**). In short, being-for-itself is not a **transcendence-in-itself**, a pure transcendence, but the transcendence of its facticity. In everyday terms, it is human projects that constitute the transcendence of being-for-itself. A person's projects always aim at a future in which he will have overcome something presently lacking, a future in which he hopes and desires to be more satisfied, fulfilled and at one with himself. Sartre argues that ultimately being-for-itself always aims at coinciding with itself, at being its own foundation, at being what he calls a **being-for-itself-in-itself**. Being-for-itself, however, can never achieve this state of self-supporting self-identity because it exists only as the negation of being-in-itself and as such is grounded upon it rather than upon itself. It is destined always to be grounded upon a being that it is not and as such can never be its own foundation. Sartre's examination of the impossibility of being-for-itself becoming being-for-itself-in-itself provides a **phenomenological** explanation of why complete satisfaction is unachievable, why, in Sartre's view, **'man is a useless passion'**.

Being-for-itself is nothing in itself, therefore it must constantly make itself be something, or rather, it must constantly aim at being something without ever being able to become it once and for all. A person can 'become' a waiter, for example, but this does not mean that he has become a waiter-thing in the way that a table is a table. He has to constantly choose to play the role of a waiter and can always choose to do otherwise (see Sartre's example of **the waiter** for further discussion of this). Being-for-itself aims at being something through **choice** and **action**. Being-for-itself has to constantly choose its way of being; it cannot not do so because to choose not to choose is still a choice. Being-for-itself is burdened with having to choose itself, with having to choose its responses to its situation. It is, as Sartre says, **'condemned to be free'**. For Sartre, being-for-itself is essentially free, and it is this aspect of being-for-itself that most interests Sartre in his writings. **Freedom**, for Sartre, is not freedom from **responsibility**, but the responsibility that being-for-itself has to choose a response to every situation. To affirm this responsibility and to live up to it is the essence of **authenticity**. To seek to evade this responsibility by choosing not to choose, by acting as though one does not have a choice, by treating oneself as an object and so on, is the essence of **bad faith**. Every being-for-itself, in Sartre's view, is capable of authenticity, but most of the time most beings-for-themselves, most people, live in bad faith as a way of evading the **anxiety** that comes from realizing that there is nothing that they are or can be in the mode of being it, that they have to choose what they are and are responsible for doing so.

Being-for-itself can be described, as it has been described above, in terms of negation, lack, consciousness, temporality, transcendence, freedom, bad faith and so on, and it is important to note that for Sartre these key **phenomena** are not characteristics of being-in-itself – it has no characteristics other than being. It is in and through the relationship between being-for-itself and being-in-itself that all the key phenomena pertaining to human reality arise. Being-in-itself is **undifferentiated being**, it is only for being-for-itself that being is differentiated, that it is manifest as **differentiated being**. See also *Being and Nothingness*, **being-in-the-world**, **Dasein**, **double negation**, **internal relation**, **transcendent subject** and **upsurge**.

being-for-itself-in-itself   Often abbreviated as 'for-itself-in-itself'. An impossible state of **being-for-itself** in which being-for-itself coincides with itself and becomes its own foundation. In truth, being-for-itself can never become its own foundation. Its foundation must be **being-in-itself** of which it is the **negation**. Being-for-itself continually strives to coincide with itself as being-for-itself-in-itself. It strives to become its own foundation and to overcome the lack that it is. Being-for-itself-in-itself is a perpetually desired but absolutely unrealizable state of being in which the negation of being becomes a negation-in-itself. It is the impossible synthesis of the **for-itself** and the **in-itself**, an impossible state of being in which the non-being that is the essence of being-for-itself exists with the full positivity of being-in-itself. **God** is the ultimate being-for-itself-in-itself in that his existence and his essence are one. (The Ontological Argument for the existence of God assumes this unity of existence and essence. For the Medieval philosopher, Anselm, the most perfect conceivable entity must have the attribute of existence. So, for Anselm, God's essence implies his existence.) Hence, the striving of being-for-itself to be being-for-itself-in-itself is a striving to be God. According to **Sartre**, every **desire** that a person has is an expression of his fundamental desire to be God, his fundamental desire to be at one with himself. See also **annihilation**, **non-being-in-itself** and **transcendence-in-itself**.

being-for-others   Those structures of a person's being that belong to the **Other** (another person or persons) and are realized from the point of view of the Other. In order to fully realize all the structures of his being a person requires the existence of the Other. Some modes of **consciousness** are not attributable simply to **being-for-itself** and must be realized from the point of view of the Other. Such modes of consciousness include shame, embarrassment and pride. These modes of consciousness, although they are *for* consciousness and exist only in so far as a person is conscious of them, are fundamentally other-related. A person's being-for-others is very much a being that he is, but he is it over there, for the Other, in so far as the Other is free to interpret and evaluate his actions as he sees fit. A person's being-for-others constitutes a whole range of (his) possibilities, but they are alienated possibilities. They are not possibilities that he maintains and controls through his own **transcendent subjectivity**, but possibilities fixed by the transcendent subjectivity of the Other. **The look** of the Other reduces a person to an object from the Other's point of view. His transcendent subjectivity is transcended by the **transcendence** of the Other. He becomes a **transcendence-transcended** until he regains his transcendence over the Other and in turn reduces him to a transcendence-transcended. **Sartre** characterizes interpersonal relations as a ceaseless, unresolvable power struggle. He is of the opinion that **conflict** is the essence of human relationships, a view that is summed up in his play *In Camera* (1944) with the assertion that 'Hell is other people'. See also **being-in-the-midst-of-the-world** and **Mitsein**.

being-in-itself   A central notion in Sartre's philosophy. Often abbreviated as 'in-itself' or simply '**being**'. Also referred to as **undifferentiated being**. Being-in-itself is the basis or starting point of Sartre's **ontology**, his theory of what exists in the most general sense and the way in which it exists. It is the starting point of Sartre's ontology, if not his entire philosophy, because every phenomenon that **Sartre** describes ultimately depends on being-in-itself for its existence. **Consciousness**, for example, or what Sartre generally refers to as **non-being** or **being-for-itself**, exists as the **negation** or denial of being-in-itself. As such, consciousness is entirely dependent on being-in-itself because it is nothing but being-in-itself denied.

All that can really be said about being-in-itself is that it *is*. It is its own foundation. That is, it is founded upon itself and not upon anything else. It is that which exists fundamentally, *in itself*, in its own right, rather than being that which does not exist in itself and is dependent upon something else for its existence. It is self-sufficient, uncreated and unchanging. It is tempting to suppose that it has always been and will always be, and even Sartre refers to eternity in describing it. Being-in-itself, however, is eternal only in the sense of being timeless. There is no before or after, **past** or **future**, for being-in-itself. **Temporality** exists only for a being that is perpetually not what it was and not yet what it will be, namely being-for-itself. It is also tempting to suppose that the existence of being-in-itself is necessary. However, to describe being-in-itself as a necessity is to characterize it as that which cannot not be, when, according to Sartre, it has no characteristics whatsoever other than *being*. Being-in-itself exists utterly, yet its existence is not necessary. It *is*, yet it need not be. This is the **contingency**, superfluity or even **absurdity** of being-in-itself that Sartre describes so powerfully in his novel *Nausea* (1938). It exists without reason or justification. It is also tempting to suppose that because being-in-itself exists it must be the realization of a possibility – 'derived from the possible', as Sartre puts it. Possibility, however, exists only for being-for-itself which cannot pre-exist being-in-itself, so being-in-itself cannot be identified or characterized as the realization of what is possible. Being-in-itself is not derived from the possible and neither does it have possibilities. Being-for-itself has a future in which to realize and actualize its possibilities. Being-in-itself, as said, has no future, or past, and therefore possibility is not a quality that can be discovered in it or applied to it.

That being-in-itself has no characteristics leads Sartre to describe it as undifferentiated being. It is not a necessity, it has no possibilities, it is not temporal or even spatial. It should not be thought of as an infinite monoblock of physical stuff, although Sartre does sometimes refer to physical objects as 'in-itself', in contrast to persons who are 'for-itself'. If being-in-itself were spatial it would be differentiated in the sense of having different regions, here and there, here as not there, and so on. Being-in-itself has no regions or parts just as it has no past or future. Unlike its negation – being-for-itself – being-in-itself is never other than itself. It is what it is, whereas being-for-itself is what it is not and not what it is (see **temporality** for an explanation of this paradox).

Hegel argues that being (he does not use the term being-in-itself) is so undifferentiated and featureless that it is in fact indistinguishable from non-being or **nothingness**. For Hegel, there is neither being nor non-being but only **becoming**. Sartre disagrees with Hegel, insisting that being-in-itself *is* while non-being or nothingness *is not*. For Sartre, being-in-itself is logically primary. All else – i.e. non-being – is logically subsequent to it, dependent upon it and derived from it.

Being-in-itself has a negation in the form of being-for-itself. It is tempting to suppose that being-in-itself gave rise to its negation, as though giving rise to its negation was a project on the part of being-in-itself. Being-in-itself, however, because it is what it is and cannot be other than what it is, cannot have projects or conceive possibilities. So, the question remains, how did being-for-itself as the negation of being-in-itself arise? Sartre insists, though not all scholars agree with him, that it is impossible to answer this question, that any attempt to account for what he describes as the **upsurge** of being-for-itself from being-in-itself produces only hypotheses that cannot be validated. For Sartre, the upsurge of being-for-itself must be accepted as axiomatic just as the being of being-in-itself must be accepted as axiomatic.

To summarize: Being-in-itself *is*. It is not created, changing, temporal, necessary, physical or spatial. It has no characteristics other than being, and it is not differentiated in any way. It has a negation that Sartre describes as being-for-itself, a negation that is entirely dependent upon it for its **borrowed being**. The emergence or upsurge of this negation from being-in-itself is, for Sartre, an unfathomable mystery. All those phenomena that comprise the human world – change, temporality, possibility, spatiality, distinct objects, **lack**, **freedom** and so on, arise through the relationship between being-for-itself and being-in-itself and exist only from the perspective of being-for-itself.

being-in-itself-for-itself   A term with the same meaning as **being-for-itself-in-itself**.

being-in-situation   **Being-for-itself** is always situated. The immediate situation of being-for-itself is the **body**. **Sartre** sometimes refers to the being-in-situation of being-for-itself as its **situatedness**. Being-for-itself does not just happen to be situated, it is fundamentally a being-in-situation. It is never other than a being-in-situation although it may strive to deny its being-in-situation and relinquish **responsibility** for it through various projects of **bad faith**. **Authenticity** involves a person taking full responsibility for his being-in-situation without blame, excuse or **regret**. See also **facticity**.

being-in-the-midst-of-the-world   A term originally employed by **Heidegger** and often used by **Sartre** to refer to a person's presence in the world as an object among other objects. As a being-in-the-midst-of-the-world a person's free **transcendence** is transcended by the transcendence of the **Other**. He becomes an object for the Other. He becomes a **transcendence-transcended** by **the look** of the Other. His possibilities belong to the Other and are subject to the Other's judgement. Being-in-the-midst-of-the-world corresponds to a person's **being-for-others**. Being-in-the-midst-of-the-world contrasts with what Sartre, following Heidegger, refers to as a person's **being-in-the-world**. In *Being and Nothingness* (1943) Sartre illustrates the switch from the latter to the former with the example of a voyeur at a keyhole. Until the voyeur is caught in the act he remains a being-in-the-world, a transcendence. He is a subject absorbed in his actions and does not judge them. Suddenly, he realizes he is seen. The meaning of his act escapes him. It now belongs to the Other for whom he has become an object, a transcended being-in-the-midst-of-the-world. Sartre's most detailed description of the nature and implications of being reduced to a being-in-the-midst-of-the-world appears in *Saint Genet* (1952), when he considers the life-defining moment Genet was caught in the act of stealing.

being-in-the-world   A term originally employed by **Heidegger** and often used by **Sartre** to refer to a person's being for himself as opposed to his being for other people – his **being-for-others**. For himself and from his own point of view a person is not an object in the world among other objects – what Sartre, following Heidegger, refers to as a **being-in-the-midst-of-the-world** – but a **transcendence**, a subject that freely transcends the world towards his own possibilities. Being-in-the-world is the mode of being of **being-for-itself** when it is transcending the world in its perpetual **temporal flight** towards the **future**.

being-towards-death   For **Heidegger**, human existence is essentially being-towards-death. A person's life is a process of projecting himself towards his possibilities and using them up. A person's ultimate or '**ownmost possibility**' is the possibility of death. The exhaustion of this possibility is the exhaustion of all possibilities. The meaning of a person's death is that he has no more possibilities. For Heidegger, death is a person's ownmost possibility because only he can die his own death. In anticipating his own death a person establishes his uniqueness and **authenticity**. Authenticity for Heidegger is primarily authentic-being-towards-death. A person who recognizes his being-towards-death and who modifies his behaviour and attitude in accordance with an awareness of his **mortality** is authentic. **Sartre** agrees with Heidegger that embracing life's finitude is a prompt to **authentic action**, but he does not agree that death is a person's ownmost possibility. As the absolute limit of all of a person's possibilities death is not itself a possibility. See also **affirmation of mortality** and **everydayness**.

being-with-others   See **Mitsein**.

Bergson, Henri (1859–1941)   French philosopher, author of *Time and Free Will* (1889), winner of the 1927 Nobel Prize for Literature and Sartre's earliest significant philosophical influence. As a teenager **Sartre** was extremely eclectic in his reading and studied with no particular direction. This dilettantism ended when he read Bergson's *Time and Free Will*. Bergson did not introduce Sartre to philosophy – Sartre's philosophy professor at the Lycée Louis-le-Grand, Colonna d'Istria, introduced Sartre to Bergson – but Bergson inspired Sartre to consider himself a philosopher first and foremost from then on.

Bergson distinguishes between divisible, scientific time and the continuous temporal flow that is intuitively experienced by **consciousness** and is so central to psychic life. In studying Bergson's theory of the relationship between time and consciousness Sartre first discovered the key idea of **temporality**. He later refined his understanding of this key idea through his study of **Husserl** and **Heidegger** (themselves influenced by Bergson) and eventually placed it at the core of his own philosophy of mind. Sartre makes periodic and respectful references to Bergson's ideas throughout his philosophical writings.

the body   See **embodiment**.

borrowed being   See **being, borrowed**.

Brentano, Franz (1837–1917)   German philosopher and psychologist. A significant influence on **Sartre**, not least through his influence on Edmund **Husserl** who attended Brentano's lectures on **phenomenology** and **intentionality**. Sartre's philosophy is essentially **phenomenological** in its approach, while the notion of intentionality lies at the heart of his theory of **consciousness**. Brentano's major work is *Psychology from an Empirical Standpoint* (1874).

buffeted consciousness (buffeted human reality)   See **consciousness, buffeted**.

— **C** —

Camus, Albert (1913–60)   French **existentialist** author. Born and raised in Algeria, Camus overcame the disadvantages of poverty to graduate in philosophy from the University of Algiers in 1936. He became a member of the Communist Party and his first book, a collection of essays entitled *Betwixt and Between*, was published in 1937. With his reputation in Algeria growing Camus moved to Paris in 1938 to work first for the anticolonialist newspaper, *Alger-Républicain*, and later, *Paris-Soir*. During World War II Camus was a member of the French Resistance Movement. His best-known novel, *The Stranger* (alternative title *The Outsider*), appeared in 1942. Like Sartre's 1938 novel, **Nausea**, which deeply impressed Camus, *The Stranger* explores the meaninglessness and **absurdity** of human existence through the eyes of its despairing, alienated and nihilistic central character, Meursault. 1942 also saw the publication of *The Myth of Sisyphus*, a philosophical essay in which Camus compares human existence to the plight of the mythical figure Sisyphus who is condemned for all eternity to push a boulder to the top of a hill only to watch it roll down again. Camus asks if life is worth living given that it is as absurd and ultimately futile as the plight of Sisyphus. In choosing to live, in refusing the ever-present possibility of suicide, a person confers value and significance on a life that has no value or significance in itself. He also assumes **responsibility** for his life in so far as he is choosing to live it rather than end it. Camus' seemingly pessimistic account of the **existential truths** of the **human condition** yields an optimistic conclusion: although life's struggle has no ultimate purpose and always the same final result, a person can still create a sense of purpose through the struggle itself and through the way he plays life's game. The affirmation of life that follows from the rejection of suicide is central to Camus' theory of authentic human existence. Sartre's own theory of **authenticity** focuses instead on the **affirmation of freedom**. Nonetheless, **Sartre** agrees with Camus that in the absence of a **God** to confer meaning on human existence, a person's life can have only the meaning the person himself chooses to give it.

Camus and Sartre had influenced each other's thought and reviewed each other's books but they did not meet until 1943 at the Paris opening of Sartre's play, **The Flies**. They became friends, Sartre helping Camus to found the Resistance newspaper, *Combat*, but after World War II political differences began to emerge between them that progressively strained their friendship. Sartre became increasingly left-wing and radical, offering moral support to various Communist regimes around the world and arguing that revolutionary violence was not only justified but inevitable. Camus, who had been politically engaged longer than Sartre, became increasingly disillusioned with Communism and began to question left-wing assumptions about the use of revolutionary violence. Their friendship finally ended in 1952 with a very public row that took place in the pages of

Sartre's journal, **Les Temps modernes**, after Sartre's protégé, Francis Jeanson, wrote a critical review of Camus' 1951 novel, The Rebel. Camus responded angrily to the review provoking Sartre to an equally angry rejoinder in which he accused Camus, amongst other things, of not having read **Hegel**, implying thereby that Camus had no real philosophical understanding of the forces and processes that shape history. The two men never spoke again.

In light of what is known today about the corruption and injustice at the heart of many of the Communist regimes that Sartre endorsed, Camus' anti-Communist philosophy of reconciliation and non-violence appears the more attractive. Sartre, however, may have been right to view Camus as politically naive, particularly with regard to his unrealistic hopes for peace agreements and compromise between French Algerians and Algerian Arabs and Berbers. While Camus dithered, criticizing but refusing to condemn French rule in Algeria, Sartre, true to the uncompromising nature of his **existentialism**, rejected half measures and campaigned vigorously for Algerian independence.

Camus won the **Nobel Prize for Literature** in 1957. He continued to write novels and to work as a journalist until his tragic and untimely death at the age of 46 in a car crash near Sens, France on January 4, 1960. See also **Gallimard**.

the champion of sincerity   In *Being and Nothingness* (1943) **Sartre** explores the various aspects of **bad faith** through a series of examples of people in bad faith. One of his examples of a person in bad faith is that of the champion of sincerity who urges his **homosexual** friend to declare himself and admit that he is a homosexual. Prima facie, it appears that the homosexual is in bad faith for denying that he is a homosexual whereas the champion of sincerity is not in bad faith because he recommends honesty and **sincerity**. In advocating honesty and sincerity, however, the champion of sincerity is as much in bad faith as the homosexual. He is in bad faith with regard to the homosexual in that he urges the homosexual to consider himself a **facticity** rather than the **transcendence** of his facticity. In urging the homosexual to consider himself a facticity, the champion of sincerity seeks to stereotype the homosexual, he seeks to deny him the **freedom** that makes him an individual and thereby to reduce him to a **transcendence-transcended**.

Transcendence is and must be the transcendence of facticity. All projects of bad faith aim at the separation and inversion of facticity and transcendence. In not considering himself to be a homosexual, the homosexual considers himself to be a pure transcendence rather than the transcendence of his facticity. He is in bad faith. In urging the homosexual to consider himself a facticity the champion of sincerity urges him to exchange one project of bad faith for another.

The Childhood of a Leader (1939)   A short story by **Sartre** contained in a collection of short stories entitled **The Wall**, *The Wall* being the lead story in the collection. Extremely detailed yet brilliantly concise, *The Childhood of a Leader* traces the emotional, psychological, social, sexual and moral development of a privileged bourgeois, Lucien Fleurier, from infancy to adulthood. Lucien is a sensitive, intelligent, imaginative child given to fantasizing and inventing games. Even as an infant he worries about his self-identity and the nature of reality. When made to wear an angel costume he worries that he might become a girl or be permanently mistaken for one. He wonders if he is real, if anything is real, if his parents and other adults are just pretending to be who they appear to be. He often feels he is asleep, that his thoughts are just mist or that he is nothing but mist himself, and he wishes he could wake up to a reality that is clear, certain and solid.

Like the young, precocious Sartre himself, Lucien is troubled by questions of identity and reality throughout his childhood. (Many of the incidental details in the story are also drawn from Sartre's own childhood as later described in his autobiography, **Words** (1964). For example, Lucien, like Sartre, ceases to be cute and becomes a 'toad' when he has his golden locks shaved off.) Lucien's childhood and adolescence are characterized by a quest to understand who he is, to find and define himself, to give himself a solidity and reality that replaces the vagueness, **indeterminacy** and insubstantiality he usually feels. In feeling indeterminate and contingent he is recognizing the **existential truth** that there is nothing that he is in the mode of being it, that, like everyone else, he must play at being what he is because he cannot simply *be* what he is. Lucien, however, like most people, does not like to have a sense of his own indeterminacy and **contingency**, it makes him uncomfortable and anxious. He tries various strategies to overcome it as he grows, eventually choosing to think and act in profound

bad faith, creating and forcing himself to believe in the illusion of his own necessity and determinacy.

Primarily, *The Childhood of a Leader* details one person's slide into the kind of chronic, cowardly, morally repugnant bad faith that, for Sartre, typifies the French (or any) bourgeois: The faith that his existence is not accidental but essential and that he has sacred rights granted by **God** and his nation, such as the right to have unquestionable opinions and prejudices and the right to have his necessary existence confirmed through the respect of others, especially the social inferiors he is destined to lead. In his novel, **Nausea** (1938), written around the same time, Sartre refers to the bourgeoisie as *salauds* (swine). *The Childhood of a Leader* complements *Nausea* in that it charts the personal development of a *salaud* who, like the *salauds* in *Nausea*, might well, as an adult, have a portrait of himself painted in which he appears grander, more significant, more substantial and infinitely less contingent than he really is.

As an adolescent Lucien becomes close friends with Berliac, a Jewish youth who is very mature and well informed for his age. Lucien and Berliac share confidences, each admitting to a childhood desire for his own mother (Oedipus Complex). In this way, Berliac introduces Lucien to Freudian **psychoanalysis**, which Lucien then studies avidly. Psychoanalysis appears to hold the answer to Lucien's worries about his identity. It seems he has been unable to find the true Lucien and his lifelong search for him has been misguided because the true Lucien is buried deep in his subconscious. He decides, like Berliac, that all his worries are just 'complexes' as diagnosed by **Freud**.

Much to Berliac's annoyance, Lucien becomes acquainted with Berliac's mentor, Bergère, a surrealist artist in his thirties whose intentions towards Lucien are sexual. Bergère awakens homosexual desires in Lucien, but partly as a result of his naivety and partly as a result of bad faith Lucien refuses to acknowledge his own homosexual tendencies or the true meaning of Bergère's advances. In this respect Lucien is comparable to Sartre's **flirt** who relinquishes **responsibility** for herself and her situation, refusing to acknowledge the sexual background of her companion's attentions. Lucien escapes the burden of his responsibility for himself by allowing himself to exist for Bergère as a flattered, pampered object, a doll. He has fantasized since childhood in a vaguely sexual way about being treated like a doll. Unable to determine himself, Lucien allows himself to be determined as the object of Bergère's desires. Bergère finally succeeds in seducing Lucien who, nervous but consenting at the time, is left feeling disgusted and ashamed of himself. He fears what will become of his respectable, middle-class reputation and his destiny to lead if he 'becomes' a homosexual. Though he is a homosexual in so far as he practises homosexuality, he nonetheless shares the anti-homosexual prejudices of his social class.

Lucien's reaction to his sexual encounter with Bergère, his reaction to his encounter with his own homosexuality, is a **radical conversion** to extreme bad faith. He immediately begins striving to deny the true meaning of this encounter, treating it as an unfortunate aberration to be blamed on circumstances and other people. He has nothing more to do with Bergère, Berliac or Freud. Raised in an anti-Semitic environment it is easy for him to convince himself that the dangerous, perverted, Jewish ideas of Berliac and Freud temporarily corrupted his mind and his moral health and led him to the episode with Bergère. His anti-Semitism is a distraction from his homosexual desires. What he really fears and therefore hates are these desires, but to hate them would be to recognize that he has them, so he hates Jews instead. In an attempt to convince himself that he is heterosexual he finds a girlfriend and loses his virginity, but it is clear that he does not really enjoy heterosexual sex. He embraces the security and respectability of his family, looking forward to the day when he will inherit his father's factory and be respected by his workers. He adopts his father's positive view of capitalism, his nationalism and above all his anti-Semitism. He joins the French Fascist movement and helps to beat up an immigrant in the street in a random, unprovoked, racially motivated attack. Membership of this aggressive, macho, anti-intellectual tribe makes him feel strong and proud and gives him a sense of belonging. He had formerly searched for his *personal* identity, but now he is happy to take on an identity granted and confirmed by the group. In fiercely despising Jews, his badge of honour among his fellow Fascists, he not only finds a scapegoat for his past actions, he sees himself as important and substantial in comparison to those he despises. He prides himself that he is not a member of a despised race, but a Frenchman with a good French name and respectable ancestry. His anti-Semitism, unreasonable and unfounded though it is, transforms him into a man of conviction. His convictions define him and give him solidity; they demand the respect of others.

Throughout the story the moustache marks out those serious-minded bourgeois who command respect for their convictions, their belief that whatever they choose to believe is true. These apparent men of substance have fooled themselves and others that they are what they are in the mode of being it – a **being-in-itself** rather than a **being-for-itself**. The transformation in Lucien's self-image, the construction of his false object-self, is finally completed when, dissatisfied with his pretty, childish face, he decides to grow a moustache. See also *Anti-Semite and Jew*.

choice   A person is continually confronted by a range of alternative courses of **action**. He has a choice as to which course of action he takes. The course of action he takes intentionally is his *choice*. This much belongs to the common understanding of the term 'choice'. **Sartre** explores the phenomenon of choice as the central feature of **existential freedom**. Denying **determinism**, he holds that people are free and that, therefore, their choices are genuine choices. People could always have chosen a different action from the action they chose. Furthermore, any course of action chosen and embarked upon can be abandoned at any time for an alternative course of action. **Being-for-itself** is indeterminate, a perpetual striving to define itself. It seeks to define itself through the actions it chooses to take in face of its **facticity**. A person is the product of the choices he has made in the **past**. A person is continually confronted by choices and obliged to choose. Freedom is unlimited in that the obligation to choose is endless (see **unlimited freedom**). A person cannot not choose because to choose not to choose is still a choice for which he is responsible. Sartre's theory of freedom is very much a theory of **responsibility** also, and he repeatedly emphasizes that people are responsible for their choices. That is, they are responsible for their actions. A person who behaves as though he is not responsible for his actions and treats choosing not to choose as though it were not a choice, a person who declares 'I had no choice', is acting in **bad faith**. Many of Sartre's critics, **Merleau-Ponty** for example, argue that responsibility and the ability to choose are less extensive than Sartre supposes and that his views on the limitlessness of freedom are so uncompromising as to be untenable. See **responsibility** for criticism of Sartre's thesis that freedom and responsibility are limitless. See also **fundamental choice, groundless choice, negative choice, positive choice** and **radical choice**.

choice, fundamental   For **Sartre**, there is nothing that a person is in the mode of being it. A person's character is not a fixed nature or essence but the product of the choices he has made during his life. His choices can be traced back to a fundamental or original choice of himself made in response to a particular childhood event that occurred at the dawning of **self-consciousness**. The event may be trivial in itself but the response to it is hugely significant in that it is the start of a process whereby a person chooses actions that affirm or deny his view of himself as a certain type of person. The actions that a person chooses in response to his fundamental choice comprise his **fundamental project**. A person's fundamental choice is arbitrary and groundless but it is nonetheless a choice of self that establishes grounds for all subsequent choosing. Each person's fundamental choice is unique and can only be discovered through a detailed exploration of their personal history. For Sartre, this exploration is the task of **existential psychoanalysis**. Sartre holds that it is possible for a person to undergo a **radical conversion** in which he redefines himself by establishing a new fundamental choice of himself. See also **Baudelaire**, **Freud** and **Saint Genet**.

choice, groundless   **Sartre** argues that every **choice** is a radical expression of **freedom** unavoidably based upon wholly arbitrary decisions. A person's beliefs, convictions and values do not provide grounds for choice because they have only the significance he chooses to give them and are themselves the product of groundless choices. Sartre illustrates his theory of the groundlessness of choice in **Existentialism and Humanism** (1946) with the example of a student of his who faced the dilemma of leaving home to fight for the Resistance or staying home to take care of his sick mother. Sartre told the student there were no grounds for deciding which course of action to take. He must simply plunge into one or other course of action without reason or justification. Sartre holds that if a choice could be guided and influenced in any way by beliefs, convictions or values it would be a caused phenomenon rather than a genuinely free choice. According to his critics, Sartre's insistence that choice is groundless reduces choice to a mysterious phenomenon. Sartre can offer no explanation of why a person faced with options that have only the value he chooses to grant them, chooses one course of action rather than another. It would, for instance, explain nothing to say that the person was like a man who based every decision on the toss of a coin because an explanation would still be lacking as to why a man chooses to attribute value to and abide by the toss of a coin. Some critics reach the damning conclusion that Sartre's theory of freedom can shed no light at all on the phenomenon of choosing unless it is modified to accommodate the view that choices can in some sense be caused yet remain choices. Along these lines **Merleau-Ponty** argues that there is a **natural self** based upon the natural limitations of the body and its basic physical relationship with the environment that limits freedom by rendering certain evaluations inevitable. The natural self provides a pre-structure or framework within which choices can be made that are more than arbitrary. See also **radical choice**.

choice, negative   The opposite of **positive choice**. Situations demand responses. They demand decisive action. A negative choice is a **choice** not to meet the demands of a situation. It is a choice not to choose on the part of a person who falsely assumes that they are exempt from the requirement to choose. **Sartre** illustrates negative choice in *Being and Nothingness* (1943) with the example of the **flirt** who chooses neither to withdraw her hand from the man who holds it or to accept the implications of holding hands. Her negative choice is a choice of herself as an object that does not have choices and responsibilities, but as to choose not to choose is still a choice she is in **bad faith**. To choose negatively is to act inauthentically. See also **ascetic ideal**, **negative freedom**, **negative will to power**, **responsibility** and **slave ethic**.

choice, positive   The opposite of **negative choice**. Decisive action in response to the demands of a situation. A **choice** whereby a person takes **responsibility** for himself in the situation in which he finds himself rather than seeking to relinquish responsibility for himself by acting in **bad faith** and choosing not to choose. To choose positively is to act authentically. See also **affirmation of freedom**, **authentic action**, **authenticity**, **noble ideal**, **positive freedom** and **positive will to power**.

choice, radical   **Sartre** argues that every **choice** is an extreme or radical choice because there are ultimately no grounds for choosing one course of **action** rather than another. A choice is not grounded upon reasons and justifications because these have only the significance a person chooses to give them. **Condemned to be free** a person cannot not choose and every choice he makes is an unconditional and radical expression of his **unlimited freedom**. Every choice is, so to speak, a radical departure. Radical choice is a notion closely akin to **groundless choice**.

concrete negation   See **negation, concrete**.

The Condemned of Altona (1959)   Alternative titles *Altona* and *Loser Wins*. A play by **Sartre** set in post-World War II Germany in the house of Gerlach, a wealthy shipping tycoon. Gerlach made a fortune building warships for the Nazis and another fortune helping to rebuild Germany after the war. Sartre uses the play to put forward the Marxist view that the wealthiest capitalists like Gerlach benefit regardless of who holds political power. Nazis or the US, it is business as usual. Gerlach is dying of throat cancer. His wealth cannot save him. His dying wish is to speak to his estranged eldest son, Franz, who has locked himself away for fourteen years in the upper rooms of the house. Franz' needs are taken care of by his sister, Leni, with whom he is having an incestuous relationship. As the play develops the story emerges of how Franz and his father became estranged and why Franz is a recluse.

Although he was not a member of the Nazi Party, Gerlach senior collaborated with the Nazis, knowingly selling them land for a concentration camp, an act he dismissed by arguing that had he not sold them the land someone else would have. Disgusted by his father's weakness and lack of conscience Franz helped an escaped Rabbi and was arrested by the SS for harbouring a Jew. Using his influence with Goebbels, Gerlach senior secured Franz' release on condition that Franz enlist in the German Army. Franz returned traumatized and defeated from the Russian front and refused to leave the house. Soon after the war he took the blame for his sister's assault on an America soldier who tried to rape her. Gerlach senior persuaded the American authorities to overlook the matter and they agreed on condition that Franz emigrate to Argentina. Rather than leave Germany, however, Franz took to hiding in the upper rooms of his father's house. In time, his father travelled to Argentina and returned with a false death certificate for Franz, completing his son's isolation. Officially dead, Franz turned his back on the outside world and became a recluse. Afraid the authorities would discover he was alive and in Germany his family allowed him to remain in isolation.

It is against this background that Gerlach senior persuades Johanna, the beautiful wife of his younger son Werner, to act as an intermediary between himself and Franz. Johanna gains access to Franz' rooms and in doing so enters a world where the insane but charismatic Franz strives to stop time while attempting to justify his war crimes to future generations. He wears chocolate medals and throws oyster shells at a portrait of Hitler. He makes recordings of his ravings and talks to the air imagining that representatives from the thirtieth century can hear him. As a former actress, Johanna is intrigued by Franz' world of make-believe and soon establishes a close relationship with him that provokes the jealously of her husband Werner and his sister Leni. Johanna eventually persuades Franz to leave his room and meet with his dying father. During their first conversation since the war Franz admits to his father that he is the 'butcher of Smolensk'. He tortured Russian prisoners to death, not because he believed in the Nazi cause but because he was tired of feeling weak and powerless. The Nazi cause simply gave him an excuse to overcome his sense of powerlessness through a decisive act of evil. His father admits that he already knew about his son's war crimes as two Russians had attempted to blackmail him over the matter three years earlier. Father and son leave the house to commit suicide by driving a Porsche into the River Elba. The play ends with Leni locking herself away in her brother's rooms.

The philosophical focus of the play is German collective guilt, or the lack of it, in face of the Nazi atrocities. Divorced from the outside world in his private rooms, hiding from daylight and the passage of time, Franz sees himself as being on trial before all eternity for his war crimes and those of his nation. He identifies one of his crimes as a crime of omission, a failure to act against the Nazis. He resisted them when he helped the Rabbi but cooperated with them afterwards. Like his father, like the majority of the German people, he gave in to the Nazis. He could have resisted them regardless of the consequences but in **bad faith** he acted as though he had no **choice** but to go along with them. Making an excuse of his weakness and his desire for self-preservation he simply despised the Nazis while acting on their behalf. When Franz' feelings of powerlessness and frustration became unbearable he overcomes them by choosing to exercise the power of a torturer. For personal rather than ideological reasons he chose to identify himself with Nazi power, and in acting like a Nazi he became a Nazi. Franz serves to illustrate why ordinary people in adverse circumstances choose to commit atrocities. Franz' choice is understandable, but it is not excusable. He is unable to excuse himself despite fourteen years of isolated soul-searching. Unlike most people who commit atrocities, Franz cannot forget or ignore that he is responsible for his actions. This much makes him a sympathetic character, unlike his father who shows no remorse.

Sartre's aim in *The Condemned of Altona* is not to attack the German people in particular. He sees the Nazi atrocities, chief among them the Holocaust, as being to the shame of all mankind, a product of man's inhumanity towards man rather than, specifically, the inhumanity of Germans towards Jews. As a Marxist, Sartre identifies capitalism as the fundamental evil, characterizing Nazism as just one more manifestation of capitalism. Nazism required capitalism in order to arm itself. In return, Nazism provided capitalism with new markets and new opportunities for growth. The Nazis fell but the capitalists, whose interests the Nazis served, marched on with the capitalist US committing atrocities comparable to those of the Nazis (Sartre gives the example of Hiroshima) and Germany soon recovering its economic prosperity to become the wealthiest country in Europe. One reason that Franz gives for his isolation from the world is his desire to maintain the belief that Germany has been permanently destroyed by the war. He thinks that the permanent destruction of Germany would be just and would to some extent atone for the war crimes of the German people. To believe that Germany has recovered, that its people have moved on, only adds to the acute sense of guilt that he continues to feel years after the war has ended. *Loser Wins*, the alternative title of the play, refers to the economic success that Germany enjoyed soon after losing World War II.

'condemned to be free'   In putting forward his theory of **existential freedom**, **Sartre** argues that we are *necessarily* free by virtue of the fact that **being-for-itself** must always choose what it is without ever being able to become what it is. We cannot choose not to be free because, as Sartre points out, to choose not to choose is already to have chosen. We are unable, by any means whatsoever, to cease being free, and in this sense we are *condemned* to be free. We are condemned to be free, not by **God**, but by the nature of our **consciousness** and our way of **being-in-the-world**. There is, in Sartre's uncompromising view, no escape from the **responsibility** of having to be free and having to choose. See **responsibility** for criticism of his uncompromising view. See also **choice**.

confession   See **sincerity**.

conflict   In expounding his theory of **being-for-others**, **Sartre** argues that conflict is the essence of all human relationships. He characterizes interpersonal relations as a ceaseless power struggle. The **freedom** that is the essence of every person endeavours to 'enslave' the freedom of the **Other**, constantly striving to transcend the Other and reduce him to a **transcendence-transcended**.

Some critics resist Sartre's claim that the essence of all relationships is conflict, not because they think it pessimistic, but because they think it is an unjustifiable generalization. They argue that Sartre's insistence on the universality of conflict is motivated by personal considerations. He speaks too much from his own experience and overemphasizes one aspect of human behaviour for dramatic effect. When he suggests that **the look** is always threatening he ignores the evidence of certain concrete situations, such as, for example, the protective–protected look between mother and child. In Sartre's defence it is important to note that he shows some appreciation of the capacity people have for being together without conflict in his account of Heidegger's notion of **Mitsein**, the 'we' subject. He acknowledges that rather than always seeking to transcend each other, people are capable on certain occasions of submerging themselves in an *us*. This submergence in an *us*, however, is often maintained through conflict with a *them* as opponent and/or hate object – Sartrean conflict at the group level. See also **hate**, *In Camera* and **love**.

consciousness   **Being-for-itself** at the **phenomenological level**. A term more or less synonymous with being-for-itself that is often used interchangeably with being-for-itself. In the view of **Sartre** and other **phenomenologists** such as **Brentano** and **Husserl** the defining feature of consciousness is **intentionality**. That is, consciousness exists only in so far as it *intends* something. It is nothing in itself and must always be consciousness *of* something. A fact summed up by the maxim **'consciousness is consciousness of __'**. Consciousness is consciousness of the world and consciousness of itself in various ways. For Sartre, there is (a) **positional consciousness** of the world, (b) implicit **non-positional consciousness** or **non-thetic consciousness** (of) consciousness without which consciousness would not be conscious and (c) explicit **positional self-consciousness** or

thetic self-consciousness in which consciousness reflects on itself. Both (b) and (c) are often referred to as **self-consciousness** but strictly speaking only (c) is self-consciousness. Consciousness (of) consciousness is not really self-consciousness. The *self* does not pre-exist the act by which consciousness reflects on itself. The self is a transcendent **psychic object** realized in and through the act of consciousness reflecting on itself. See **self-consciousness** for a full explanation of the difference between consciousness (of) consciousness and self-consciousness. See also *The Transcendence of the Ego*.

'consciousness is consciousness of ___' A maxim used by **Sartre** and other **phenomenologists** to describe the nature of **consciousness**. Consciousness, or what Sartre often refers to as **being-for-itself**, has no being of its own. It exists only as the **negation** of **being-in-itself** and as such is dependent upon being-in-itself for its **borrowed being**. It follows that consciousness is nothing in itself. It is not a mental substance, as **Descartes** supposes, existing in its own right and then entertaining thoughts. Consciousness exists only in so far as it is consciousness *of* something, only in so far as it *intends* something and is *about* something. It is a relationship to the world it is consciousness *of* and nothing beyond that. Like a reflection in a mirror it is comprised of what it reflects and nothing more. See **aboutness** and **intentionality**.

consciousness, buffeted (buffeted human reality) For **Sartre**, a person is a buffeted consciousness if he sees himself as a given or fixed entity buffeted and swept along by circumstances. A buffeted consciousness is a **consciousness** in **bad faith**. To cease being a buffeted consciousness and achieve **authenticity** a person must realize that he is not a given or fixed entity, a **facticity**, but only ever his *response* to the facticity of his current situation. Rather than act as though his situation is not his situation or complain that it should not be, he must take full **responsibility** for his **being-in-situation** without **regret**. An example of a buffeted consciousness is Lulu in Sartre's short story, *Intimacy* (1939).

consciousness, disembodied Sartre argues that **consciousness** must always be embodied (see **embodiment**). The body is the immediate and necessary situation or **facticity** of consciousness. Consciousness is never its own **transcendence** but always the transcendence of the body.

Sartre denies the possibility of disembodied consciousness, ruling out the existence of ghosts and spirits. His view is opposed to Cartesian dualism. **Descartes** supposes that the mind is fundamentally distinct from the body and can exist independently of it.

consciousness, false   A term referring to the consciousness of a person who is fooling himself in some way, for example, by refusing to confront his **facticity** and face the facts of his situation. A person in a state of false consciousness is in **bad faith**. The terms 'false consciousness' and 'bad faith' are often used synonymously.

consciousness, non-positional   See **consciousness, non-thetic**.

consciousness, non-thetic   Implicit and continual consciousness (of) consciousness without which **consciousness** would not be conscious. Also called non-positional consciousness, pre-reflective consciousness and pre-reflexive consciousness. Strictly speaking, non-thetic consciousness (of) consciousness should not be confused with **self-consciousness**. Consciousness (of) consciousness underpins all consciousness including self-consciousness but is not itself self-consciousness. See **self-consciousness** for a full explanation of the difference between non-thetic consciousness (of) consciousness and self-consciousness.

consciousness, positional   **Consciousness** of the world. Con-sciousness of **intentional objects**. Consciousness of the world is always from a particular position or perspective. Consciousness is non-positionally conscious (of) itself – **non-positional consciousness** or **non-thetic con-sciousness** – but is also capable of positional consciousness of itself – **positional self-consciousness** or **thetic self-consciousness** – in which it reflects on itself as an intentional object.

consciousness, pre-reflective   See **consciousness, non-thetic**.

consciousness, pre-reflexive   See **consciousness, non-thetic**.

consciousness, reflected-on   **Being-for-itself** reflected on. That which is reflected on in the act of self-reflection. Reflected-on consciousness exists only in so far as it is reflected on by **relective consciousness**. It is not, therefore, distinct from reflective consciousness. Reflective and reflected-on consciousness are internally related (see **internal relation**). The relationship between reflective and reflected-on consciousness is the same as the internal relationship between **past** and **future**. Reflected-on consciousness is past for reflective consciousness which must transcend reflected-on consciousness towards the future in order to reflect on it. See also **consciousness** and **self-consciousness**.

consciousness, reflective   See **self-consciousness, thetic**.

consciousness, reflexive   See **self-consciousness, thetic**.

consciousness, thetic   **Consciousness** is capable of positional or thetic consciousness of itself – **thetic self-consciousness** – in which it reflects on itself as an **intentional object**. This is **self-consciousness** proper as opposed to **non-thetic consciousness** (of) consciousness. See **self-consciousness** for a full explanation of the difference between consciousness (of) consciousness and self-consciousness.

contingency   The state of being contingent, unnecessary, accidental. That which is contingent is not logically necessary, it need not be or be so. **Sartre** identifies contingency as a fundamental **ontological** feature of existence and explores the phenomenon in detail, not least in his philosophical novel **Nausea** (1938), a work he nicknamed his 'factum on contingency' while drafting it.

Although for Sartre **being-in-itself** is uncreated and not dependent on anything else for its being, its being is not necessary. As that which exists without reason for being, being-in-itself cannot be derived from a necessary law. As that which has no determinants or characteristics, being-in-itself cannot have the characteristic of being that which cannot not be. Being-in-itself *is*, but it is unnecessary, and in being unnecessary it is contingent. For Sartre, being-in-itself is contingent in the sense of being absurdly superfluous. Being-in-itself exists for no reason and for no purpose.

The intense awareness of existence that Sartre describes as 'the nausea' in the novel *Nausea* is a terrifying apprehension of the utter contingency,

absurdity, pointlessness, meaninglessness and futility of existence. Moreover, this terrifying apprehension belongs to a **consciousness** that has no being of its own and exists only as a *relation* to this contingency – a relation by **negation**. For a person to suffer the nausea is for him to experience a state of naked, superfluous existence that not only surrounds him but with which he is continuous by virtue of his **body**. Human society, and most human endeavour, aims to overcome contingency by imposing meanings and purposes on the world. This is achieved largely by naming and categorizing things. In naming something people believe they have made sense of it, ascribed meaning to it, grasped its essential essence, removed the contingency of its raw, nameless existence. But the truth, according to Sartre, is that things only have meaning and purpose relative to other things – words immediately link a thing to other things through language – and the whole only has the relative meaning and purpose that our ultimately pointless activities give it. Seen for what they are in themselves, apart from the **system of instrumentality** that defines them or the framework of meaning that explains and justifies them, objects are incomprehensible, peculiar, strange, even disturbing in their contingency. Contingency for Sartre is mysterious and to be aware of contingency is to be aware of the unfathomable mystery of being.

Sartre's challenge as a philosopher expounding an ontological theory of contingency is to use language to try to convey a sense of a world stripped of language and meaning. He clearly feels that literature, with its scope for description, its levels of irony, its capacity to convey ideas through action, atmosphere and streams of consciousness, is more effective than straight-forward philosophy at achieving this difficult feat. This, arguably, is the main reason why his major work on contingency, *Nausea*, is presented as a novel rather than as a theory maintained in argument.

Sartre is not recommending that people should be like the central character of *Nausea*, dwelling obsessively on contingency and striving to live always under the aspect of eternity in a meaningless and absurd world. That way lies madness. Sartre himself, like most people most of the time, lived and acted very much in the world of relative meanings and purposes. Like most people most of the time, he kept his sanity and sense of perspective by directing his attentions to the task in hand, to the daily round and so on. Nonetheless, he clearly held that an occasional or background awareness of contingency is vital if a person is to achieve any degree of

authenticity and to avoid living a lie. Sartre's philosophy is characterized by an abiding hatred and distrust of people (typically bourgeois) who seem totally unaware of life's contingency; people who, having once glimpsed life's contingency and been terrified by it, are fleeing from it. He portrays the development of such a person in his short story, **Childhood of a Leader** (1939). The **fundamental project** of such people is to evade their own contingency and that of the world by acting in **bad faith**. The world, they tell themselves, is not contingent but created with humankind as its centrepiece. They assume that they have an immortal essence, that their existence is inevitable and that they exist by divine decree rather than by accident. They believe that the moral and social values to which they subscribe are objective, absolute and unquestionable. Society as it is, as that which, in their view, is grounded in these absolute values, is seen by them to constitute the only possible reality. All they have to do to claim their absolute right to be respected by others and to have the respect of others sustain the illusion of their necessity is to dutifully fulfil the role prescribed to them by society and identify themselves totally with that role. At worst, like the *salauds* (swine) in *Nausea*, they arrogantly lie to themselves and others that they are utterly necessary and indispensable by having portraits of themselves produced in which they appear taller, grander, wealthier, more significant, more substantial and infinitely less contingent than they really are.

co-presence   A relationship existing between objects from the point of view of **being-for-itself** when being-for-itself is equally present to them. Sartre's philosophy swings between **transcedental idealism** and **realism**, exhibiting a serious inconsistency that is seemingly impossible to resolve. When swinging towards transcendental idealism, **Sartre** argues that no relations exist between objects independently of being-for-itself. Objects have no co-existence, only co-presence for the **for-itself** when the for-itself is present. At other times, when swinging towards realism, he assumes that objects co-exist independently of the for-itself with various relations holding between them quite apart from the for-itself. Whatever his inconsistencies, he is certainly constant in his view that the for-itself is not co-present with **being-in-itself**. The for-itself exists as a **temporal flight** from being in the **present** towards being in the **future**. It has no being in the present and therefore no capacity for co-presence with being-in-itself. See also **temporality**.

Crime Passionnel   See **Dirty Hands**.

Critique of Dialectical Reason, Volume One: Theory of Practical Ensembles (1960) and **Volume Two: The Intelligibility of History** (Unfinished, posthumously published 1985)   The most ambitious and important work of the later **Sartre** in which he draws together the overall development of his philosophical thought since **Being and Nothingness** (1943), the major publication of his early career, and responds to criticisms of the theory of **existentialism** expressed in that work by attempting to synthesize it with Marxism. *Critique of Dialectical Reason* has a not entirely undeserved reputation for being over-long and very difficult to penetrate even by Sartre's standards of complexity. One critic has described it as 'baggy monster' of a book. Volume One alone is 755 pages of dense, multi-layered argument, and Sartre scholars tend to agree that had Sartre had the time or inclination after the titanic effort of actually writing it, the *Critique* would have benefited from extensive editing. As to those complexities that would doubtless remain despite the most meticulous editing, it can be said in Sartre's defence that a degree of complexity is sometimes unavoidable in any worthwhile work of philosophy and that the synthesis of two vast philosophical theories is no mean under-taking. Who but Sartre would or could have dreamed of undertaking it, although even he, at times, felt daunted by the task. It has become part of the folklore of the *Critique* that Sartre had to dose himself with ampheta-mines to accomplish the task. Certainly, apart from his usual daily stimulants of coffee, whisky and tobacco, Sartre, now in his mid-fifties, damaged his health chewing countless Corydrane tablets, a mixture of aspirin and racemic amphetamine. The *Critique*, however, should not be dismissed, as some have attempted to dismiss it, as the drug-fuelled ramblings of an ageing, declining philosopher. Sartre scholars who have had the time and the knowledge of both existentialism and Marxism required to really penetrate the *Critique* tend to hold that it is an important work that achieves its goal of synthesizing two major philosophies.

After World War II Sartre became increasingly Marxist, both in his philo-sophical outlook and in his political activities. Pro-existentialist critics argued that he should abandon his new-found Marxism as incompatible with his existentialism, while pro-Marxist critics argued that he should abandon his existentialism as incompatible with his new-found Marxism. Few thinkers besides Sartre seemed to think that the two theories were, or could be made to be, compatible. The tension grew around and within Sartre until in the late 1950s he felt compelled to show critics on all sides, as well as prove to himself, that existentialism and Marxism were not contradictory philosophies. The incompatibility, or *apparent* incompatibility, concerns **freedom**. Existentialism is a theory that above all maintains that human freedom is inalienable, whereas, according to many Marxists of Sartre's time, Marxism is a deterministic theory of human history at the centre of which is the notion of dialectical materialism.

For Marx (1818–83), mankind is a product of his dialectical relationship with the material world. Since his earliest evolution mankind has constantly shaped and been shaped by his environment. What mankind has been, is and will become is the result of an historical process. **Hegel**, Marx's major influence, identifies this historical process with the dialectical development of ideas towards perfect rationality. Marx, turning Hegel's **idealism** on its head, identifies this historical process with the dialectical development of matter by mankind and mankind by matter. What is all-important in this historical process as Marx sees it is *production*. Mankind acts purposefully on the world – *praxis* – with the means available to him, means that are a product of earlier *praxis*, to produce new materials, tools and technologies. These new products change man by changing the way people interact with the world and with each other. The Internet, for example, a product of many earlier developments, has made new kinds of productive activity possible (as well as made others obsolete) and has allowed if not forced people to interact with each other in new ways. Marx recognizes that every technological revolution, every change in what he calls 'the means of production', brings about a social revolution, changes in what he calls 'the relations of production', changes in who has effective power and control over what and who.

Sartre agrees with Marx. What he does not agree with is what some Marxists have seen as the main implication of Marx's theory, namely, that it is deterministic and that there is no place in it for human freedom. Sartre's reading of Marx is that his theory of dialectical materialism gives an all-important role to human **consciousness** and, by implication, human freedom because freedom is an essential characteristic of consciousness. Sartre argues that it is a misreading of Marx to suppose that his materialism is a reductionist theory that proposes the development of matter by matter with humans being nothing more than a material product of the process. Of course, humans cannot play a role in the development of matter without having material bodies, but this is not to say that they are merely material. The reductionist view of dialectical materialism is more properly called mechanical materialism. It was proposed by Dühring and attacked by Marx's colleague, Engels, in *Anti-Dühring* as early as 1877. It nonetheless persisted as a crude interpretation of Marx. Stalin, a great enemy of all human freedom but his own, endorsed it in the 1930s and in 1960 Sartre felt obliged to respond to some post-Marxists by accusing them of proposing a simplistic 'dialectic without men'. Sartre treats 'dialectical materialism', with its reductionist connotations, as a corrupted term, preferring instead the term 'historical materialism' which reflects more accurately the materialism Marx actually proposed.

So, Sartre begins to synthesize existentialism and Marxism by arguing that it is a misunderstanding of Marxism to view it as utterly materialistic and deterministic, as fundamentally opposed to any theory of human freedom, individuality or even consciousness. Sartre goes on to argue that Marxism can accommodate the **existentialist** view of human freedom and indeed must do so if it is to make sense. A person is a part of the material world by virtue of his **body** but he could not exist in a dialectical relationship with matter unless he was able to distinguish himself from matter and be a point of view on it. By 'matter' Sartre and Marx do not mean raw matter. They both note that the material world people encounter is almost always worked matter, the product of earlier *praxis*. Sartre refers to this worked matter as the *practico-inert*. The *practico-inert* is a **system of instrumentality** facilitating *praxis*, but it is also an obstacle resisting *praxis*. The *practico-inert*, however well worked, continues to manifest an 'active inertia' that resists human projects. Tools break or are unfit for purpose. *Praxis* towards one objective has consequences that hinder *praxis* towards another. Conflict arises, particularly over scarcity of resources. Sartre has a lot to say in the *Critique* about the huge influence of scarcity on human history. Sartre's notion of the *practico-inert* is a refinement of his notion of **facticity**.

As a **negation** of **being** consciousness remains rooted in matter and could not exist without matter. Nonetheless, as a negation it is never at one with the matter it negates. Consciousness transcends matter towards the **future** (see **transcendence**), and in so doing realizes the future possibilities of matter, possibilities that are none other than the future possibilities of a consciousness existing in relation to matter. In *Being and Nothingness* Sartre denies the possibility of dialectical processes existing in nature apart from consciousness. In the *Critique* he allows that they might exist, only then to argue that the historical dialectic, the development of matter through man and man through matter, cannot be accounted for in terms of blind, mechanical dialectical processes that do not involve consciousness. Man is made by history, but it is also man that *makes* history by responding practically to his present historically derived situation. Through *praxis* man projects himself beyond the present situation towards *his* future situation (see **situatedness**), towards future possibilities that will be realized when a future state of matter is produced. This future state of matter will, in turn, provide the conditions for further projection, that is, for further projects of production. Marx and Engels say, 'Men make their history upon the basis of prior conditions.' They do not mean, as some Marxists take them to mean, that men are mechanisms conditioned by circumstances to act in a certain determined way, but that men make their history by *choosing* their *response* to their conditions. Man is the product of his own productive activity but he is never just a product among products because he is the only product capable of realizing that he is a product. Sartre argues that Marxism is not only a theory of history that requires a notion of human consciousness and therefore freedom, Marxism *is* 'history itself become conscious of itself'.

Marx famously advocates that people should strive for their political freedom. 'The workers have nothing to lose but their chains. They have a world to gain.' This presupposes that people are at least psychologically free in the Sartrean sense. What value or meaning could political freedom have for beings that were entirely subject to deterministic laws? In the *Critique* Sartre recognizes far more than he does in *Being and Nothingness* that a person, a whole social class of people, can be without freedom in any real practical sense as a result of political and economic oppression. A person's existential freedom remains inalienable, he cannot not choose, but his freedom does not amount to much if his only **choice** is, for example, to endure drudgery and exploitation in a factory for a subsistence wage or to die. This view is, in a sense, a development rather than a departure from views expressed in *Being and Nothingness* in so far as Sartre recognizes in that work that the most serious threat to a person's freedom is the freedom of the **Other**. Just as one person can transcend another and reduce him to an object, to a **transcendence-transcended**, so one social class can, through economic and social exploitation, transcend another social class and reduce its members to objects. In this way the Sartre of the *Critique* develops his theory of **being-for-others**, a central plank of existentialism, into a *Marxist* theory of man's alienation by man.

Sartre is fully prepared to place existentialism at the service of Marxism in this way. He identifies Marxism as the dominant philosophy of the age and existentialism as a subordinate theory the purpose of which is to function within Marxism positively influencing its future development towards the realization of a classless, harmonious society. Such a society, according to Sartre, is possible but not inevitable. See also *Search for a Method*.

— **D** —

Dasein   The central notion of Heidegger's philosophy as detailed in his major work, *Being and Time* (1927). Dasein refers to the essential **situatedness** of a person in the world, his **being-in-the-world**. For Dasein, to be and to be situated are one and the same. The most common translation of 'Dasein' from the German is 'being-there'. However, although 'sein' certainly means 'being', 'Da' does not always mean 'there'. 'Da' can mean 'neither here nor there, but somewhere in between'. The essential **indeterminacy** of Dasein is temporal. The being of Dasein in the world is to be a temporal movement away from the **past** towards the **future** (see **temporality**). **Sartre** was heavily influenced by **Heidegger**. Sartre's central notion of **being-for-itself** relates closely to Heidegger's central notion of Dasein.

de Beauvoir, Simone (1908–86)   French **existentialist** philosopher, novelist and feminist. **Sartre** and de Beauvoir met as undergraduates in Paris in 1929 and remained lifelong friends, enjoying a close personal and intellectual relationship. Popular accounts often misrepresent their intellectual relationship. Claims based on little more than supposition are made along the lines that Sartre took all his ideas from de Beauvoir and put them forward as his own, or de Beauvoir took all her ideas from Sartre and put them forward as her own. Equally uninformed is the claim that they came to fundamentally disagree with each other and developed radically different philosophies. Such claims are inspired by various prejudices and ideological assumptions about what the relationship between a male and female philosopher must inevitably be like, or they are simply a product of indolence in face of the effort required to understand the subtleties of a very particular and special association.

The best way to dismiss the nonsense and gain a proper understanding of the intellectual relationship between de Beauvoir and Sartre is to view it in its historical context. De Beauvoir and Sartre inherited the same philosophical tradition at the same time in the same place. That is, they studied together at the École Normale Supérieure in Paris (de Beauvoir was in the year below Sartre) at a time of great social and political change between two world wars. From the moment they met they shared and developed the philosophical ideas of **Descartes**, **Kant**, **Hegel**, Marx and others that they were learning about as students, testing these ideas against their shared reality and using them to explain it. De Beauvoir and Sartre each went on to make their own distinct contributions to **existentialism**, developing the **phenomenology** they inherited from **Husserl** and **Heidegger** in different directions, but they never ceased to agree on fundamental principles; not because one slavishly followed the other, but because each remained personally convinced of the efficacy of the methods and concepts of phenomenology for describing and explaining the **human condition**.

For instance, in one of her most important works, *The Ethics of Ambiguity* (1947), de Beauvoir readily acknowledges her agreement with Sartre (and with **Kierkegaard** and Hegel as well) regarding the **indeterminacy** or **ambiguity** of the self. She then takes the notion of the ambiguity of the self as a starting point for establishing an **existentialist ethics**. Ethics is only possible, she argues, because the self is ambiguous. If a person has a defined or fixed nature, if he is something given, there can be no notion of his having-to-be something, no notion of his freely striving to achieve a certain state, moral or otherwise. De Beauvoir agrees with Sartre's maxim that **'man is a useless passion'**, that it is impossible for a person to achieve coincidence with himself as a **being-for-itself-in-itself**, but she is nonetheless positive about the implications of this 'uselessness'. A person fails to coincide with himself, but it is precisely this failure that makes him exist as a person, that gives him genuine **choice** and makes him free. He is able to disclose being because he is not being, he is able to venture out, challenging, improving and overcoming himself precisely because he does not have a fixed nature or essence. His essence, as de Beauvoir argues repeatedly, is to have no essence. Above all, by virtue of his ambiguity, a person is capable of **authenticity**, of affirming his **freedom** as an ultimate value rather than denying and regretting it.

De Beauvoir's ideas on authenticity, developed from ideas that she held in common with Sartre, no doubt influenced and inspired Sartre's own thoughts on authenticity. Then again, Sartre wrote about authenticity in his *War Diaries* and in his letters to de Beauvoir as early as 1939. Who first thought what is generally not a particularly useful game to play when considering de Beauvoir and Sartre, although it is a game that some people are all too fond of playing. Precisely because they were such fiercely independent thinkers they were never reluctant to exchange thoughts and opinions with each other and there was a constant interplay and refinement of ideas between them. Throughout Sartre's career de Beauvoir meticulously checked every one of his manuscripts before it was published, making corrections and offering suggestions for improvement. Each philosopher was constantly the midwife of the other's thoughts and as a result each greatly influenced the philosophical ideas and personal and political values of the other.

Certainly, de Beauvoir influenced Sartre towards a greater appreciation of the social aspects of human existence, not least through her most famous, important and controversial work, *The Second Sex* (1949), in which she analyses from multiple perspectives – existentialist, Marxist, historical, anthropological, biological, psychoanalytic and literary – the secondary role assigned to women by society. Man, she argues, is defined as *subject* in relation to woman who is relegated to being man's **Other**. De Beauvoir calls for an end to this long-standing oppression, demanding the necessary socio-political conditions be created for woman's emancipation and the re-establishment of her selfhood. *The Second Sex* heralded a feminist revolution. In seeking to influence Sartre towards a greater appreciation of the social aspects of human existence she did not charge him with being blind or resistant to the notion, instead she recognized that in

his major work **Being and Nothingness** (1943) Sartre had been preoccupied with describing individual existence and experience. Duly influenced,
Sartre eventually wrote **Critique of Dialectical Reason** (1960), an
ambitious work in which he seeks to synthesize existentialism, with its
concern for the individual, with the socio-political philosophy of Marxism.

De Beauvoir may emphasize one point and Sartre another, and there are
themes that Sartre explores that never appear in de Beauvoir's writings and
vice versa, but their thinking always has a common **phenomenological**
root. Sartre may have become increasingly involved with Marxism and de
Beauvoir with feminism but this is not to say that they had ceased to agree
with or influence each other, or that they had lost interest in each other's
deliberations.

They did, of course, not always agree. They disagreed with each other
frequently with a passion, but this disagreement was always a respectful,
ultimately constructive debate that sought to thrash out thesis and
antithesis so as to produce a synthesis of ideas that could be accommo-
dated within the body of existentialist and later on Marxist thought.

Though Sartre was, of course, quite capable of standing up for himself,
de Beauvoir was always willing to defend him against his critics, especially
when she felt a fundamental misunderstanding or misrepresentation of
Sartre's philosophy had occurred. Most notably, in an article, 'Merleau-
Ponty et le Pseudo-Sartrisme' (1955), she argues that the Sartre
Merleau-Ponty takes to task in his *Phenomenology of Perception* (1945) is
a Sartre of his own invention; a pseudo-Sartre. She accuses Merleau-Ponty
of overlooking certain key passages in *Being and Nothingness* and of taking
others out of context. The result being a misrepresentation of Sartre's
philosophy that fails to give full credit to Sartre's notion of **facticity**,
confounds his notions of **consciousness** and subjectivity and largely
ignores his references to the importance of the **past**. One of de Beauvoir's
novels, *The Mandarins* (1954), also alludes to the relationship between
Sartre and Merleau-Ponty as colleagues at the journal **Les Temps**
modernes and the strain placed upon that relationship by Sartre's initial
reluctance to accept post-war revelations about the brutality of Stalin's
Soviet regime.

In 1981, one year after Sartre's death in 1980, de Beauvoir published
Adieux: A Farewell to Sartre, a moving biography of the last decade of
Sartre's life. In 1983 she published the many letters she had received from

him and her *Letters to Sartre* appeared in 1992. De Beauvoir died in Paris on April 14, 1986, having made an enormous contribution to existentialist and feminist thought. She was buried next to Sartre. Without her influence Sartre's philosophical contribution would certainly have been different and probably diminished, and vice versa. She remains an important and much discussed thinker, both in relation to Sartre and in her own right.

death   See **affirmation of mortality, being-towards-death, everydayness, mortality** and **ownmost possibility**.

deceiver–deceived duality   The **psychic duality** required for genuine deception to take place. This duality exists in the case of two separate consciousnesses but not, according to **Sartre**, within a single **consciousness**. It is impossible for the deceiver also to be the deceived because it is impossible for a person both to know and not know something at the same time. If a person cynically attempts to lie to himself he will always catch himself in the act. It is the essence of a lie that the liar knows the truth he is hiding. It is a common misconception that **bad faith** is **self-deception** and it often appears that it is, but as self-deception is impossible this cannot be the case. Sartre's description of bad faith avoids the suggestion that it is self-deception involving a deceiver–deceived duality. In Sartre's view, bad faith is akin to **self-distraction** rather than self-deception, it is a project of evasion rather than a project of deception in the strict sense of the word. See also **Freud** and **translucency**.

deception   See **self-deception**.

Descartes, René (1596–1650)   French philosopher and mathematician. Known as the father of modern philosophy. Descartes revived the spirit of scepticism and genuine free enquiry that had characterized the philosophy of the Ancient Greeks. In his *Meditations on First Philosophy* (1641) Descartes takes his philosophizing back to basics, doubting everything that can possibly be doubted in the hope of discovering something absolutely certain. Through this 'method of doubt' he establishes the proposition 'I think therefore I am' as fundamental and indubitable. His overall approach leads him to characterize mind and body as externally related (see **external relations**), as two distinct substances each having being in its own right. Perhaps the major preoccupation of Continental philosophy since Descartes has been to identify and overcome the problems of his **dualism** and offer a more coherent philosophy of mind. **Sartre** is part of this tradition. He describes himself as a post-Cartesian, acknowledging Descartes as the founder of the debate in which he is engaged. Though Sartre's own conclusions are often directly opposed to Descartes', he nonetheless recognizes him as a great influence and inspiration.

In comparing Sartre and Descartes, Sartre scholars have described Descartes as an indirect realist and Sartre as a direct realist. Cartesian indirect realism holds that (1) The world can exist without any minds in it and (2) Mind can exist without any surrounding material world. If mind exists independently of the world and is directly aware of ideas rather than the world then it is not certain that ideas correspond to anything external to the mind. Indirect realists insist that ideas of the world are caused by the world but they have no way of proving this and hence no way of avoiding what Sartre calls 'the reef of solipsism'. **Solipsism** is the view that one's own mind is all that exists. The fact that it inevitably collapses into solipsism is one of the central, irretrievable flaws of Cartesian dualism/indirect realism. Sartre's response to Descartes is to reject claim (2) of his indirect realism and retain claim (1), arguing that minds exist only in relation to the world and only in so far as they intend objects (see **intentionality**). For Sartre, mind, or what he prefers to call **consciousness**, is nothing in itself and must be consciousness of a surrounding world in order to be. Sartre's direct realism contains no 'proof of an external world' as such, but if his theory of consciousness as a relation to the world is convincing then the threat of solipsism ceases to be an issue. See also **quasi-duality** and **realism**.

desire   See **lack, love, 'man is a useless passion', pseudo-irreducibles, sexual desire** and *Sketch for a Theory of the Emotions*.

despair   See **abandonment, absurdity, Camus, Kierkegaard,** *Nausea*, **nihilism** and *The Wall*.

determinism   The theory that all human actions are causally determined and that there is no such phenomenon as free will. Determinism implies that there are no genuine choices because if all actions are determined then it was not possible for a person to have taken an alternative course of action from the one he took. Sartre's theory of **existential freedom** is opposed to determinism. See also **anti-determinism** and **choice**.

differentiated being   See **being, differentiated**.

Dirty Hands (1948)   Alternative title *Crime Passionnel*. A play by **Sartre** in which a young man, Hugo Barine, is sent to assassinate Hoederer, a leader of the radical, left-wing political party to which they both belong. A faction within the party wants Hoederer assassinated because of his plans to form a national coalition government with liberals and conservatives. Such a compromise, any compromise, is considered an intolerable deviation from official party policy. Hugo's own motives in wishing to carry out the assassination are questionable. Are they political or personal? Hugo is in **bad faith** in so far as he seeks to convince himself that his motives are political. As the play reveals, he is not so much driven by political idealism as by a desire to change himself and thereby the way others view him. Hugo is deeply dissatisfied with his **being-for-others**. Other party members dismiss him as a young, bourgeois intellectual, the ordinary people laugh at his political views and his campaigning, his wife Jessica treats him like a child and his father sees him as a failure. He is so desperate to be taken seriously that he is prepared to kill. He hopes and believes that by killing he will become a man of substance, a decisive man of action who will be feared and respected for his ruthlessness and admired for the apparent firmness of his convictions. Like the central character of Sartre's short story ***Erostratus*** (1939), Paul Hilbert, who also becomes a killer, Hugo wants to take final and complete control of his being-for-others through a decisive act that will define him beyond question. As he says at the end of the play, 'I wanted to hang a crime round my neck, like a stone.' Hugo wants to exchange the insubstantiality and **indeterminacy** he feels so strongly as a **being-for-itself**, for the solidity and substantiality, not of a **being-in-itself**, but of a **being-for-itself-in-itself**.

Not unlike Lucien Fleurier, the central character of Sartre's short story, ***The Childood of a Leader*** (1939), and many other characters in Sartre's stories and plays, Hugo is struggling with issues of self-identity. Sartre recognizes that this is true of all people to some extent. As he says of himself in **Words** (1964), the autobiography of his childhood, until he decided to become a writer he felt as though he was travelling on a train without a ticket; travelling through life without justification for his absurd existence. Sartre also recognizes that every person, every being-for-itself, is striving in vain to become a being-for-itself-in-itself – a being that is founded upon itself rather than upon the world of which it is conscious. Fortunately, unlike Paul Hilbert, Lucien Fleurier and Hugo Barine, most people do not seek to obtain this goal through violence, although many do. Hugo wants to feel significant, necessary and indispensable, and he sees winning positive regard from others as a way of achieving this. Unfortunately, he is incapable of winning positive regard from others by reasonable, constructive means because he is self-obsessed and shows others too much resentment for them to warm to him. In desperation he decides to *demand* positive regard from others, or at least grudging respect, by becoming a killer.

Ironically, the only character in the play that shows Hugo respect and is prepared to take him seriously is Hoederer. Hugo finds himself drawn to Hoederer who is strong, intelligent and respected and seems to possess the heroic substantiality Hugo lacks. Above all, Hoederer is decisive. He is prepared to get *dirty hands* acting with expediency against the endlessly theorizing idealists and political purists in his party to secure a genuine practical advantage. By acting alongside Hoederer, Hugo has the opportunity to change the person he is and become a true revolutionary, but he does not have the imagination or will to commit himself to such a project. As Hoederer is finally obliged to point out, Hugo will never become a true revolutionary because he has no love for people. He is an intellectual who hates men because he hates himself. 'An intellectual is never a true revolutionary; he's only just good enough to be an assassin.'

Hoederer's words are proved right when Hugo eventually shoots him in a fit of jealously after Jessica develops an infatuation for him. Hugo's killing of Hoederer is not the cold-blooded assassination Hugo wanted it to be, but neither is it truly a crime of passion. Hugo is motivated by a sense of his own inadequacy and insubstantiality far more than by any passion he has for Jessica.

Two years later Hugo is released from prison. The party has U-turned and adopted Hoederer's policy of collaboration, the policy for which they once

condemned Hoederer to death. Hoederer's reputation has been rehabili-
tated. The party want to cover up the fact that they sent Hugo to kill him.
They want Hugo to take on a new identity, to forget that he ever knew
Hoederer or killed him, to deny his past and Hoederer's. During his time in
prison Hugo has become increasingly ashamed that he killed Hoederer in a
fit of jealousy. He wishes he had killed him for being a collaborator, that his
motives had been moral and political. That way he would feel less
ashamed. He decides that he would feel even more ashamed denying that
he killed Hoederer at all. To deny that he killed Hoederer would make it
appear Hoederer died by accident and for nothing. Hugo decides he owes
it to Hoederer to assert that he was sent by the party to kill him, thus
emphasizing that Hoederer did not die for nothing but for his ideals and his
policy; that he was a great man responsible for his own death. In a sense,
the party give Hugo the opportunity to finally kill Hoederer for the political
reasons for which he was sent to kill him in the first place. The party enable
Hugo to redeem his past and to achieve **authenticity** like his hero
Hoederer. At the end of the play, like Hoederer, Hugo stands up for his
beliefs and asserts his **freedom** even in face of the execution he will suffer
because of his refusal to follow party orders.

disembodied consciousness   See **consciousness, disembodied**.

Disorder and Genius   See ***Kean***.

double negation   See **negation, double**.

double property   A human being is both a subject and an object. This
is his double property. He is a subject, a **being-for-itself**, a **transcendence**, a **being-in-the-world** in so far as he transcends the world towards
his possibilities. He is also an object, a **facticity**, a **being-in-the-midst-of-
the-world** in so far as he has a physical body that exists as an object
alongside other objects from the point of view of other people. **Sartre**
most often uses the term 'double property' when referring to facticity and
transcendence. A person is both a facticity and a transcendence, or, more
precisely, he is the transcendence of his facticity. **Bad faith** involves various
attempts to manipulate and distort the double property of the human
being.

double reciprocal incarnation See **sexual desire**.

dualism The view, most commonly associated with **Descartes**, that mind and body are distinct entities existing independently of each other. Descartes identifies the body as *res extensa* (extended in space) and the mind as *res cogitans* (mental substance having ideas). Dualism assumes that the relationship between mind and body is like the relationship between two objects, external rather than internal. In assuming that mind and body are independent and externally related, dualism raises a number of intractable problems. For example, it is unable to offer a satisfactory explanation of how mind and body interact. Descartes resorts to arguing that mind and body interact in the pineal gland at the base of the brain, which fails to answer the question of *how* they interact. Though **Sartre** considered himself to be a Neo-Cartesian, a French philosopher in the tradition of Descartes, Sartre's theory of **consciousness** is opposed to dualism and driven by a desire to circumvent it. For Sartre, mind, consciousness or **being-for-itself** is not a mental substance, a distinct entity with its own independent existence, it is *intentional*, it exists only in so far as it *intends* objects (see **intentionality**). As Sartre says, **'consciousness is consciousness of ___'**. As nothing but the negation of **being-in-itself** consciousness is internally related to being-in-itself and entirely dependent on it for its **borrowed being**. This view of mind and body, consciousness and world, avoids the problems of dualism. See also **external relations** and **internal relation**.

— **E** —

ekstasis **(of time)** Greek for 'standing out from'. **Sartre** refers to each of the three dimensions of time – **past, present** and **future** – as an *ekstasis*, in that each dimension stands outside of itself in the other two and has being only in terms of the other two. The past is a **past-future**, the future a **future-past** and the present the **presence** of **being-for-itself** to **being-in-itself** as a perpetual **temporal flight** from the past towards the future. Sartre refers to this temporal structure as *ekstatic*. See **temporality**.

Elkaïm-Sartre, Arlette (c. 1936–)   Algerian Jewish writer and musician. Sartre's adopted daughter and heiress to his estate. Arlette Elkaïm first met **Sartre** in the mid-1950s when she called at his apartment to discuss *Being and Nothingness* (1943) for her philosophy dissertation. They became close friends, travelling widely and Sartre eventually adopted her in 1965, 'So that, when I'm old, you'll push my wheelchair'. Sartre was approaching sixty and knew that when he died Arlette would manage his estate, his legacy and the posthumous publication of various works. She has done so, perhaps somewhat over-protectively, since his death in 1980.

embodiment   For **Sartre**, **being-for-itself** is not a being that happens to be attached to the human body, as though it could exist independently of the human body. Being-for-itself is *necessarily* embodied in that it exists only as the **transcendence** of the **facticity** of its immediate bodily situation and not as a transcendent being in its own right. The body is always the immediate and inescapable situation of being-for-itself. See also **disembodied consciousness**, **incarnation**, **Merleau-Ponty** and **situatedness**.

The Emotions: Outline of a Theory   See *Sketch for a Theory of the Emotions*.

epochē   See **Husserl** and *Transcendence of the Ego*.

Erostratus (1939)   A short story by **Sartre** contained in a collection of short stories entitled *The Wall*, *The Wall* being the lead story in the collection. The narrator and central character of the story is Paul Hilbert, an alienated, cold-hearted, misanthropic loner with dangerous psychotic tendencies. Though Paul has no interest in people on a personal level – he despises them and finds them physically repulsive – he wants to impress mankind with an act of infamy for which, like Erostratus, he will always be remembered. Erostratus was an Ancient Greek who, lacking the talent to immortalize his name in any other way, burnt down the temple of Ephesus, one of the seven wonders of the ancient world.

Paul decides that he will go out into the streets of Paris and indiscriminately shoot six people with a revolver. Not unlike Hugo Barine in Sartre's play, ***Dirty Hands*** (1948), Paul wants to perform a decisive act the consequences of which cannot be undone. He believes that the supremely decisive act of killing will make him a less indeterminate, more substantial person who is universally feared and respected. He aspires to become a **being-for-itself-in-itself** – a being that is founded upon itself rather than upon the world of which it is conscious. Paul becomes obsessed with his plan, he fantasizes, sometimes sexually, about shooting people or blowing them up with a bomb. He neglects his office job until he is dismissed. He sends letters to 102 French writers explaining what he is going to do and why. He lives expensively, intending to carry out his shooting spree when all his money has gone.

With only 17½ francs left he takes his revolver and leaves his room in a state of high **anxiety** intending to kill. Overcome by fear and confusion in the large crowd he is unable to do the deed. He returns to his room and stays there for three days without eating or sleeping, psyching himself up for the 'execution'. Angry, excited and anxious he returns once again to the street. Again he is overcome by fear and confusion, he hardly knows where he is going or what he is doing, but finally he manages to shoot a big man three times in the belly. He runs away in a direction opposite to that he had planned, firing two more shots to disperse the crowd. He locks himself in the lavatory of a café as a crowd gathers outside. It seems to him that the crowd are waiting outside the door for him to shoot himself. He resents this. He puts the barrel of the gun in his mouth but lacks the courage to squeeze the trigger. He throws the revolver down and opens the door.

Erostratus enters the mind of a psychopath, detailing, from his own point of view, the relentless progression of his obsessive misanthropy from fantasy to violent action. Paul tells his story in a sparse, matter-of-fact way, offering us little or no insight into the past that may have shaped him. He tells us only that he was born hating the human spirit that most men love and has no idea why he is like he is. With no authorial voice passing judgement on Paul the reader is left to draw his or her own conclusions about him from an analysis of his words and deeds.

His loathing of the **Other**, the focus of all his thoughts, is arguably a distraction from the deep self-loathing that is at the root of his mental condition. Symptomatic of his self-loathing is the fact that he will not allow the prostitutes he hires to touch him or pay him any attention. He wants, by the way he looks at them and the way he makes them move, to reduce them to objects, to their **being-in-the-midst-of-the-world**. He meticulously avoids running the risk that they will transcend his **transcendence** and reduce him to an object, to a **transcendence-transcended**. He cannot abide others because he cannot abide his **being-for-others**. He wants to annihilate others so as not to exist as a being for them. Furthermore, because he knows he cannot annihilate all others, he wants to take final and complete control of his being-for-others by defining himself as a 'black hero', as an infamous villain, a definition he believes others will accept and never question.

Modern times have seen a huge increase in the number of indiscriminate shootings and bombings conducted for personal and/or political motives. The reasons for this trend are complex but undoubtedly the emergence of a global mass media has made an enormous contribution to it. Any psychopath can achieve instant, world-wide recognition for himself or the cause he identifies himself with if he succeeds in slaughtering enough innocent people. In light of this, *Erostratus* has particular contemporary resonance.

eternal recurrence   **Nietzsche** hypothesizes that given infinite time everything recurs eternally. Whether or not eternal recurrence is the case, however, is less important to Nietzsche than the fact that the idea of eternal recurrence provides a means by which a person can evaluate his life. A person who genuinely desires to live his life all over again in every detail affirms his life to the highest degree by taking full **responsibility** for it without **regret**. He does not desire that any moment of his life had been different, and to the extent that he is the sum total of his experiences, he does not wish he was someone else. He is authentic. Nietzsche recommends that every person adopt as his **formula for greatness** an aspiration to live in such away that he desires eternal recurrence. Sartre's philosophy contains no notion of eternal recurrence but his views on **authenticity** compare with the views that Nietzsche expresses through the idea of eternal recurrence. Like Nietzsche, **Sartre** holds that authenticity involves taking full responsibility for oneself and one's **past** and living without regret. See also **noble ideal** and **will to power**.

everydayness   Mediocrity. **Heidegger** argues that human existence is essentially **being-towards-death**. **Death** is a person's **ownmost possibility** and each person is the unique possibility of his own death. In anticipating his own death a person realizes he is a unique individual and not just another person. In realizing he is unique he escapes the mediocrity of ordinary, everyday life wherein people take themselves for granted and carry on as though they were just another person destined to live the predictable, everyday, seemingly endless existence prescribed to them by social expectations. Outwardly, the life of the person who has embraced his mortality may be no different from that of his neighbour who has not, but in embracing his mortality he has made his life uniquely his own, he has achieved **authenticity**, at least in the Heideggerian sense of authentic-being-towards-death. A person who lives his life in anticipation of his own death will be motivated to live life to the full and to get the most out of it rather than to hold back in timid and ultimately futile self-preservation. Heavily influenced by Heidegger's views, Sartre's **existentialism** certainly recognizes what Heidegger refers to as 'everydayness'. **Sartre** holds that mortality, as one of the **existential truths** of the **human condition**, must be acknowledged if a person is to escape mediocrity and **bad faith** and achieve authenticity. Sartre, however, disagrees with Heidegger that human existence is essentially being-towards-death on the grounds that death is the *limit* of all possibility rather than itself a possibility. See also **affirmation of mortality**.

'existence precedes essence'   A maxim often used to summarize the core principle of Sartre's **existentialism**. Existence (the world, **being-in-itself**) is logically prior to essence (**being-for-itself, consciousness**, ideas, meaning). **Sartre** holds that existence is fundamental and that essence is logically subsequent to existence and arises through the **negation** of existence. Although Sartre himself uses the phrases 'existence precedes essence' and '*existence* comes before *essence*' in *Existentialism and Humanism* (1946), the terms 'existence' and 'essence' are somewhat misleading in the context of his philosophy. The term 'existence' does not allow for the important distinction Sartre draws between being-in-itself or **undifferentiated being** and **phenomena** or **differentiated being** and could always refer to either of them. Being-in-itself *is*, whereas phenomena are founded upon **non-being**. That is, phenomena emerge for being-for-itself, which is the negation of being, when it negates being (see **double negation**). As for the term 'essence', Sartre normally avoids it because of its metaphysical connotations. It suggests that whatever is common to a series of particular things exists independently of them in a formal, abstract, metaphysical sense. Sartre denies abstract essences and is fond of arguing against idealist philosophers like Plato that there is 'nothing beyond the series' of particular things. *Existentialism and Humanism* was originally a lecture delivered at a popular literary event and when Sartre uses the phrase 'existence precedes essence' he simply means to convey that a person, unlike a created object made according to a plan, exists first and defines himself, his 'essence', afterwards. For the sake of giving people a ready handle on his **existentialism** he was prepared to use terms that they would immediately understand even though his philosophy was somewhat distorted in the process. He clearly thought this was a price worth paying and it is undeniable that explaining and discussing Sartre's famous maxim is a good way of introducing people to his philosophy and inspiring them to investigate further. See also **ontology** and **idealism**.

existential   Of or relating to **existentialism**. Existing, actual, real, concrete or personal, as opposed to theoretical, formal, ideal, abstract or impersonal. Legitimate, authentic or genuine: an existential threat, for example, as opposed to a possible or supposed threat. That which is existential need not be physical, corporeal, material. An absence, for example, can be an **existential absence** rather than a **formal absence**. What makes an existential absence, or any other such **lack**, *existential* is that it defines and characterizes the concrete situation of a particular person or persons. 'Existential' also refers to the fundamental, irrevocable, inescapable features of existence, particularly human existence: the **existential truths** of the **human condition**. With regard to an emotion such as **anxiety**, the adjective 'existential' is meant to emphasize that the emotion is not a mere feeling rooted in physiology but a central feature of a person's relationship with his world. **Existential psychoanalysis** aims to understand a person's behaviour and disposition by investigating his unique personal history. It avoids applying impersonal psychological categories to his behaviour and disposition; labels, as **Laing** points out, that do not serve to explain him so much as explain him away.

existential absence   An absence or **lack** that characterizes a person's concrete situation as opposed to a **formal absence** that is a mere abstract idea having no real bearing on the situation. In *Being and Nothingness*

(1943), **Sartre** gives an example in which he is waiting in a café for his friend Pierre who is late. Pierre's absence is an existential absence that defines the situation for the person expecting him. Pierre's absence is not merely *thought*, it is an actual event in the café that characterizes the café as the place from which Pierre is absent. Expectation is not simply a feeling but the way in which a person encounters his world as presently lacking something for him. See also **existential**.

existential freedom   See **freedom, existential**.

existential project   A term originally employed by **Merleau-Ponty** referring to an individual or collective project involving spontaneous action to bring about actual concrete changes in circumstances. An existential project is distinct from what Merleau-Ponty refers to as an **intellectual project**. Specifically, Merleau-Ponty views social revolution as an existential project and accuses **Sartre** of treating it as an intellectual project.

existential psychoanalysis   A form of psychoanalysis founded by **Sartre** that places emphasis on the detailed exploration of a person's personal history in order to discover the nature of his unique **fundamental choice** of himself and his resulting **fundamental project**. Sartre agrees with the traditional psychoanalysis founded by **Freud** that personality is predominantly shaped by early experiences, but he disagrees with the emphasis that traditional psychoanalysis places on certain supposedly fundamental or irreducible drives and desires – **pseudo-irreducibles** – in its attempts to explain personality. Freud, for example, appeals to **sexual desire** to explain many complex behavioural phenomena while treating sexual desire itself as an irreducible. For Sartre, a person's sexual desire and sexuality are not fundamental or irreducible but complex phenomena that require analysis and deconstruction. Sartre's biographies, ***Baudelaire*** (1946), ***Saint Genet*** (1952) and ***The Family Idiot*** (1971–2) are detailed psychological case studies that employ and exhibit the methods of existential psychoanalysis. See also **Laing**.

existential truths   The fundamental inescapable truths of human existence: **abandonment, freedom, responsibility,** change, **lack, indeterminacy, desire, mortality, contingency, being-for-others** and so on. **Bad faith** involves obscuring the existential truths and living as though they are not the case. **Authenticity**, on the other hand, involves confronting the existential truths and living in a manner that affirms rather than denies them. See also **Camus** and *Truth and Existence*.

existentialism   A broad intellectual movement of largely Continental philosophers, psychologists, novelists, dramatists, artists and filmmakers that developed in the nineteenth and twentieth centuries and remains influential today. The movement is defined by its shared concerns rather than by a set of common principles to which all **existentialist** thinkers subscribe, although there are principles common to many of them. Existentialism is primarily concerned with providing a coherent description of the **human condition** that fully recognizes and incorporates the fundamental or **existential truths** pertaining to that condition. **Freedom**, **responsibility**, **indeterminacy**, **desire**, guilt, the existence of others (see **being-for-others**), **mortality**, the elusiveness or non-existence of **God** and so on. In the nineteenth century these truths became the concern of the Christian philosopher Søren **Kierkegaard**, and the atheist and romantic philosophers, Arthur Schopenhauer (1788–1860) and Friedrich **Nietzsche**, who, in their different ways, set the agenda for what later became known as existentialism. The concerns of Kierkegaard, Schopenhauer and Nietzsche were taken up during the first half of the twentieth century by Karl Jaspers (1883–1969) – who coined the phrase 'existence philosophy' – Martin **Heidegger**, Jean-Paul **Sartre**, Simone **de Beauvoir**, Maurice **Merleau-Ponty** and Albert **Camus**. Their writings established existentialism as a distinct branch of philosophy. The ideas of these philosophers converge to form a largely coherent system of thought. At the heart of their system is the maxim **'existence precedes essence'**. This maxim encapsulates a view that is fundamentally opposed to **idealism**, the view that there are no metaphysical essences giving reality or meaning to particular things. There are particular things and there is nothing beyond the series of particular things other than **consciousness**, which is nothing but consciousness *of* particular things. With specific regard to people, 'existence precedes essence' refers to the view that each person exists first, without meaning and purpose, and strives thereafter to give himself meaning and purpose. A person's essence is to have no essence other than the one he must continually invent for himself. Mainstream existentialism, then, is anti-idealist, anti-metaphysical and atheistic. It sees mankind as occupying an indifferent universe that is meaningless to the point of **absurdity**. Any meaning that is to be found must be established by each person from within the sphere of his own individual existence. A person who supposes that his meaning comes ready-made or that there is an ultimate purpose to human existence established externally by a deity or deities is deluded and a coward in face of reality. As indicated, not all thinkers who deserve existentialist credentials will endorse all of these viewpoints. The novelist Fyodor Dostoevsky (1821–81), for example, clearly an existentialist thinker in many respects, is evidently, like Kierkegaard, not an atheist. Existentialism is a broad church that includes religious thinkers such as Paul Tillich (1886–1965), Martin Buber (1878–1965), Karl Barth (1886–1968) and Gabriel Marcel (1889–1973), and atheist thinkers such as Samuel Beckett (1906–89). The director Bernardo Bertolucci (1940–) explores existentialist themes in his films and the psychologist R.D. **Laing** defines the mental conditions of psychosis and schizophrenia in existential-ist terms. Shakespeare (1564–1616), in retrospect, particularly the mature Shakespeare of the great tragedies, is recognizably, even profoundly, exis-tentialist. Existentialism, as a way of viewing the human condition, has been around much longer than the term itself. Sartre initially rejected the term, preferring '**phenomenological ontology**' or 'philosophy of existence', but soon adopted it in face of popular insistence upon it.

Existentialism and Humanism (1946)   A short philosophical work by **Sartre** that was originally delivered as a lecture at a fashionable literary event in Paris on October 29, 1945 at the Salle des Centraux. It is reported that there was fainting in the audience when Sartre first referred to **existentialism** as a humanism – as endorsing **atheism** and so on – although other sources suggest that the fainting was simply due to the heat. Sartre's desire to shock and entertain his bourgeois audience, which is evident throughout the work, unfortunately led him to distort and over-simplify some of his views. A common position among Sartre scholars is that the work is somewhat unrepresentative, and Sartre himself came to regret its publication and even rejected some of its conclusions in later writings. Despite its various faults, *Existentialism and Humanism* remains one of Sartre's most popular philosophical works. Its brevity and accessibility, its brusque and provocative style, make it an undeniably useful introduction, not only to existentialism, but also to Sartre himself as a challenging, icono-clastic philosopher. The work creates an exciting and thought-provoking first impression that often inspires people to pursue the far more detailed and accurate understanding of existentialism to be gained from Sartre's far less brief and accessible work, **Being and Nothingness** (1943).

Existentialism and Humanism undertakes to defend existentialism against various criticisms that have been levelled against it by Christians, rationalists and other advocates of conventional moral and social values. Sartre argues that existentialism is not, as it is accused of being, a pes-simistic philosophy that dwells on **anxiety** and **despair**, but in fact an optimistic philosophy that sets out to empower people by revealing to them that they are masters of their own destiny. Existentialism argues that people are abandoned in a Godless universe (see **abandonment**), but it draws from this apparently despairing position the positive conclusion that people are free to choose and responsible for the choices they make. In one of the most useful passages of *Existentialism and Humanism*, as regards under-standing the basics of existentialism, Sartre argues that the non-existence of a divine creator means that, for humans, **'existence precedes essence'**. Unlike a knife, for example, the idea or essence of which is in the mind of the artisan before it comes into existence, a person exists first and must choose his essence – his meaning and purpose – thereafter. In arguing that human existence precedes human essence, Sartre rejects the idea of a universal **human nature**, the view that there is a fixed and determined essence common to all people. He does, however, argue that there is a universal **human condition**, in so far as everyone, regardless of their particular circumstances, is free, mortal and so on.

According to Sartre, people become anxious when they realize that they must choose what they do, what they are and what is of value to them. This anxiety or anguish leads some to 'deceive' themselves that they lack **freedom**. They act in **bad faith**, doing as they are told and adopting without question the values that are given to them by society and religion.*

---

*In his major work *Being And Nothingness* (1943), Sartre clearly distinguishes bad faith from **self-deception**, arguing that even though bad faith looks like self-deception, it is not. Self-deception is impossible, and to describe bad faith as self-deception is, at best, a convenient oversimplification. In *Existentialism and Humanism*, however, he speaks of self-deception *rather* than bad faith, deliberately oversimplifying his philosophy in response to the various situational constraints of the original lecture. Such inaccuracies are the reason why the work must be read with caution.

Existentialism and Humanism contains by far the best-known illustration of Sartre's radical or **groundless choice** thesis in any of his writings. Sartre gives the example of a student of his who faces the dilemma of leaving home to fight for the Resistance or staying home to take care of his afflicted mother. There is no question that the student must reach a decision, yet there are, according to Sartre, no grounds for deciding which course of **action** to take. Ethical formulae are unhelpful as these have only the value he chooses to give them. The student is **'condemned to be free'** and must, therefore, make an arbitrary decision. He must plunge into one or other course of action without reason or justification. Sartre's general claim is that ultimately **choice** is always and unavoidably based upon arbitrary decisions. His view is that if a choice could be guided and influenced in any way by beliefs, convictions or values it would be a caused phenomenon rather than a genuinely free choice. Sartre, mistakenly according to critics such as **Merleau-Ponty**, does not allow that choices can in some sense be caused and yet remain choices. Unfortunately, Sartre's groundless choice thesis cannot be treated as a mere aberration, as the result of the relative superficiality of *Existentialism and Humanism*, as it is a view he expresses consistently elsewhere.

Apart from his naively positive beliefs regarding the political status of the proletariat in Russia in 1945, Sartre's most infamous error in *Existentialism and Humanism* is his claim that when a person chooses a course of action, marriage for example, he chooses it for everyone in so far as he asserts by his choice that everyone ought to do as he does. This moral theory is not only a confused version of Kant's theory of the Categorical Imperative, it is inconsistent with the central claims of Sartre's own existentialism (see **Kant**).

existentialist   Of or relating to the intellectual movement known as **existentialism**. A person, **Sartre** for example, whose work and ideas contribute to existentialism. Anyone who broadly subscribes to the theories and outlook of existentialism or attempts to live according to its principles.

existentialist ethics   **Sartre** repeatedly insists in various works that taking **responsibility**, affirming **freedom** and striving for **authenticity** are good, while **bad faith** in its various forms is bad, and he certainly had a very strong personal sense of right and wrong that led him to take up many moral and political crusades. He is, however, less certain when it comes to invoking the authority of philosophical ethics to support his moral sentiments and opinions. Sartre's promise at the end of ***Being and Nothingness*** (1943) to produce a fully developed **existentialist** theory of ethics, consistent with the central claims of his **existentialism**, was never really fulfilled, although between 1945 and 1948 he made extensive notes on ethics many of which were published posthumously in 1983 as ***Notebooks for an Ethics***. These notebooks have become the main basis of informed speculation by Sartre scholars as to what a Sartrean existentialist ethics might have looked like had he succeeded in fully formulating one. The direction of Sartre's thought in that work is towards the view that ethics is other-related authenticity and involves people respecting and affirming each other's freedom.

In ***Existentialism and Humanism*** (1946), a work more or less contemporary with *Notebooks for an Ethics*, Sartre, in his quest for an existentialist ethics, flirts with an ill-formed version of Kantian or deontological ethics (see **Kant**). Sartre argues that in choosing a particular course of action a person is advocating that everyone should choose it. For example, if a man gets married he is advocating that all men should get married. Sartre soon rejected this particular theory as confused and unconvincing, although he continues to flirt with Kantian ethics in other respects in his *Notebooks for an Ethics*.

existentialist ideal   For most **existentialist** philosophers, including **Sartre**, the ideal life is one of sustained authentic existence (see **sustained authenticity**). In ***Saint Genet*** (1952) Sartre portrays the writer Jean Genet as a hero who manages through sustained effort to come very close to achieving the existentialist ideal. Although sustained authentic existence appears to be unachievable, certainly for the vast majority of people, the suggestion is that it is nonetheless an ideal worth aiming at. See also **authenticity** and **noble ideal**.

external relations   The kind of relationships that hold between objects from the point of view of **consciousness**. Spatial or causal relationships. The relationships with which the empirical sciences deal. Relationships that are posited by consciousness in its experience of the world. For example, A is to the left of B. A is not to the left of B in itself, but to the left of B for a consciousness that posits this external relation between A and B from a particular point of view. Consciousness posits external relations, but its own relation to the world, the relation that it is, is not an external relation but an **internal relation**. The philosophy of **Descartes**, his **dualism**, is fundamentally flawed in treating the relationship between mind and world as external when in fact it is internal. Following **Hegel** and **Husserl**, **Sartre** treats the relationship between mind and world as internal.

— **F** —

facticity   The resistance or adversity presented by the world that free **action** constantly strives to overcome. The concrete situation of **being-for-itself**, including the physical **body**, in terms of which being-for-itself must choose itself by choosing its responses. The **for-itself** exists as a **transcendence**, but it is not a pure transcendence, it is the transcendence of its facticity. In its transcendence the for-itself is a **temporal flight** towards the **future** away from the facticity of its **past**. The past is an aspect of the facticity of the for-itself, the ground upon which it chooses its future. In confronting the **freedom** of the for-itself facticity does not limit the freedom of the for-itself. The freedom of the for-itself is limitless because there is no limit to its obligation to choose itself in face of its facticity. For example, having no legs limits a person's ability to walk but it does not limit his freedom in that he must perpetually choose the meaning of his disability. The for-itself cannot not be free because it cannot not choose itself in face of its facticity. The for-itself is necessarily free. This necessity is a facticity at the very heart of freedom. Comparable to Sartre's notion of facticity is his notion of the *practico-inert* as described in his **Critique of Dialectical Reason** (1960). See also **being-in-situation, choice, present-at-hand** and **situatedness**.

faith of bad faith   See **bad faith, faith of**.

faith of nihilism   See **nihilism, faith of**.

false consciousness   See **consciousness, false**.

The Family Idiot, Vols 1–3 (1971–72)   (The English translation is divided into five volumes.) A book by **Sartre** about the French novelist, Gustave Flaubert (1821–80), author of *Madame Bovary* (1857) and other works. Sartre's longest work at 2801 pages and his last significant work before his eyesight failed in 1973. His blindness meant that he was unable to write a planned fourth volume focusing on *Madame Bovary*.

As with Sartre's other books about writers – **Baudelaire** (1946) and **Saint Genet** (1952) – *The Family Idiot* is not so much a biography of Flaubert, detailing the main events of his life in chronological order, as an exhaustive psychological study, an exercise in **existential psychoanalysis**. It is also and at the same time an exhaustive sociological study from a Marxist perspective that seeks to explain Flaubert as both a product of, and a reaction to, the immediate social circumstances of his family life and the broader social circumstances of his age and culture. Sartre describes his method of investigation as 'regressive-progressive', a method he first outlined in **Search for a Method** (1960). The regressive phase of the method involves an analytical/psychoanalytical investigation of Flaubert's personality, while the progressive phase involves synthesizing the results of the psychoanalytic investigation with the results of a sociological investigation of Flaubert's economic, political, historical and cultural context. Sartre moves deftly between analysis and synthesis as required in order to *totalize* Flaubert, in order to comprehend Flaubert as a *totality*, as a unified whole. Sartre's view of most biographies, unsuccessful biographies, is that in simply listing lots of facts and events relating to a person they fail to grasp the person as a totality.

In attempting to classify *The Family Idiot* Sartre scholars have taken the notion of *totalization* and applied it to the work itself. Arguably, not only does this ambitious work seek to totalize Flaubert, it seeks to totalize Sartre's own philosophy in the process. That is, it seeks to synthesize all the central Sartrean elements and concerns – **phenomenology**, imagination, existential psychoanalysis, Marxism, literature, literary theory, biography – in order to answer Sartre's most abiding philosophical question: what is it to be a person?

Some Sartre scholars argue that in so far as *The Family Idiot* involves Sartre seeking to understand both what it is to be a person and the purposes of his own philosophy – he saw himself as inseparable from his writing – it is really Sartre seeking to understand himself. In short, *The Family Idiot* is Sartre's autobiography in disguise, the sequel to his 1964 autobiography, **Words**. Sartre denied this, pointing out that his childhood was unlike Flaubert's. He, for example, was doted on while Flaubert was 'underloved'. Far from seeing himself in Flaubert, Sartre claims he was fascinated with Flaubert as his opposite. Sartre, for example, was prolific, he wrote quickly, he always had more than one project on the go. Flaubert, on the other hand, was painstakingly slow, he could take years to write a book, endlessly researching and revising it. It remains a matter of debate how much of himself Sartre projects on to Flaubert both intentionally and unintentionally, but what is certain is that his biography of Flaubert returns to the central theme of *Words*: writing as a choice of being. The thesis that *The Family Idiot* is Sartre's autobiography in disguise is not really credible, but it is a work in which Sartre is obsessed with the *choice* to be a writer, a choice of self that was very much his own.

Sartre's preoccupation with the choice to be a writer explains why he chose a writer as the subject of his most ambitious case study. But why Flaubert and not, for example, Dostovesky? (In **Being and Nothingness** [1943], while drawing conclusions about existential psychoanalysis, Sartre proposes studies of both Flaubert and Dostoevsky.) The answers to this question are largely practical. Sartre had to choose someone, so why not Flaubert? There is a wealth of documentation by and about Flaubert that facilitates any investigation into his life, and Sartre had been intimately acquainted with Flaubert since childhood, having first encountered his work in the form of a small, cloth-bound book in his grandfather's library. Not least, Sartre identifies Flaubert as the 'creator of the modern novel', a response to the literature of the previous 150 years, and therefore as highly relevant to the history of eighteenth- and nineteenth-century literature that he spends so much time discussing in *The Family Idiot*, both for its own sake and as part of his extensive sociological investigation of Flaubert's context.

Sartre says of the young Gustave Flaubert, 'His family is a well, he is at the bottom.' He can rise up the well, but he remains imprisoned in it. The walls of the well were, as they are for every child, built before he was born.

Gustave's grandmother died giving birth to his mother, Caroline. His grandfather was heartbroken. The guilt Caroline felt over killing her mother was reinforced by the death of her father when she was ten. The father had not loved the daughter enough to want to go on living. Caroline resurrected her father and so eased her guilt by marrying his double, Achille-Cléophas Flaubert, a stiff, domineering, successful doctor several years her senior. At first the marriage was happy. Caroline doted on her husband and a son, Achille, was born. By the time Gustave arrived, however, Caroline had lost a number of children and her husband was having affairs. Caroline wanted a daughter, a female companion to compensate for her lonely childhood, so Gustave was a disappointment. Not only that, but as the two siblings who immediately preceded him had died, Gustave was not expected to survive. There was little maternal affection in the skilful care that the disappointing, futureless child received; it aimed only at pacifying him. Sartre identifies Flaubert's passivity as his **fundamental choice** of himself, at least until he underwent a **radical conversion** in his twenties. He was not encouraged to respond, to feel that he had a purpose, to feel that he could be something more than an object his mother was obliged to care for. Gustave fared no better with his father, whose attentions and hopes were directed towards Gustave's older brother, Achille, who eventually became a successful doctor like his father and of whom Gustave was deeply jealous. Pacified, overlooked as a person, Gustave's intellectual development was slow. He was unable to read at the age of seven. His family further reinforced the low self-esteem at the heart of his ennui by viewing him as an idiot.

Gustave was eventually taught to read by the local priest. Though still passive in his general demeanour and given to meditative stupors that made him appear a simpleton, Gustave took possession of his new-found ability and by the age of nine was writing stories. Dr Flaubert decided that his son would become a lawyer. Passive as ever, Gustave followed this plan, all the while developing a nervous disorder of a psychosomatic nature. The defining moment of Gustave's life occurred in 1844 when he suffered a nervous crisis, possibly an epileptic fit. Incapacitated by this crisis he was unable to pursue the career his father had chosen for him. His crisis, arguably self-induced, was the opportunity for Gustave to finally free himself of his father's domination and become a writer. The invalid, being no good for anything better, was left to write. The idiot was at last free to transform himself into a genius. For Sartre, Flaubert's crisis was a radical conversion to **authenticity**, an act of self-assertion in which he finally dispensed with his passivity, his choice not to choose, his **bad faith**. Through an act that had the outward appearance of a collapse, but was in fact a positive **affirmation of freedom**, he ceased to exist primarily for others and began to exist for himself.

To some *The Family Idiot* is Sartre's crowning glory, a work in which he brilliantly fuses together all the key elements of his life's work, to others it is a self-indulgent monstrosity that cobbles together a grotesque portrait of Flaubert with little regard for established facts. Oddly enough, there appears to be some credibility in both these claims, though the real truth lies somewhere in between. Undoubtedly, it is a work rich in insight, an impressive demonstration of a powerful method of investigation, an earnest and sustained effort by a great philosopher to solve the riddle of what makes a person.

Flaubert, Gustave   See *The Family Idiot*.

The Flies (1943)   A play by **Sartre** based on the Ancient Greek legend of Orestes. Written and first performed in Paris during the German occupation the play was an implicit commentary on the political situation.

Calling himself Philebus, Orestes returns as a young man to Argos the town of his birth. Orestes was sent away as a child fifteen years earlier when Aegistheus murdered Orestes' father, King Agamemnon, and married Orestes' mother, Clytemnestra. Argos has become a dismal place plagued by flies. The flies epitomize the sin and corruption of the people of Argos and the collective remorse they continue to suffer for failing to defend Agamemnon or avenge his murder. Orestes has only recently become aware of his personal history and his links with Argos so initially he is not inclined to take revenge on Aegistheus. Orestes plans to leave Argos without interfering and is encouraged to do so by the god Zeus who enjoys the misery and repentance of the people of Argos and wants the situation to remain as it is. Orestes, as Philebus, meets his sister Electra. She tells him how Clytemnestra treats her as a slave in her own home for refusing to honour Aegistheus. Orestes, still as Philebus, then meets Clytemnestra. She has no remorse for her part in the murder of Agamemnon but confesses that she has been racked with guilt for fifteen years for sending her child

Orestes away. She says that **confession** is the national pastime of Argos and that the endless guilt and repentance of the people is like a pestilence. This pestilence reaches its height once a year on the Day of the Dead when the ghosts of the dead are believed to rise up from the underworld to torment the people of Argos. Inspired by the arrival of Orestes, though she still does not know who he is, Electra dances with joy on the Day of the Dead defying the ghosts to attack her. She tells the people that ghosts are just shadows of remorse imagined by the living. The people start to believe her until Zeus frightens them back into their state of remorse by moving a large boulder. Orestes offers to help Electra escape Argos but she refuses to run away. He realizes that he too must stay, he must avenge his father's death and rid Argos of its pestilence of remorse. Though he is an intellectual who has never killed a man he realizes he must become a warrior and take decisive **action**. He reveals his true identity to Electra. Acting against the will of Zeus, Orestes kills Aegistheus and Clytemnestra, refusing to feel any remorse for his actions yet taking full **responsibility** for them. Electra is not so strong-willed. She succumbs to guilt and is reduced to begging Zeus for forgiveness for her part in the killings. Orestes reveals himself to the people as the son of Agamemnon and the rightful king of Argos but he refuses to take the throne. He leaves the town taking the pestilence of flies with him.

The play explores the key **existentialist** themes of **freedom** and responsibility through the radical conversion of Philebus the peace-loving intellectual into Orestes the warrior. A person may not be prepared for present crises by his past experiences, but it is nonetheless **bad faith** for him to declare, 'I was not meant for this' or 'This should not be happening to me'. Orestes resists bad faith and achieves **authenticity** by rising to the demands of his circumstances and fully realizing his **being-in-situation**. Orestes is free to choose not to choose and to walk away from Argos and its troubles, but instead he chooses to act positively, to avenge his father's death and to live with the consequences of killing his mother. Orestes triumphs over **God** and guilt, becoming a true existentialist hero. He asserts his free will against the will of God, revealing the limitlessness of human freedom. He takes full responsibility for his past deeds accepting that he is the sum total of all his actions and in so doing overcomes **regret**, the desire to repent and the desire to be forgiven.

Published and first performed during World War II, *The Flies* is a call to arms that seeks to illustrate the inadequacy of pacifism in face of extreme situations that require decisive action. To be authentic a person must rise to the occasion in which he finds himself. He must fight violence with violence if necessary and take full responsibility for his actions without remorse. See also *The Trojan Women*.

flight   See **surpassing, temporal flight** and **temporality**.

the flirt   In *Being and Nothingness* (1943), **Sartre** explores the various aspects of **bad faith** through a series of examples of people in bad faith. One of these examples is that of the flirt or coquette. Sartre describes a situation in which a man compliments a young woman and pays her polite attentions that she takes at face value refusing to acknowledge their sexual background. Eventually the man takes the young woman's hand creating a situation that demands from her a decisive response, but she chooses to flirt, neither withdrawing her hand nor acknowledging the implications of holding hands. She treats her hand as though it is not a part of herself, as though it is an object for which she is not responsible, and she treats her act of omission of leaving her hand in the hand of the man as though it is not an **action**.

The woman knows her hand is held and what this implies, yet somehow she evades this knowledge, or rather she is the ongoing project of seeking to evade it and distract herself from it. The woman distracts herself from the meaning of her situation and the disposition of her limbs by fleeing herself towards the **future**. Each moment she aims to become a being beyond her situated self, the meaning of which would not be her current situation. She aims to become a **being-for-itself-in-itself**. Such a being would not be subject to the demands of the situation. It would not be obliged to choose and to act. She abandons her hand, her whole **body**, to the **past**, hoping to leave it all behind her. Yet, in the very act of abandoning it, she re-apprehends the situation of her body as a demand to choose. To take the man's hand willingly or to withdraw, that is the **choice**. But she meets this demand for **positive choice** with a choice of herself as a being that would-be beyond the requirement to choose. It is this **negative choice** that exercises and distracts her and stands in for the positive choice she knows her **being-in-situation** demands. She avoids making this positive choice by choosing herself as a person who is about to completely transcend her

responsibility for her embodied, situated self; she chooses herself as a being who is about to completely escape its **facticity**.

While she is involved in this precarious project of bad faith the woman treats the facticity of her situation, in terms of which her choices of herself should be exercised, as a transcendent power over her. That is, she treats her facticity as though it is a **transcendence**. At the same time, she treats her transcendent consciousness as though it is its own transcendence; as though it is a **transcendence-in-itself** rather than the transcendence of the facticity of her situation. That is, she treats her transcendence as though it is a facticity. Sartre's example of the flirt establishes the crucial point that bad faith is achieved through attempted selective inversions of facticity and transcendence. See also **self-distraction**.

for-itself   An abbreviation of '**being-for-itself**'. Unless reference to being-for-itself is specifically required, **Sartre** and his commentators generally use the expression 'the for-itself' as it is less lumbering.

for-itself reflected-on   See **consciousness, reflected-on**.

for-itself-in-itself   An abbreviation of **being-for-itself-in-itself**.

formal absence   An absence of something that is not genuinely *lacking* and does not characterize the concrete situation of a **being-for-itself**. An absence that is a mere abstract idea and has no real bearing on the situation. Formal absence contrasts with **existential absence**. In *Being and Nothingness* (1943), **Sartre** contrasts the formal absence of the Duke of Wellington from a café with the existential absence of a friend, Pierre, whose arrival is expected.

formula for greatness   **Nietzsche** argues that the ability to want everything in all eternity to be just as it is, the desire for **eternal recurrence**, is the mark of true greatness, the mark of the truly authentic person. In so far as a person is the sum total of his experiences, for him to **regret** anything is for him to wish that he could be someone else. For a person to wish that he could be someone else is inauthentic and in Sartre's terms **bad faith**. See also **authenticity**, **eternal recurrence**, **noble ideal** and **will to power**.

freedom   A central concept of Sartre's **existentialism** with a specific and detailed meaning rather than a broad meaning. By 'freedom' **Sartre** almost always means '**existential freedom**' rather than 'liberty, 'lack of restrictions' and so on. See **freedom, existential**.

freedom, affirmation of   Sartre argues that people are unavoidably and limitlessly free. They can seek to deny that they are free by acting in **bad faith** or they can affirm that they are free by continually striving to take **responsibility** for their choices. To affirm or assume **freedom** is to accept without **regret** that freedom is one of the **existential truths** of the **human condition**. The affirmation or assumption of freedom involves a person recognizing his freedom and living accordingly. To affirm or assume freedom is to treat freedom itself as a source of values. Affirming or assuming freedom is central to the project of **authenticity**. The authentic person is one who affirms or assumes his freedom. A person who has lived in bad faith who begins to assume his freedom is said to have undergone a **radical conversion** to authenticity. In his *Notebooks for an Ethics* (1947–48, published posthumously 1983), Sartre suggests that in affirming his own freedom an authentic person would also respect and affirm the freedom of other people. Thus, he indicates a possible link between authenticity and ethics, suggesting that ethics is other-related authenticity. See also **authentic action**, **noble ideal**, **positive choice**, **positive freedom** and **positive will to power**.

freedom, existential   One of the central concepts and most abiding concerns of Sartre's **existentialism**. Free will, **choice** and **action** as defined by existentialism, as distinct from other theories of free will, particularly those that merely seek to refute **determinism** rather than offer a positive account of free will (see **anti-determinism**). Arguably, Sartre's theory of freedom, rooted as it is in his **ontological** theory of the relationship between **being-in-itself** and **being-for-itself**, not only makes room for free will, it explains it, showing not just how it is possible but how it is *necessary* given the nature of **consciousness**.

For **Sartre**, freedom is the fundamental, necessary and inalienable possession of every conscious human being, every being-for-itself. Being-for-itself is a paradoxical and indeterminate being that is never at one with itself and never identical with itself. As the **negation** of being-in-itself it is not founded upon itself but upon what it is not, and is therefore nothing in itself; nothing in the **present**. Being-for-itself is never in the present. It exists only as a perpetual **temporal transcendence**, a **temporal flight**, a **temporal surpassing**, away from the **past** towards the **future**. As a temporal transcendence it stands outside the causal order. The causal order, that which is, that which cannot be other than it is once it has come to pass, belongs to a past which being-for-itself realizes by constituting itself as the future of that past. The past exists only for a **for-itself** that transcends it towards the future. The for-itself exists only as a **transcendence** of the past towards the future. The for-itself is the future of the past, which is to say, it is the future possibilities of the past. As nothing but a being towards the future, as nothing but the future possibilities of the being that it transcends, the for-itself has to be these possibilities. It cannot not be an opening up of possibilities. The freedom of the for-itself consists in the perpetual opening up of the possibilities of being. The for-itself discovers itself in a world of possibilities that it creates by being a temporal transcendence towards the future. The for-itself is not *in* the future, the future exists only as the 'not yet' towards which the for-itself flees. Furthermore, the future can never be reached because to 'reach' the future is to immediately render it past. Hence, Sartre describes the future as a **future-past** and the past as a **past-future**. Nonetheless, it is in the future at which the for-itself aims that the for-itself is free, free in the sense of having future possibilities which it realizes for itself, possibilities among which it must choose by its actions. The for-itself projects itself through bodily action towards its chosen possibilities, transforming those possibilities – the possibilities that are the for-itself as a being towards the future – into actuality. The transformation of possibility into actuality is the transformation of future-past into past-future, the transformation of the possibilities that constitute the for-itself into a past being for further transcendence.

The fact that, at the **ontological level**, the for-itself has to be a temporal transcendence in order to exist at all, the fact that it cannot not be an opening up of possibilities, implies that, at the **phenomenological level**, it cannot not choose – which is to say, it cannot not be free. Although the for-itself is contingent in that it need not be, given that it exists, it is a necessary attribute of its existence that it is not free to cease being free. People are necessarily free, or, as Sartre puts it, people are **'condemned to be free'**. The for-itself can never surrender its freedom. It can never render itself an object causally determined by the physical world, for the very project of surrender, the very attempt to render itself causally determined, must be a free choice of itself. The for-itself cannot render itself determined by the world, for whenever or however it attempts to do so, it must choose to do so. A person's freedom does not consist in a kind of 'freefall' or a lack of obligation, it consists in the constant **responsibility** of having to choose who he is through the actions he chooses to perform in response to the **facticity**, adversity and resistance of his concrete situation. For Sartre, there is no end to the responsibility of having to choose. Just as freedom is necessary, so it is also limitless. Not limitless in the sense that a person is free to do anything, fly though he has no wings, etc., but limitless in the sense that the obligation to be free is unremitting (see **unlimited freedom**).

People employ various strategies to convince themselves and others that they are not free and to fool themselves and others that they need not choose or have not chosen. Sartre refers to this phenomenon as **bad faith**. Bad faith is not the opposite of freedom, it is freedom that gives rise directly to the possibility of bad faith. Bad faith is a project of freedom whereby freedom aims at its own suppression and denial.

Many of Sartre's critics, **Merleau-Ponty** for example, argue that responsibility and the ability to choose are less extensive than Sartre supposes and that his views on the limitlessness of freedom are so uncompromising as to be untenable. See **responsibility** for criticism of Sartre's thesis that freedom and responsibility are limitless. See also **affirmation of freedom**, **negative freedom**, **positive freedom** and **temporality**.

Freedom, negative The opposite of **positive freedom**. **Freedom** that exercises itself in denying, checking and repressing itself rather than positively affirming itself through decisive action in response to the **facticity** of its situation (see **affirmation of freedom**). Choosing not to choose. **Bad faith**. The person who exercises negative freedom exercises **negative will to power**. See also **ascetic ideal**, **negative choice** and **slave ethic**.

freedom, positive The opposite of **negative freedom**. **Freedom** that affirms itself through decisive, responsible, **authentic action** in response to the **facticity** of its situation. Freedom that refuses to exercise itself in denying itself. A person exercises positive freedom when he does not attempt to relinquish **responsibility** for himself by choosing not to choose, when he does not act in **bad faith**. The person who exercises positive freedom exercises **positive will to power**. See also **affirmation of freedom**, **authenticity**, **noble ideal** and **positive choice**.

freedom, unlimited   For **Sartre**, our **existential freedom** is limitless in the sense that there is no limit to the **responsibility** of having to choose who we are through our **choice** of **action** in any given situation. Although the options in any situation are limited, there is no limit to the responsibility of having to choose an option in every situation. What is not possible is not to choose because, as Sartre notes, to choose not to choose (**bad faith**) is still a choice. Sartre does not mean that our freedom is limitless in the sense that we are free to perform impossible actions: fly unaided or walk on water. He does not equate freedom with ability. For example, a person without legs is not free (able) to walk, but his freedom is nonetheless limitless in that there is no limit to his responsibility to choose responses to the **facticity** of his situation, the facticity that is his disability. He may well not be responsible for his disabled condition but he is responsible for choosing the *meaning* of his condition. This is what Sartre means when he says, 'I cannot be crippled without choosing myself as crippled.' Many of Sartre's critics, **Merleau-Ponty** for example, argue that responsibility and the ability to choose are less extensive than Sartre supposes and that his views on the limitlessness of freedom are so uncompromising as to be untenable. See **responsibility** for criticism of Sartre's thesis that freedom and responsibility are limitless.

Freud, Sigmund (1856–1939)   Austrian physician and psychiatrist. Founder of psychoanalysis. In analysing the thoughts, dreams, sexual desires, neuroses and early experiences of his patients, Freud formulated a theory of the psyche in which the mind is divided into conscious and unconscious elements. According to Freud, the unconscious is the seat of the **Id**, the source of primitive drives and urges, particularly **sexual desire**. The conscious part of the mind is the seat of the ego or self. According to Freud, the personality is shaped by the tensions existing between the Id and the ego. The Id provides the ego with much of its motivation for action, while the ego seeks to control, censor and censure the Id.

Although a major influence on **Sartre**, Sartre is highly critical of Freud. While accepting the importance of early experiences in shaping personality, Sartre rejects Freud's notion that personality is shaped by irreducible drives such as sexual desire (see **pseudo-irreducibles**). In response to Freud, Sartre formulated **existential psychoanalysis**, an approach that seeks to understand personality through the detailed exploration of a person's personal history and the discovery of their **fundamental choice** and **fundamental project**.

Sartre's biggest disagreement with Freud regards Freud's notion of the **psychic duality** of conscious and unconscious. Sartre rejects the notion, arguing that because **consciousness** exists only in so far as it is conscious of itself, an unconscious consciousness is impossible (see **translucency**). More specifically, Sartre rejects Freud's claim that the ego is able to selectively repress certain distasteful truths, beliefs and desires emerging from the Id and keep them down in the unconscious. Sartre argues that to act with discernment the censor would have to be *conscious* of what it was repressing, implying that **self-deception** is impossible. Sartre explains as forms of **bad faith** the attitudes and behaviours that Freud explains as products of a psychic duality. See also *Sketch for a Theory of the Emotions*.

fundamental choice   See **choice, fundamental**.

fundamental project   The series of actions that a person chooses in response to and as a result of his **fundamental choice** of himself. The abiding aim of the fundamental project is the affirmation or denial of the fundamental choice. As a **lack** of being a person must choose some particular project or other through which he can aim to overcome the lack of being that he is. A person's fundamental project is his life history viewed as a ceaseless effort to overcome his own particular lack of being as defined by his fundamental choice of himself. Through its fundamental project every **being-for-itself** ultimately strives to be **God**. That is, it strives to become a **being-for-itself-in-itself**, a being, like God, that is founded upon itself rather than upon the **being-in-itself** it negates. As such a state of being is impossible, the ultimate goal of the fundamental project is unachievable.

future   See **future-past** and **temporality**.

future-past   The future described in **phenomenological** terms as a future that will become the **past**. A term that captures the fact that what is now a person's future will, in the future, become his past. For **Sartre**, each of the three dimensions of time – past, **present** and future – stands outside of itself in the other two and has being only in terms of the other two. The future of a **being-for-itself** is the future-past of that for-itself; a future-past that, in the future, will be the **past-future** of that for-itself. See also *ekstasis*, **existential freedom**, **temporality** and **transcendence**.

futurizing intention   Being-for-itself is a **temporal flight** towards the **future**. It continually intends the future realization of the possibilities that constitute it and so can be described as being or having a futurizing intention. See also **existential freedom**, **temporality** and **transcendence**.

— G —

Gallimard   Editions Gallimard, Paris. Sartre's publishers, responsible for the publication of the vast majority of his works in their original French and therefore present custodians of his literary legacy. **Sartre** signed a contract not long before his death giving Gallimard exclusive rights to all his unpublished manuscripts. Sartre is among the ten all-time most profitable products of this major French publishing house. Gallimard also publish many of Sartre's contemporaries including Simone **de Beauvoir**, Albert **Camus** and Maurice **Merleau-Ponty**.

Gaston Gallimard (1881–1975) founded the journal *La Nouvelle Revue Française* in 1909, after a false start in 1908, with the help of the authors André Gide and Jean Schlumberger. Editions Gallimard began in 1911 as an offshoot of the journal and became an independent enterprise in 1919. Editions Gallimard became one of the major French publishing houses and remains so today. As the publisher of so many important French intellectuals, including several who accepted or declined the Nobel Prize for Literature (Gide 1947 accepted, Camus 1957 accepted, Sartre 1964 declined) it is not surprising that an article in the *Guardian* newspaper once described Gallimard as having the world's best backlist. It was Gaston Gallimard himself who came up with **Nausea** as the title of Sartre's first novel after its original title, *Melancholia*, was rejected. In 1960 Michel Gallimard, the nephew of Gaston Gallimard, crashed his car, killing his passenger Albert Camus. Michel Gallimard died a few days later.

Genet, Jean See *Saint Genet, Actor and Martyr*.

God **Sartre** is an atheist who denies the possibility of a conscious, personal, moral God that created the universe. Essentially, in Sartrean terms, theists conceive God to be a **being-for-itself**; a conscious, knowing being. God's **consciousness**, however, is held to exist fundamentally rather than as a relation or a **negation**. That is, God's existence and essence are held to be one, or in Sartrean terms, God's being-for-itself is held to exist in itself. In short, God is held to be the ultimate **being-for-itself-in-itself**. The Ontological Argument for the existence of God assumes this unity of existence and essence. For the Medieval philosopher Anselm, the most perfect conceivable entity must have the attribute of existence. So, for Anselm, God's essence implies his existence. Sartre argues that every **for-itself** desires to be God in that every for-itself strives to be a being-for-itself-in-itself that has achieved identity with itself. That is, every for-itself strives to be a **non-being** that *is* its own non-being so as to escape being a non-being that *has to be* its own non-being as the negation of **being-in-itself**. Sartre argues that the unity of being-for-itself and being-in-itself is impossible to achieve because being-for-itself must always be the negation or denial of being-in-itself. Negation can never coincide with or achieve unity with the being it negates. For Sartre, the impossibility of this unity is the impossibility of the existence of God.

Sartre also argues against creationism. If being was conceived in the divine subjectivity of God it remains a mode of God's subjectivity and cannot even have a semblance of objectivity, it cannot exist in its own right, independently of God, as a genuine creation. Moreover, if being is perpetually created, as some creationist theories suppose, then being would have no substantiality of its own, its being would be perpetually derived from the being of God. Once more, it would remain a mode of God's subjectivity having no objectivity. Sartre concludes that even if being was created it is inexplicable as a creation. Being must be absolutely independent of God in order to be that which is, and must be, its own foundation. Being assumes its being beyond creation. See also **abandonment**, **atheism**, **Kierkegaard**, *Lucifer and the Lord*, **Nietzsche** and **nihilism**.

good faith   In so far as 'good faith' is opposed to '**bad faith**' it can be taken to have the same meaning as '**authenticity**'. However, this use of 'good faith' can create confusion in that 'good faith' is synonymous with '**sincerity**', a term that, for **Sartre**, refers to a form of **bad faith**. Indeed, Sartre argues that all faith is bad faith, although even he allows that there are some uses of 'sincerity' or 'good faith' that refer to the kind of straightforward honesty that does not involve bad faith. The meaning of any particular instance of the term 'good faith' requires an appreciation of the context in which it appears. For Sartre 'good faith' refers predominantly to sincerity, which for him is a form of bad faith.

grace   See **sadism** and **sexual desire**.

groundless choice   See **choice, groundless**.

— H —

hate   **Sartre** explores the phenomenon of hate as an aspect of **being-for-others**, as a feature of our 'concrete relations with others'. He argues that any act on the part of the **Other** that puts a person in the state of being subject to the **freedom** of the Other can arouse hatred. A person who is subjected to cruelty is likely to respond with hatred, but a person who is shown kindness may also respond with hatred rather than the expected gratitude. Both cruel acts and kind acts, in subjecting a person to the freedom of the Other, prevent that person from ignoring the Other.

Love, **sexual desire**, even **masochism** and **sadism**, aim at some form of union with the Other, whereas hatred is the abandonment of any attempt to realize union with the Other. The person who hates does not want his freedom to be a **transcendence** of the Other, he wants to be free of the Other in a world where the Other does not exist. To hate is to 'pursue the death of the Other'. This is not to say that hatred must involve actively plotting the death of the Other, and usually it does not. Rather, the person who hates seeks to realize for himself a world in which the hated Other does not feature and has no significance, past, present or future. To hate is to want the death of the Other, but moreover it is to want that the Other had never existed.

Hatred should not be confused with contempt. Not least, there is often humour in contempt as displayed by ridicule, but hate, though it often struggles to disguise itself as contempt by pretending to laugh at the Other, takes the Other very seriously and is not amused. Hate does not abase the Other and to hate is not to have contempt for some particular aspect of the Other such as his appearance. To hate is to resent the existence of the Other in general.

To hate the Other is to perceive him as an object, but the Other as hate-object remains nonetheless an object haunted by a transcendence that the person who hates prefers not to think about or acknowledge. This avoided transcendence lurks as a potential threat to the freedom of the person who hates, it threatens to alienate him and the hatred by means of which he strives to be free of the Other.

In hating, the person who hates strives to be free of the Other, strives to inhabit a world in which the Other does not exist and has never existed as a free transcendence. But the very fact that he hates the Other implies that he recognizes the freedom of the Other. Hatred strives to deny the freedom of the Other by projecting the non-existence of the Other, but precisely because hatred is a striving to deny the Other it is an implicit affirmation of the Other. Seemingly consistent with Sartre's analysis of hatred is the view that hatred fuels itself in so far as this implicit affirmation of the Other is given grudgingly and is therefore resented. I hate the Other all the more because my hatred of him obliges me to recognize his freedom. I blame the Other for the fact that my hatred of him cannot be the pure denial of him I wish it to be.

Hatred fails as an attempt to abolish the Other because it cannot help being an implicit affirmation of the Other. Even if the hated Other dies or is killed by me he is not abolished for me. Death does not make it that the Other had never existed and for my hatred to attempt to triumph in the death of the Other requires me to recognize that he *has* existed. I desire the death of the hated Other in order to be free of him, but with his death what I was for him becomes fixed in a past that I am as having-been-it. The fact that I cannot influence what I was for the Other once he is dead means that he continues to alienate me from his grave.

Hatred is hatred of the Other as Other. As the hatred of otherness hatred is, as Sartre points out, hatred of all others in one Other. Hate is a revolt against one's being-for-others in general. However, even if a person could entirely suppress or destroy all others (as tyrants attempt to do) he would not thereby reclaim his being-for-others or free himself from others. Once a person has been for others he will be forever haunted by his awareness that being-for-others is a 'permanent possibility of his being'. To have been for-others is to have to be for-others for life. See also *In Camera*.

Hegel, George W.F. (1770–1831)   German idealist philosopher. Hegel was heavily influenced by the ideas and methods of his predecessor **Kant**. In his turn, Hegel heavily influenced many subsequent philosophers, particularly within the Continental tradition, **Sartre** among them but most notably Marx, another significant influence on Sartre. Like Kant before him and Sartre after him Hegel seeks to explain, particularly in his major work, *Phenomenology of Spirit* (1807), the nature of the mind and its relationship to the world. He takes from Kant the notion that experience is a synthesis of **consciousness** and what is presented to consciousness. However, he adds an historical and social dimension to Kant's philosophy of mind, arguing that human reason is an historical development and that history itself is the progressive development of human reason towards perfect rationality. Ideas, Hegel argues, develop dialectically. A thesis confronts an antithesis and together they eventually give rise to a synthesis – a new higher, more refined idea. Reason develops the institutions that comprise the human world while reason itself is developed by these institutions. For Hegel, mind and world, or what he prefers to call subjective and objective mind, are not distinct entities but internally related aspects of a single whole, each reflecting the other.

Sartre became increasingly Hegelian as his career progressed in the sense that, via Marx, he came to more or less endorse the central Hegelian notion of the historical development of human reason. Sartre's earlier writings on the nature of consciousness also repeatedly reflect Hegel's influence. Hegel and Sartre agree that the mind exists as a relationship to the world and that it is nothing in itself. They agree that the mind is a **negation**. In his major work, ***Being and Nothingness*** (1943), Sartre explicitly endorses Hegel's key claim that 'the mind is the negative'. Despite their agreement on this crucial point, however, a fundamental disagreement exists between them regarding the nature and status of **being** and its negation – being and **non-being** – although it is by directly opposing Hegel's position that Sartre is able to develop his own position regarding being and non-being.

Hegel argues in his *Science of Logic* (1816) that being and non-being are mere abstractions of thought, that there is neither being nor non-being but only becoming. '*Being* as little *is*, as nothing *is*, or, all *flows*, which means all is *becoming*.' Against Hegel, Sartre argues that being *is* and non-being is not. Being, or what Sartre calls **being-in-itself**, must exist in order for non-being to exist as the negation of being, as an emptiness of being. Emptiness is always emptiness of something. For Sartre, being is fundamental and does not depend on anything else for its being, whereas non-being, the negation of being, is entirely dependent on being for its borrowed existence (see **borrowed being**). 'We must recall here against Hegel,' says Sartre, 'that being is and nothingness is not.' See also ***Critique of Dialectical Reason*** and **Kierkegaard**.

Heidegger, Martin (1889–1976)   German **existentialist** philosopher. Heidegger adopted and developed the **phenomenological** method of his teacher, Edmund **Husserl**. Heidegger succeeded Husserl as professor of Philosophy at the University of Freiberg in the late 1920s. A supporter of National Socialism, although he left the party in 1934, Heidegger sought to distance himself from Husserl who was Jewish. Heidegger's Nazism is something he shared with millions of Germans caught up in the mass hysteria generated by the National Socialist movement. More damning is his failure after 1945 to retract pro-Nazi opinions expressed in 1933–34. This failure is unfortunate as it continues to cast a shadow over a philosopher whose thought is original, profound and highly influential.

Heidegger's main philosophical concern is with **ontology**, questions concerning **being** and what it is 'to be'. In his major work, *Being and Time*

(1927), he argues that since the Ancient Greek period philosophy has largely neglected questions concerning being. Heidegger investigates being by investigating the mode of being that reveals being, namely the embodied, situated, active, questioning, social, mortal being that each person instantiates. He refers to this mode of being as **Dasein** (being-there). Heidegger's philosophy is largely an exploration of Dasein's *way* of being. Heidegger's philosophy, as a questioning of Dasein, is in perfect keeping with the nature of Dasein in that Dasein is a perpetual questioning as to the nature of its own being. The being of Dasein is indeterminate. The **indeterminacy** of Dasein is rooted in the fact that it is not fixed in the **present** but is essentially a temporal movement away from the **past** towards the **future**. Heidegger repeatedly stresses that understanding **temporality** is the key to understanding Dasein and to answering the deepest questions of **phenomenological ontology**. As he says, *'The central problematic of all ontology is rooted in the phenomenon of time.'*

All these ideas were hugely influential on **Sartre** and it is fair to say that Heidegger is Sartre's biggest single influence after Husserl. Some commentators even choose to see Sartre's **Being and Nothingness** (1943) as a more accessible if not diluted re-write of Heidegger's *Being and Time*. This is unfair as *Being and Nothingness* contains many original insights and Sartre is never shy of raising disagreements with Heidegger when he sees fit. Nonetheless, Sartre's ideas concerning **being-for-itself** echo to a great extent Heidegger's ideas concerning Dasein. Sartre also shares Heidegger's view that understanding temporality is the key to understanding the **human condition**, though he accuses Heidegger of failing to provide an adequate account of the **ontological** origin of the temporality of the self. He argues that Heidegger overlooks the fact that temporality is ontologically subsequent to being in that it arises through the **original negation** of being-in-itself that constitutes the being of **consciousness**. Heidegger overlooks the fact because he does not focus sufficiently on the phenomenon of consciousness and the original negation that gives rise to consciousness.

Authenticity is a central theme for both Heidegger and Sartre and it is clear that Sartre's views on the phenomenon are heavily influenced by Heidegger's. Both Heidegger and Sartre hold that the project of authenticity involves affirming the inescapable truths of the human condition – indeterminacy, **freedom**, **mortality** and so on. There are, nonetheless, differences in emphasis regarding authenticity and at least one significant disagreement. Sartre's account of authenticity emphasizes the **affirmation of freedom** whereas Heidegger's account emphasizes the **affirmation of mortality**. For Heidegger, authenticity is primarily authentic **being-towards-death**, with death being each person's **ownmost possibility**. Sartre rejects this, arguing that although the affirmation of mortality inspires **authentic action**, death, as the limit of all possibility, is not itself a possibility.

'hell is other people'   See *In Camera*.

the homosexual   In *Being and Nothingness* (1943) **Sartre** explores the various aspects of **bad faith** through a series of examples of people in bad faith. One of his examples of a person in bad faith is that of the homosexual who denies that he is a homosexual. The homosexual does not deny his homosexual desires and activities, such deliberate **self-deception** is impossible, rather he denies that homosexuality is the meaning of his conduct. Rather than take **responsibility** for his conduct he chooses to characterize it as a series of aberrations, as a game, as bad luck, as the result of curiosity rather than the result of a deep-seated tendency. He believes that a homosexual is not a homosexual as a table is a table. This belief is justified in so far as a person is never simply what he is in the mode of being it. A person *has to be* what he is, he chooses it through his actions, he aims at it and so on. The homosexual is right that he is not a homosexual *thing*, but in so far as he has adopted a pattern of conduct defined as the conduct of a homosexual, he is a homosexual. That he is not a homosexual in the sense that a table is a table does not imply that he is not a homosexual in the sense that a table is not a chair. Sartre argues that the homosexual plays on the word *being*. He surreptitiously interprets 'not being what he *is*', as 'not being what he is not'.

The homosexual attempts to deny that he is his **facticity**, when, in fact, he is his facticity in the mode of not being it; in the mode of no longer being it. That is, though he is not his facticity – his **past** – in the mode of being it, he is his facticity in so far as it is the past being which he affirms as belonging to him by virtue of the fact that he must continually transcend it towards the **future**. He assumes in bad faith that he is a pure **transcendence**; that his facticity, being past, has vanished into the absolute nothingness of a generalized past that has nothing to do with him. The truth of the matter, however, is that far from being a pure transcendence he is and must be the transcendence of his facticity. The homosexual, in his project of bad faith, attempts to create within himself a divide between facticity and transcendence.

The homosexual has a friend, the **champion of sincerity**, who urges the homosexual to declare himself and admit that he is a homosexual. The champion of sincerity is another of Sartre's examples of a character in bad faith.

horizons   Husserl's term for those aspects of an object that are not currently appearing (to someone) but which could appear. Horizons are possible **appearances**. **Sartre** agrees with **Husserl** that actual appearances, those appearances or aspects of an object that are presently appearing, do not indicate an underlying object-in-itself but rather an infinity of possible appearances that are not presently appearing but which by turns could do so. Sartre refers to these possible appearances, these horizons, as **transphenomenal**.

human condition   **Sartre** argues that people do not have, or share in, a fixed **human nature** or essence. Instead, what people have in common is their human condition; the fact that by virtue of being in the world as embodied, conscious, free, mortal, active beings they are all unavoidably subject to the same fundamental demands, limitations and restrictions. Every person, whatever his particular situation, finds himself in a world where **being-for-others** and his own **death** are inevitable, where his own **body** is inescapable, where he has to make choices, where he must perform actions to achieve ends, where he must be a **futurizing intention** and so on. The human condition is inseparable from the fundamental **existential** conditions, the **existential truths**, to which all people are inexorably subject. Sartre contrasts the notions of human condition and human nature in *Existentialism and Humanism* (1946).

human nature   **Sartre** denies the existence of human nature, the existence of a fixed universal essence common to all people. A person's nature or essence is to have no nature or essence. There is nothing that a person *is*. A person must always choose what he is without ever being able to coincide with his **choice** of himself. These claims are consistent with Sartre's **unlimited freedom** thesis, his view that human **freedom** is limitless because the obligation to make choices is limitless, but they have been widely disputed. His contemporary, Maurice **Merleau-Ponty**, for example, argues that people do have a human nature rooted in the demands and limitation of the **body** and its basic physical relationship with the environment. Merleau-Ponty refers to this as the **natural self**. Some critics have argued that because all people are free, freedom itself consti-tutes a universal human nature, but Sartre rejects this claim, arguing instead that freedom is a feature of the universal **human condition**. Sartre contrasts the notions of human nature and human condition in *Existen-tialism and Humanism* (1946).

Husserl, Edmund (1859–1938)   German mathematician and **phen-omenologist**. Husserl was arguably Sartre's biggest single philosophical influence both directly and through the influence of Husserl's student **Heidegger**, who **Sartre** also studied closely. Sartre became fascinated with Husserl when his friend Raymond Aron introduced him to Husserl's **phenomenology** at a legendary meeting in a Parisian café in the spring of 1933. Aron, who was then studying Husserl in Germany, showed Sartre how he could begin philosophizing simply by considering the object in front of him. According to **de Beauvoir**, who was also present, the object in question was an apricot cocktail; according to Aron they drank only beer. Starting with Emmanuel Levinas' *The Theory of Intuition in Husserl's Phenomenology* (1930), which he bought immediately after his meeting with Aron, Sartre read everything by and about Husserl he could, hardly studying another philosopher for six years. Sartre's fascination with Husserl led him to swap places with Aron for a nine-month sabbatical at the French Institute in Berlin beginning in the autumn of 1933.

Husserl developed the phenomenology of **Brentano**, placing Brentano's notion of **intentionality** at the heart of his theory of **consciousness**. In his *Cartesian Meditations* (1931) Husserl describes his own approach as Neo-Cartesianism. He praises **Descartes** for focusing in on the *cogito* or ego via his method of doubt, but he rejects Descartes' realist conclusion that the ego is a substantial entity that can exist apart from its thoughts. In place of Descartes' subjective realism, Husserl offers transcendental subjectivism, the view that the ego is not real but transcendental. He argues that the ego is not a part of the world. It is nothing in itself and exists only in so far as it intends objects. For Husserl objects are a unified synthesis of **appearances** and the ego is the unifying principle of these appearances and nothing beyond that. In this respect Husserl's transcendental subjectivism is comparable to the **transcendental idealism** of **Kant**. A central feature of Husserl's phenomenology is the *epochē* or 'suspension', the procedure of 'bracketing off' existence. The procedure sets aside all questions regarding reality and existence and focuses instead on questions concerning the defining characteristics of **phenomena** as they appear to consciousness. The aim of this **phenomenological** reduction is to produce a description of phenomena as they appear to consciousness that reveals their essential nature as appearances.

Sartre criticizes Husserl's transcendental subjectivism in one of his earliest published works, *The Transcendence of the Ego* (1937). Sartre endorses Husserl's phenomenological programme in so far as it involves the exploration and description of different types of **intentional object**. He argues, however, that Husserl posits a transcendental ego that stands behind the activities of consciousness. If the transcendental ego stands behind consciousness, intentional objects become a product of the activity of the transcendental ego upon contents of consciousness rather than upon appearances themselves. In Sartre's view, Husserl's phenomenological programme falls short of its primary objective of getting back to the appearances themselves. Instead, the objects intended by the ego are constructed from a hybrid stuff contained in consciousness – Husserl's hylé – that is somehow capable of representing the objects intended by the transcendental ego. Sartre insists that there is no ego standing behind consciousness or within consciousness. The ego is an intentional object for consciousness. That is, the ego is an appearance for **reflective consciousness** existing entirely as the transcendent unity of previous states and actions.

Sartre's disagreements with Husserl were instrumental in the development of his own theory of consciousness that he later put forward in his most important work, *Being and Nothingness* (1943).

Id   A key term in the psychoanalytic theory of **Freud** referring to the unconscious or subconscious mind; the seat of primitive drives, desires and instincts. **Sartre** denies the existence of the unconscious or subconscious mind on the grounds that it supposes an impossible **psychic duality** or **deceiver-deceived duality** within a single **consciousness** whereby one part of consciousness can be concealed from another. Sartre argues for the **translucency** of consciousness, the view that consciousness is consciousness through and through, and he rejects as contradictory any notion of an unconscious consciousness.

idealism   A term most commonly used to refer to belief in or pursuance of ideals, to the attitude of the idealist who desires, believes in and strives for a world that is morally and politically perfect. 'Idealism' retains this meaning in philosophy and some philosophers are idealists as described above. However, in philosophy, the term is most often used to refer to the view that ideas or metaphysical essences are the primary and fundamental features of reality. This view can be summed up in the maxim, 'essence precedes existence'. According to the idealist philosopher Plato, for example, true reality is comprised of perfect, mind-independent, meta-physical Ideas or Forms, while the physical world is a mere appearance or shadow cast by the true reality of the Forms. Another idealist philosopher, George Berkeley, holds that objects are actually collections of ideas that must be perceived by a mind in order to exist. Sartre's **existentialism**, as its name suggests, is opposed to idealism and is summed up in the maxim, **'existence precedes essence'**. For **Sartre**, it is not ideas, essences or minds that are primary but pure existence in the form of **being-in-itself**. Being-in-itself does not depend on anything else for its being, whereas **being-for-itself**, the basis of **consciousness** and ideas, arises through the **negation** of being-in-itself. As such being-for-itself is dependent upon and subsequent to being-in-itself – it is *preceded* by being-in-itself.

Sartre also argues that there is nothing beyond any series or collection of particular things. For Sartre, general ideas or essences do not exist prior to particular things and therefore cannot give rise to particular things as Plato argues. In Sartre's view, general ideas or essences are merely generalizations about particular things produced by consciousness following an empirical examination of particular things. The idea of the perfect circle, for example, does not exist independently of particular circles in the world and is not the origin of particular circles in the world. Rather, the idea of perfect circularity, as expressed in geometry, is the broadest possible generalization about all the circular things in the world. It is a mere abstraction from the series of actual circles and is nothing beyond the series. See also *Existentialism and Humanism* and **realism**.

ignorance   See *Truth and Existence*.

illusion of immanence   A phrase used by **Sartre** in *The Imaginary* (1940) to refer to the view common in both philosophy and **psychology** that mental images have the quality of **immanence**, that they are actually *in* **consciousness** like pictures in a picture gallery. This view has since come to be known by Sartre scholars and philosophers in general as the picture gallery model of the mind. Sartre rejects the picture gallery model on various grounds, not least that it is impossible to have a picture, spatial by definition, within a mind that is not material. For Sartre, **consciousness is consciousness of** ___. It is nothing in itself. It exists only in so far as it *intends* objects (see **intentionality**). Sartre thinks that the very term 'mental image' is confusing, arguing that the so-called 'mental image of x' is in fact 'the imaginative consciousness of x'. To have a mental image of the Eiffel Tower, for example, is not to have a picture of the Eiffel Tower in the mind but to intend the Eiffel Tower. It is the Eiffel Tower itself that is the object of imaginative consciousness. When a person 'conjures up an image' of the Eiffel Tower, which is to say, when he directs his imaginative consciousness towards the Eiffel Tower, he does not have to, and often does not, reflect on his imaginative consciousness as such. He does not necessarily reflect, 'I am thinking about a mental image of the Eiffel Tower'. This is because he is not thinking about an image of the Eiffel Tower but about the Eiffel Tower. He can, of course, begin at any moment to reflect upon the fact that he is thinking about the Eiffel Tower. It is then and only then that his thinking about/imagining the Eiffel Tower becomes the **intentional object** of his consciousness rather than the Eiffel Tower itself. This is not to say that an immanent image of the Eiffel Tower is now occurring in his mind for his contemplation, but rather that he reflects on his intentional consciousness of some feature of the world (in this case the Eiffel Tower) with a further act of intentional consciousness – an act of **self-reflection** or **thetic self-consciousness** – that takes consciousness itself as its intentional object.

The Imaginary: A Phenomenological Psychology of the Imagination (1940)   Alternative title, *The Psychology of Imagination*. A relatively early philosophical work by **Sartre**, drafted in 1937, in which he conducts a **phenomenological** investigation of the imagination and mental images through the application of the theory of **intentionality** he inherited from **Brentano** and **Husserl**. The work reiterates and develops ideas put forward in his first published work, *Imagination: A Psychological Critique* (1936). Sartre's main aim in *The Imaginary* is to show that, however matters may appear prima facie, mental images are not in consciousness. He attacks what he calls the **illusion of immanence**, the view common in both philosophy and psychology that mental images are quasi-objects, pictures in a picture gallery of the mind. He argues that a so-called 'mental image of x' is in fact 'the imaginative consciousness of x'. To have a mental image of x, to think about x, is not to focus on a mental picture, but to *intend* x. To have a mental image of Peter, for example, is not to have a picture of Peter in the mind but to intend Peter. It is Peter himself that is the object of imaginative consciousness of Peter. Mental images, Sartre continues, have no existence of their own. They consist of nothing but the intentional directedness of consciousness towards a particular object. For this reason, Sartre argues, mental images never surprise us or teach us anything, they have only what our intentions give them.

Sartre explains a good deal about the nature of imagining and mental images by comparing these **phenomena** with perception and objects of perception. An object of perception has an infinite number of possible, hidden, **appearances** – what Husserl calls **horizons** and Sartre, later in his career, calls the **transphenomenal**. An object of perception can be viewed over time from an infinite number of different perspectives. It is never given all at once and the longer it is examined the more it reveals. For this reason, perception does not produce instant understanding. Understanding a perceived object, says Sartre, is like serving an apprenticeship. We learn more about it the longer we perceive it, the more aspects we explore and so on. A mental image, on the other hand, has no hidden appearances, no transphenomenal aspects. It *reveals* nothing because it has only the appearances a person's intentions give it at the time he gives them. To take one of Sartre's examples, an imaginary rotating cube does not reveal, as it rotates, sides that were hidden. The sides that appear were not hidden before they appeared, they simply did not exist, they were nothing at all. Unlike a real rotating cube, a mental image of a rotating cube occurs all at once. There is never more of it to emerge and what may appear to emerge is only what is added by the rotating-cube-intending consciousness concerned. A mental image, then, is understood all at once, there is no apprenticeship to be served with regard to knowing it because there is nothing in it that is not put into it by consciousness.

Sartre moves on to explore what he calls 'the image family' – portraits, caricatures, signs, schematic drawings, naturally occurring resemblances such as faces in a fire and the hallucinatory hypnagogic images that people believe they 'look at' with their eyes closed especially while intoxicated or half-asleep. What is common to them all phenomenologically is that they all intend that which is *not present* for the consciousness perceiving them, or *apparently* perceiving them. (A hypnagogic image is a particularly vivid mental image and as such is not perceived.) Having established this common principle Sartre is able to show that the mental image is a legitimate member of the image family, that it is essentially no different from the other members of the image family in that it too, as the imaginative consciousness of an *absent* x, intends that which is not present. Of course, as already argued, the mental image is not an object of perception like a portrait with an existence independent of the intentional directedness of consciousness, but it is in essence the same as the object members of the image family in that like them it serves as the positing of an object in the absence of that object. Like portraits and caricatures the mental image is an analogue, all be it an analogue that, as Sartre points out, fades away completely leaving no examinable residue when consciousness ceases to be directed towards the object the mental image is an analogue of.

Having given a phenomenological account of imagining and the image family, Sartre undertakes to interpret or qualify various claims made about the imagination by physiologists, psychologists and psychiatrists in such a way that these claims are revealed as consistent with his phenomenological account. Sartre shows himself to be particularly knowledgeable about the empirical findings of clinicians investigating different types of mental disturbance. He was a personal friend of Daniel Lagache, author of *Verbal Hallucinations and Speech* (1934), and his own analysis of verbal hallucinations or 'hearing' voices owes a lot to Lagache's work. Sartre visited Lagache at the hospital where he worked to find out more about the phenomenon of hallucinations verbal and visual. To that end, in January 1935, Lagache injected Sartre with the powerfully psychoactive drug mescaline. Sartre had a bad trip and never took hallucinogenics again, but the experience served to give him an understanding of hallucinations that he makes use of in *The Imaginary*. Sartre says that his hallucinations existed by stealth on the margins of his consciousness; that they disappeared when he turned his full attention on them. That his hallucinations disappeared when he turned his full attention on them suggested to Sartre that he was in some sense dreaming them. He concludes that hallucinations occur when perception crumbles and a person, having become unreal to himself, begins to dream the world of perception. In other words, hallucinations occur when the distinction between perceiving and dreaming becomes blurred for a person experiencing a loss of self. His loss of self will be due in large part to the most consistently reported feature of the hallucinogenic drug experience, a dislocation of time and space.

The *Imaginary* can at times seem laboured and repetitive but this is because it is meticulous in exploring all aspects of the imagination and accounting for them within a single, unified theory. Sartre's capacity to employ the phenomenological method of approach to grasp the essence of apparently obscure phenomena is impressive. An important work of philosophy in its own right, *The Imaginary* can nonetheless be seen as preparing the way for Sartre's major philosophical work, **Being and Nothingness**, which was published three years later in 1943. *The Imaginary* develops many ideas and themes that are central to the theory of consciousness expounded in *Being and Nothingness*; ideas and themes such as intentionality, transphenomenality, the rejection of immanence in favour of **transcendence** and the dismissal of the Freudian unconscious (see **Freud**).

Imagination: A Psychological Critique (1936)   Sartre's first published work. A **phenomenological** investigation of the imagination inspired by Sartre's study of the **phenomenology** of **Husserl** at the French Institute in Berlin during 1933–34. The key ideas of *Imagination* are taken up and developed in Sartre's better-known and more significant work, *The Imaginary*, drafted in 1937 and published in 1940.

immanence   The condition or quality of existing, operating or remaining within. Inherence. Contrasts with **transcendence**, the condition or quality of being outside or beyond. For **Sartre**, **consciousness** is essentially transcendent rather than immanent. In particular, to hold that thoughts, ideas and mental images are quasi-objects contained within consciousness is to be misled by an **illusion of immanence**.

In Camera (1944)   Alternative title *No Exit*. A play by **Sartre** in which Garcin, Inez and Estelle, three strangers who have nothing in common with each other, find themselves trapped together in a room forever. They have died and the room is Sartre's vision of hell. A place without sleep, dreams, blinking, books, windows or distractions of any kind save unattractive Second Empire furniture. There are no mirrors to help the characters see themselves as others see them. There are no devils to torture them. They torture themselves with self-reproach and attempted self-justification regarding the life they have lived, they torture each other with criticisms and with the knowledge they soon acquire of each other's faults. Each suffers their **being-for-others** as they attempt in vain to control the opinions the others form of them. Towards the end of the play Garcin sums up its central message: 'There's no need for red-hot pokers. Hell is other people.' Not least, this famous maxim reflects Sartre's view that the basis of all human relationships is **conflict**.

The play also seeks to reveal the absurdity of human existence and human concerns under the aspect of eternity. It makes the case that annihilation is better than eternal life as the person one is, although it does so by supposing an eternal life that consists of a single dreary room with no other distractions but the company of unpleasant people. See also **hate**, **the look** and **transcendence-transcended**.

inauthenticity   **Bad faith**. The antithesis of **authenticity**.

incarnation   To arouse oneself or the **Other** to an awareness of the **body** as passive flesh. To cause to exist as passive flesh. See **masochism**, **sadism** and **sexual desire**.

indeterminacy   Generally refers to the indeterminate, ambiguous nature of **being-for-itself**, the being of which is to be what it is not and not to be what it is. See also **ambiguity**.

indifference   An attitude towards others in which a person is wilfully blind to the being of the **Other** as a **transcendence** and thereby to his own **being-for-others**. The indifferent person does in fact comprehend that the Other exists and that he is a being for the Other, but he practises evading this comprehension through a blindness maintained in **bad faith**. He does not suffer his blindness as a state, he continually makes himself blind. He practises a sort of **solipsism**, acting as if he were alone in the world. He engages with the Other as an instrument or avoids the Other as an obstacle, recognizing only the Other's function or lack of function. He refuses to imagine that the Other can **look** at him, that he can be an object for the Other's subjectivity, that the Other can render him a **transcendence-transcended**. He looks at the Other's look as a modification of the mechanism that the Other is for him, as something that expresses what the Other is rather than what he is for the Other. He certainly does not look at the Other's look to stare the Other down and render him a transcendence-transcended. He has perfected a studied indifference towards the transcendence of the Other and has no interest in a battle of wills with the Other.

The indifferent person appears to have discovered a way of no longer being threatened by the Other's transcendence, but in fact it is because he is so threatened by the Other's transcendence that he persists in his indifference. As he is indifferent to the Other, he cannot be shy, timid or embarrassed before the Other, and so comes across as self-confident. But his self-confidence is not a confidence before the Other as Other – he will not allow the Other to exist for him in that way – it is rather a confidence in his practised ability to manage the instrument or obstacle that the Other is for him. Indifference, then, is premised upon a deep insecurity and involves a profound isolation. The indifferent person is alienated by his alienation of the Other. In cutting himself off from the Other he is cut off from what he could be for the Other and from what the Other could make him be.

His indifference to the transcendence of the Other means that he can neither transcend the Other's transcendence to become a subject for the Other, or be transcended by the transcendence of the Other to become an object for the Other. He can only be the unjustifiable subjectivity that he is for himself. He is stuck with himself, unable to find any relief from his **contingency** and **ambiguity** in what the Other makes of him.

Sartre famously argues that **'hell is other people'**, meaning that it is hell to exist for the Other and to be at the mercy of the Other's judgements. In his analysis of indifference, however, Sartre recognizes the hell of refusing to exist for the Other and of isolating oneself in one's own subjectivity. Being-for-others is a source of distress but it is also a source of relief and pleasure. Only by acknowledging the existence of the Other, and in so doing his existence for the Other, can a person feel proud or flattered, for example. In allowing himself to be reduced to an object by the Other's look he may be pleased to discover that he is a pleasing or fascinating object for the Other, and so on. The Other is a source of positive as well as negative evaluations, but the Other cannot be a source of *any* evaluations unless his otherness is admitted. See also **hate** and **love**.

in-itself   An abbreviation of '**being-in-itself**'. Unless reference to being-in-itself is specifically required, **Sartre** and his commentators generally use the expression 'the in-itself' as it is less lumbering.

insanity   See *The Condemned of Altona*, *Erostratus*, **Laing**, *Nausea* and *The Room*.

insincerity   The opposite of 'sincerity' as ordinarily defined. Dishonesty. However, Sartre's radical redefining of 'sincerity' as a form of **bad faith** results in 'insincerity' ceasing to function as the opposite of 'sincerity'. In a sense, 'insincere' and 'sincere' come to have the same meaning in Sartre's philosophy in so far as sincerity is equated with bad faith, bad faith with dishonesty and dishonesty with insincerity. The redefining of 'sincerity' means that use of the term 'insincerity' would lead to confusion in most contexts within Sartre's work, the main reason why he does not use the term very often. See **sincerity**.

instrumental complex   See **system of instrumentality**.

instrumental system   See **system of instrumentality**.

instrumentality   See **system of instrumentality**.

intellectual project   A term originally employed by **Merleau-Ponty** referring to an individual or collective project involving deliberate theorizing and intellectualizing about means and ends. By itself an intellectual project is insufficient to bring about concrete changes in circumstances. Change can only be brought about by what Merleau-Ponty refers to as an **existential project**. Specifically, Merleau-Ponty views social revolution as an existential project and accuses **Sartre** of treating it as an intellectual project.

intention   See **action** and **choice**.

intentional object/s   An intentional object is whatever **consciousness** is of or about, be it perceived, imagined, believed or felt emotionally. **Self-consciousness** involves consciousness reflecting on itself as an intentional object. An intentional object does not exist independently of consciousness intending it. It is comprised of a series of **appearances** that consciousness collects together and treats as the appearance of a particular given phenomenon. A person's hatred of an enemy, for example, does not exist in its own right but consists of the feelings of revulsion, cruel desires, negative memories and so on associated with that enemy. **Sartre** refers to this kind of intentional object as a **psychic object**. From a **phenomenological** perspective a physical object is also an intentional object, though not a psychic object. It is an intentional object in so far as it is a collection of appearances to consciousness rather than a thing in itself. In the same way that a person's experience of a phoenix is not of a physical thing but of an intentional object comprised of various appearances (literary references, artistic images and so on), so his experience of a coin is the experience not of a physical thing but of an intentional object comprised of various appearances. A coin appears large close up and small further away, different sides appear successively as it rotates, its colour appears to alter with the light and so on. When reduced to its appearances in this way a physical object does not appear, but is rather a succession of aspects. **Phenomenology**, instead of equating the physical object with a supposed ground or substratum, equates the physical object with all of its appearances, actual and possible. See also **intentionality**.

intentionality   According to **phenomenologists** such as **Brentano**, **Husserl** and **Sartre**, intentionality is the defining feature of **consciousness**. Consciousness is nothing in itself. It is a relationship to the world that exists only in so far as it *intends* something. To perceive is to perceive something, to believe is to believe something, to imagine is to imagine something and so on. Sartre argues that **consciousness is consciousness of** ___. He means that consciousness is only ever consciousness of whatever phenomena it is directed towards, concerned with or about and is never anything beyond that. The intentionality of consciousness is sometimes referred to as the **aboutness** of consciousness, though not by Sartre. Phenomenologists refer to all the various types of phenomena intended by consciousness as **intentional objects**. Whatever consciousness intends is an intentional object for consciousness. See also *Transcendence of the Ego*.

internal negation   See **negation, internal**.

internal relation   A phenomenon is internally related to another phenomenon when it exists by virtue of its relation to that phenomenon and cannot exist independently of that phenomenon. That is, an internally related phenomenon has no being other than as a relation to another phenomenon. Its internal relation is a logical relation; it is logically dependent. For **Sartre**, the fundamental internal relation is that existing between **non-being** (**being-for-itself**) and **being** (**being-in-itself**). Non-being is not the opposite of being. To speak of 'opposition' implies that non-being exists in its own right independently of being and subsequently becomes externally related to being by existing in opposition to it (see **external relations**). Rather, non-being is the **negation** of being. Non-being *is* being-denied. As being-denied it cannot be separated from being and is nothing in itself. 'Opposition' implies a fundamental independence whereas 'negation' implies a fundamental dependence.

Being-for-itself is internally related to being-in-itself because being-for-itself is completely dependent on being-in-itself for its being as a negation, for its negative, **borrowed being**. In short, being-for-itself is nothing but the negation of being-in-itself. Its being as a negation is logically internal – as opposed to logically external – to the being it must perpetually negate in order to make itself be. **Consciousness**, as a being-for-itself, is internally related to the world. As an internal relation to the world consciousness posits **external relations** between objects in order to experience the world. (Note that being-in-itself, as Sartre conceives it, is not internally or externally related to being-for-itself. Being-in-itself is what it is and does not exist in relation to another being. All relations arise from the point of view of being-for-itself.)

Through the fundamental, logically internal relationship existing between being-for-itself and being-in-itself arise other internally related phenomena that are inalienable features of the relationship between being-for-itself and being-in-itself as it is manifested at the **phenomenological level**. **Past** and **future** are internally related, for example, as are **facticity** and **transcendence**. Past and future do not exist as distinct phenomena. The past exists only for a being-for-itself that flees it towards the future. The future exists only for a being-for-itself fleeing its past. In order to emphasize the internal relation and logical dependence of past and future, Sartre describes the past as a **past-future** and the future as a **future-past** (see *ekstasis* and **temporality**). As for facticity and transcendence, transcendence cannot be the transcendence of itself but must always be the transcendence of facticity. As such, transcendence is logically dependent upon facticity for its being as a transcendence. It is internally related to facticity as the perpetual negation of it. See also **original synthesis**.

Intimacy (1939)   A short story by **Sartre** contained in a collection of short stories entitled **The Wall**, *The Wall* being the lead story in the collection. The same collection of short stories was later repackaged as *Intimacy*, *Intimacy* becoming the lead story in the collection.

Set in Paris in the 1930s the story tells of Lulu's half-hearted and ultimately unsuccessful attempt to leave her dull, oafish, impotent husband, Henri. Lulu is young, physically attractive, irresponsible and sexually repressed. Partly to relieve her boredom, partly because she is too weak-minded to resist, she allows herself to be drawn into love affairs with dominant, decisive men whose virility both intrigues and intimidates her. Her current lover, Pierre, wants her to run away with him to Nice but she is reluctant to leave the mundane, predictable, domestic, slightly grubby intimacy she has with Henri. Henri's impotence, his physical inertia particularly in bed, the lack of challenge he presents as a person generally, make Lulu feel safe and secure. Encouraged by her friend Rirette, Lulu manages to leave home with a packed suitcase, but even while she prepares to go to Nice, she deliberately shops where Henri will see her. Sure enough, much to Rirette's annoyance, Henri sees Lulu and demands that she return to him, not because he loves her but because she is his wife and belongs to him. Rirette and Henri struggle over Lulu who is 'limp as a bag of laundry' between them, until Rirette finally manages to get Lulu into a taxi and away from Henri. The split, however, is only temporary and Lulu returns to Henri that night after Pierre leaves her alone in a hotel room. She spends the remainder of the night with Henri before returning to the hotel in the morning. Finally, she is retrieved from the hotel by friends, the Texiers, and taken back to Henri before Pierre returns. She sends Pierre a letter telling him that she is staying with Henri because he is so unhappy, but that she will continue to meet with Pierre as usual.

Intimacy is essentially a character study of a physically attractive, irresponsible, passive yet manipulative young woman who is in **bad faith** in various ways. Lulu is indecisive, apparently incapable of making important decisions or of committing herself to a clear course of **action**. Even her final decision to stay with Henri is a **choice** not to choose between Henri and Pierre and to persist with a life of deception and double standards. She not only chooses not to choose, she views her actions as though others are responsible for them, as though she is a **facticity** acted upon rather than a **transcendence** acting. She stays because Henri and the Texiers want her to; she planned to leave because Pierre and Rirette wanted her to. She is what Sartre describes elsewhere as a **buffeted consciousness**, a person who sees herself as a fixed entity buffeted and swept along by circumstances, a person who believes she cannot really help what she does. In bad faith she believes that everything happens *to* her. In reality, relying largely on her physical attractiveness to others, she *makes* herself the passive centre around which others gather and scheme with regard to her. As others want her as an object for their own ends she is ultimately able to manipulate circumstances in her favour by being the object that they want her to be. Lulu's bad faith is comparable in certain respects to the bad faith of Sartre's **flirt**, and certainly Lulu is a flirt. With no real commitment to doing so she flirts with the idea of leaving Henri for the sake of a love affair that is itself a mere flirtation, a self-indulgent hobby that she finds more upsetting than exciting when she cares to reflect on it. She does not want to commit herself emotionally to Pierre and is not capable of doing so. She craves only the unemotional, domestic intimacy she has with Henri. She craves it because it is predictable and reassuring and places no demands on her.

Some critics have accused Sartre of misogyny, and Lulu is certainly the first of several negative, inauthentic female characters that appear in his writings. In Sartre's defence, it can be argued that most of his male characters are negative and inauthentic also. Sartre's constant theme is the human frailty that disposes most people, men and women, to diverse projects of bad faith.

Iron in the Soul (1949)   Alternative title *Troubled Sleep*. The third volume in Sartre's trilogy of novels, **Roads to Freedom**. It is June 1940, twenty-one months after the events of the second volume in the trilogy, **The Reprieve**. The Germans have occupied Paris and France is defeated. The defeat of a nation is the central theme of the novel, defeat as it is suffered, celebrated or refused by a variety of characters, many of whom have been introduced earlier in the trilogy.

The novel begins in New York the day after the fall of Paris. The exiled Spanish general and painter, Gomez, sweats profusely in the humid New York heat as he seeks a job as an art critic. Preoccupied with their own concerns, the Americans are unmoved by the plight of France and hardly give the war in Europe a thought. For his part, Gomez gloats over the fall of Paris on the grounds that the French did nothing when Franco entered Barcelona during the Spanish Civil War. Gomez is vain and selfish and hardly gives a thought to his Jewish wife, Sarah, and their son, Pablo, left behind in France. The novel cuts to Sarah and Pablo who are fleeing Paris. Their taxi runs out of petrol and they are forced to continue on foot along with thousands of other refugees as Nazi planes roar overhead. We are not told what becomes of Sarah and Pablo, or Gomez for that matter. Until the novel comes to focus entirely on Mathieu, the central character of the trilogy, then finally Brunet, it makes relatively brief visits to various characters before abandoning them inconclusively to their war-torn circumstances and the choices they must make. Real life seldom ties up loose ends and true to life *Iron in the Soul* does not do so either. Those characters that do not die are left as they were found earlier in the triology, struggling with their lifelong burden of **ambiguity** and **freedom**, most of them resorting to **bad faith**.

Boris is in a military hospital recovering from peritonitis. As he has failed to be 'decently and neatly killed' in action he is wondering what to do with his life. Should he marry his long-time girlfriend Lola and become a teacher or should he take the opportunity to escape to England in a plane to fight another day? He consults with Lola as to what he should do, hoping for her permission to abandon her for war a second time. Boris sees Lola only in relation to his own concerns, but she has concerns of her own – a life-threatening tumour of the womb – and is no longer particularly interested in him.

Ivich, Boris' capricious sister, longs for the death in action of her boring, wealthy husband, Georges, and to be free of her interfering in-laws. Always unrealistic, she begs Boris to rescue her from a situation of her own making, proposing, even though she detests Lola, that the three of them live together on Lola's money.

Daniel walks the streets of a largely deserted Paris that awaits the arrival of its conquerors. He rejoices in an intoxicating sensation of power and freedom, triumphing in the defeat of a city and a people that despised and alienated him for his homosexuality. He comes across Philippe, an attractive young deserter who is contemplating throwing himself from a bridge. He proceeds to seduce Philippe, enticing him to his apartment.

Jacques, Mathieu's bourgeois lawyer brother, is fleeing Paris with his wife, Odette. Jacques refuses the adventure of driving all night and they park in a lane to sleep. It emerges that it was Jacques' idea to flee Paris – Odette had wanted to stay – but in a bad-faith-ridden effort to conceal his cowardice from himself, Jacques craftily manipulates Odette into 'accepting' that *her* fears had been their motive for leaving. Dismissing Jacques as worthless and predictable, Odette dwells on her love for Mathieu.

With the Nazis advancing rapidly, Mathieu's division is abandoned by its officers. Without leadership or hope the men languish in the misery of their defeat, blurring reality with drink or religion as they wait to be taken prisoner. A small unit determined to fight arrives on the scene and Mathieu joins them, following the example of a young soldier, Pinette, who dreads returning home defeated. Without reflecting too deeply, Mathieu makes a series of momentous choices: he picks up a discarded rifle, he takes up a position on a church tower with Pinette and a few others and engages the enemy. Mathieu makes his choices not because he wants death or heroism, but to refuse the defeat that has undermined the dignity and mastered the destiny of his fellow soldiers. We learn in *The Reprieve* that Mathieu welcomes conscription as an opportunity to become committed and responsible. To accept defeat and capture would be to abandon his chosen path at the hour of reckoning and thus render all his previous actions meaningless. His brief stand against the Nazis is all but futile in military terms, but for him it is an uncompromising and decisive act that is the ultimate affirmation of his freedom. With each shot he fires he dispenses with **regret**, vacillation, scruples, all his former bad faith, and finally takes full **responsibility** for his **being-in-situation**. Unlike most of the other characters in the novel, who remain submerged in bad faith, Mathieu achieves **authenticity**. We are not told what becomes of him, but given that the exit from the tower becomes blocked with fallen beams and Brunet sees the tower collapse, we are invited to assume Mathieu is killed.

The final 120 pages of the novel, which draw heavily on Sartre's own experiences as a prisoner of war, focus on the capture, imprisonment and eventual deportation to Germany of Brunet, a zealous, tough, self-disciplined and self-possessed Communist. Like Mathieu, Brunet has learnt to accept his being-in-situation without complaint or regret and strives to act positively and decisively in his situation. He is, or strives to be, authentic.

Brunet and thousands of other captured soldiers are marched to a prison camp where they are left to starve for several days. Believing rumours that food will soon arrive, the men lounge about grumbling and waiting to be fed. They fight like dogs over a few scraps of bread thrown mockingly by a German soldier. Brunet grinds a piece that falls at his feet into the dust. He commands his body to obey him and tries to fight his hunger by running around the camp, but he eventually collapses, remaining sick for several days until finally fed.

Brunet views his fellow prisoners with contempt. With a few exceptions they are slovenly, weak-minded dreamers, lacking self-discipline and in need of someone to obey. They are like children or monkeys with their idle chatter and false hopes. Brunet's analysis of them is correct but he is nonetheless harsh and judgemental. As a Communist Brunet wants to liberate mankind from oppression but he has no particular love or empathy for any individual. He thinks about 'making use of people', viewing them as instruments for achieving greater political ends. Schneider, a man with some Communist sympathies who is Brunet's equal in composure and intelligence and his only real friend, accuses Brunet of acting like a surgeon at a post-mortem. As events unfold Brunet acquires some compassion for his fellow prisoners, but he is nonetheless irritated by their adherence to self-indulgence and idiocy. The few activists he recruits to the Communist cause report that if the prisoners were released there would be 'twenty thousand additional Nazis'. Their weak-mindedness and need for authority leads the prisoners to identify with their captors. They need to believe in Nazi organization and decency, and above all that they will be released and not deported to Germany as forced labour. Brunet is resented by the majority for not sharing their delusions. Their false belief that they are to be released is maintained even when they are packed onto a train. They act in bad faith, reassuring one another with unconvincing arguments and angrily dismissing all counter claims until it is beyond doubt that they are going to Germany. A young man is shot for jumping from the train in a bid for freedom and at last the prisoners discover real anger towards the Nazis. 'For the first time since September '39 this was war.' Brunet believes that now the prisoners have learnt to hate oppression he can recruit them to the Communist cause and influence the course of history.

— K —

Kant, Immanuel (1724–1804)   German transcendental idealist philosopher. A central figure of Western philosophy whose ideas and philosophical method redefined the work of his predecessors and profoundly influenced all subsequent philosophical thinking, particularly in the Continental tradition. Kant significantly influenced **Sartre** both directly and through his enormous influence on the German philosophers **Hegel**, **Husserl** and **Heidegger**, a triumvirate that Sartre studied closely at different times in his career. One of Sartre's earliest published works, ***The Transcendence of the Ego*** (1937), is essentially a critique of Husserl's transcendental subjectivism, a philosophy of mind that draws heavily upon Kant's transcendental idealism.

In his *Critique of Pure Reason* (1781) and other works, Kant synthesizes the rationalism of **Descartes** and Leibniz with the empiricism of Locke and Hume to produce a comprehensive theory of the relationship between the mind and the world known as transcendental idealism. He argues that the world of **phenomena** we experience is shaped at the most fundamental level by the mind. Essential features of human experience such as **time**, space and causation do not belong to the world in itself but are instead concepts that are applied to the world by the mind in order to make sense of it. These concepts are not learnt from experience as experience gives us no impression of them, they are known a priori (prior to experience). For Kant, the essential features of human experience are conceptual categories imposed on the world by reason in order to render the world meaningful.

Sartre sometimes and rather inconsistently espouses **realism** as opposed to transcendental idealism, arguing that **appearances** are mind-independent and so on, but at its **ontological** core his philosophy of mind is markedly similar to Kant's, endorsing transcendental idealism and the view that appearances are appearances to __. Sartre's crucial distinction between **being-in-itself** and phenomena, for example, directly echoes Kant's distinction between **noumenon** (the thing-in-itself) and phenomena, and Sartre's claim that phenomena arise for **consciousness** through the **negation** of **undifferentiated being** is a thoroughly post-Kantian notion.

Sartre was also influenced by Kant in his least credible attempt to derive a consistent moral theory from the basic principles of his **existentialism**. In *Existentialism and Humanism* (1946) Sartre insists that when a person chooses a certain course of action for himself he chooses it for everyone in so far as he asserts by his **choice** that everyone ought to do as he does. Sartre's position appears prima facie to be similar to Kant's theory of the Categorical Imperative: 'I ought never to act except in such a way *that I can also will that my maxim should become a universal law.*' Closer examination, however, reveals that the two positions have little if anything in common. Kant argues that morality consists of refraining from those actions that cannot be universalized without contradiction. The practice of lying, for example, cannot be universalized without destroying the convention of truth-telling upon which lying depends for its parasitic existence. Kant argues that I ought not to do things that establish maxims that cannot be universalized. He certainly does not insist, as Sartre does, that I ought only to do things that I believe everyone ought to do. Kant's emphasis is on 'ought not', where as Sartre's is on 'everyone ought'. The moral theory that Sartre puts forward in *Existentialism and Humanism*, if it can be said to amount to a theory, is not only a confused version of Kant's moral theory, it is inconsistent with the central claims of his own existentialism. Sartre's considered views on **freedom**, choice and **responsibility** simply do not imply that a man who chooses to marry, for example, is asserting by his choice that everyone ought to do likewise. Arguably, an **existentialist** is far more likely to insist that everyone can do what suits them so long as they are prepared to take full responsibility for the consequences of their actions without **regret**. The pseudo-Kantian theory Sartre puts forward in *Existentialism and Humanism* can fortunately be seen as something of an aberration and need not be taken too seriously. Sartre was guilty of distorting and oversimplifying his views in his desire to shock and entertain his audience at a fashionable literary event and he soon rejected the theory in question as confused and unconvincing, He continued, however, to flirt with Kantian ethics in other respects in his ***Notebooks for an Ethics*** (1947–48, published posthumously 1983).

Kean or Disorder and Genius (1954)   A play by **Sartre** about the great Shakespearian actor Edmund Kean (1789–1833), based on a play of the same name written in 1836 by Alexandre Dumas, *père* (1802–70). Kean was a womanizing alcoholic whose intense and turbulent personality spilled over into his brilliant performances of Shakespeare's tragic heroes. Kean was highly paid and hugely popular but his lifestyle gradually took its toll on his finances, health and reputation. He collapsed on stage in 1833 playing Othello to his son's Iago and died a few weeks later.

Sartre's play largely preserves the farcical plot and comical, melodramatic tones of Dumas' original. Repeatedly drunk, pursued by creditors and increasingly broke, Kean is having, or attempting to have, a love affair with Elena, Countess de Koefeld, wife of the Danish Ambassador. Kean is jealous of the attentions shown to Elena by his friend and patron, the Prince of Wales. Under the guise of making a wager, the Prince offers to pay Kean's debts if he ends his affair with Elena, claiming that it is damaging diplomatic relations between England and Denmark. Meanwhile, Kean is pursued by a beautiful young heiress, Anna Danby, who desires to be his lover and protégée. She and Kean are both pursued by her fiancé Lord Neville. The play climaxes with Kean playing Othello to Anna's Desdemona at Drury Lane Theatre while Elena and the Prince watch from a box close to the stage. Elena is jealous of Kean's attentions to Anna while Kean is jealous of the Prince's attentions to Elena. Anna cannot remember her lines and the Prince starts to discuss the failing performance with Elena. Motivated by jealously, Kean orders the Prince to be quiet and to let him do his job. He insults the Prince before a packed house, telling him that although he may be a prince he, Kean, is king when on stage. In a performance that the Prince describes as 'magnificent', Kean goes on to harangue his audience before leaving the stage. It appears that Kean is ruined but the play contrives a happy ending in which the Prince forgives Kean, Elena returns to her husband and Kean departs for America with Anna.

For Sartre, as for Dumas, the play is primarily a study of the character of Edmund Kean. Kean does not know who he really is. He suspects that he is nothing more than the part he is playing, that even when he is not acting on stage he is playing the part of Edmund Kean the great actor. 'I am nothing my child. I play at being what I am.' Kean plays the part of Hamlet or Kean just as the Prince of Wales plays the part of the Prince of Wales. Sartre uses the play to explore in further detail themes first raised in **Being and Nothingness** (1943) concerning the nature of self-identity. In *Being and Nothingness* Sartre describes a **waiter** who plays at being a waiter because it is impossible for him, or for anyone, to be a waiter in the mode of being one. As a **negation** of **being-in-itself** that must perpetually negate being in order to be, **being-for-itself** is not a fixed entity. A person is never what they are, they have to constantly aim at being what they are without being able to become it. Kean even comments that he is not an actor. He only ever strives to be an actor through acting. An actor is not what he is, acting is simply what he does. A person who supposes that he is a fixed entity is in **bad faith**. In so far as Kean is always acutely aware that he is not a fixed entity he is authentic (see **authenticity**). At times, when the endless change of masks threatens to overwhelm him, when he feels he is respected only as an actor and not as a person, or that nobody takes him seriously, Kean expresses the desire to give up acting and become a cheesemonger or a jeweller, but he recognizes that he would still have to act these parts and would not simply be able to become them. His desire to give up acting is another act, as are his infatuations, his bouts of apparent insanity and his attempts at **sincerity**. Kean is able to convince others, at least for the duration of his performance, that he is Hamlet or Othello, but he is unable to convince himself that he is Kean. His life would be less turbulent and disorganized, though perhaps less exciting and attractive to others, if he could achieve the bad faith required to impose some coherence upon his personality. His personality is so incoherent that he objects to having to accept the consequences of his past actions. He is utterly irresponsible and does not, for example, see why he should pay for jewellery ordered six months before for a woman he no longer loves. He has played many parts since then and loved several women and is certainly no longer the person he was. The law, of course, insists that he is and holds him accountable for his actions.

Sartre's exploration of Kean's character is an exploration of the **indeterminacy** of being-for-itself. His exploration of Kean's relations with others is an exploration of **being-for-others** and those modes of being, such as **love**, that are aspects of being-for-others. Sartre's depiction of the love between Kean and Elena expresses his **existentialist** view of love generally. Kean's love for Elena is an act. Elena loves Kean the actor and as such her love is conditional. It is evident that if Kean ceased to be a stage actor Elena would cease to love him. As Kean *is* the parts he plays, Elena's love for him is love of the parts he plays. Moreover, as the parts he plays are subject to Elena's interpretation, she is in love with her own idea of Kean rather than Kean himself. After all, she cannot be in love with Kean himself when Kean has no self.

Sartre also makes the point that people often exist more clearly and distinctly for others than they do for themselves. This is because a person is able to believe more easily that the being of another person is fixed and substantial than he is able to believe that his own being is fixed and substantial. Kean is more real to an audience as Lear or Hamlet than he is to himself as Kean. For others, Kean is the Great Kean, the great performer, and he must constantly command their love and attention in order to be reassured that he exists. Similarly, Elena is the beautiful Elena for others and the Prince of Wales is the noble prince for others. Nobody can be great, beautiful or noble alone.

The play is also a commentary on the corrupting and destructive influences of fame. Flattered and over-indulged, famous people often become like Kean, spoilt and irresponsible. Furthermore, the adoration they crave ultimately disappoints them because it is not directed towards them but towards their public persona. The more closely they identify themselves with their public persona the more intensely they suffer the capriciousness of their audience. If they distance themselves from their public persona they grow to resent it as a grotesque caricature that distorts and obscures them, a being-for-others that others hold them responsible for even though it is not them.

Kierkegaard, Søren (1813–55)   Danish philosopher, theologian and early **existentialist**. Kierkegaard is famed for breaking off his engagement to Regine Olsen in 1841 to devote himself to philosophy. For the remaining years of his relatively short life, often publishing under pseudonyms, Kierkegaard produced a huge body of philosophical and theological writing that in time inspired both **existentialism** and modern Protestant theology. Among his most notable works are *Either-Or* (1843), *Fear and Trembling* (1843) and *The Sickness Unto Death* (1849). Many of the central themes and concepts of existentialism originated in the writings of Kierkegaard – **freedom**, **choice**, **responsibility**, **anxiety**, **despair**, **absurdity**.

Kierkegaard was an important influence on **Sartre** both directly and through his profound influence on **Heidegger**. Unlike Sartre and Heidegger, who are noted for their **atheism**, Kierkegaard was a Christian, albeit a maverick Christian who was increasingly at odds with orthodox Christian views generally and the Danish State Church in particular. It is Kierkegaard's radical approach to Christianity, his views on faith and religious commitment and his rejection of a rationalist approach towards the religious life that make him a true existentialist.

Kierkegaard despises the rationalism of **Hegel**. He argues that in making human thought the product of an historical process Hegel ignores the human individual who does not experience himself primarily, if at all, as part of history, but rather as a free, anxious, despairing being troubled by moral concerns and existing without any purpose that reason can discover. Kierkegaard is also critical of traditional Christian theology for claiming that God's existence and nature can be established objectively and that religious and moral beliefs are, therefore, a matter of reason. For Kierkegaard, God's existence cannot be proven or even shown to be probable as no amount of finite reasoning can establish anything at all about the infinite. Religious faith is not a matter of objective reasoning or a matter of going along with the reasoning of others through the complacent acceptance of Church doctrine, but rather a matter of a highly personal, subjective and freely chosen commitment to believe.

For Sartre, all faith is **bad faith** and he would identify in Kierkegaard's views on religious faith the manifestations of a **primitive project** of bad faith whereby a person chooses to believe what suits him. The kind of bad faith that, as Sartre argues in *Being and Nothingness* (1943), is able 'to count itself satisfied when it is barely persuaded, to force itself in decisions to adhere to uncertain truths'. Sartre would certainly question the religious direction of Kierkegaard's philosophy, but not his view that every person is an indeterminate and necessarily free being striving to fulfil himself and to give meaning to his absurd existence. Sartre, following Heidegger, places great emphasis on Kierkegaard's view of the self as indeterminate and ambiguous (see **indeterminacy**). A person is nothing other than what he chooses to be. He is free and he cannot cease to be free. He cannot become a fixed, determinate being that no longer questions the nature of his being. As Kierkegaard notes in *The Sickness Unto Death*, the self despairs, unto death, of achieving oneness with itself, just as it despairs of being rid of itself as a self that despairs of achieving oneness with itself. Kierkegaard's notion of the self despairing both of being itself and of escaping itself was highly influential on Sartre's own notion of **being-for-itself**. Echoing Kierkegaard, Sartre argues that being-for-itself is an indeterminate being that constantly strives to be at one with itself as a **being-for-itself-in-itself**. This unachievable desire to be at one with itself is at the same time a desire to escape itself as a paradoxical being that is always what it is not and not what it is.

Perhaps Kierkegaard's most important contribution to the existentialism of Heidegger, Sartre and others is the notion that a person's inescapable freedom is a source of anxiety or anguish. Sartre echoes Kierkegaard when he notes that anxiety and fear are fundamentally different. A person's fear is his concern for his objective self, his **body**, whereas his anxiety is his concern for his subjective, ambiguous self and the fact that he must constantly determine himself through the exercise of choice. Sartre illustrates the difference between fear and anxiety with an example of a person walking along a precipice. He fears he might fall, but he is anxious and suffers vertigo because he is free to jump. Both Kierkegaard and Sartre note that a great deal of human behaviour can be explained as an attempt to avoid the anxiety of being free. A person employs various strategies to fool himself that he is not free. He seeks to evade his freedom and relinquish responsibility for himself by pretending to himself that his actions are determined by circumstances rather than by himself. He pleads the excuse of following orders or doctrine, he treats his body as though it were a mere object to be acted upon, he acts as though he is a machine and so on. It is these various strategies that Sartre details in his account of bad faith, an account inspired in no small part by the ideas of Kierkegaard.

$$— \mathbf{L} —$$

lack   As the **negation** of **being-in-itself**, **being-for-itself** is constituted as a lack of being. Being-for-itself lacks identity with itself. In short, it lacks itself. The **for-itself**, however, is not a lack in itself. If it was a lack in itself it would be identical with itself as lack, it would be pure nothingness and as such would be annihilated. Rather, it is that which cannot achieve identity with itself as a being or as a lack of being. The for-itself *has to be* its own lack without being able either to become it or to overcome it by achieving complete fulfilment.

The for-itself must be situated in order to be (see **situatedness**). The for-itself, for which the situation is a situation, exists as the negation of its situation. Every situation of the for-itself is understood not in terms of what it is but in terms of what it lacks, in terms of what the for-itself desires, and what every situation lacks is the for-itself. A situation does not lack anything in itself but every situation lacks something for the for-itself for which it is a situation. As a perpetual **temporal flight** towards future fulfilment the for-itself always encounters every situation as lacking something in the present. Every **action** of the for-itself is undertaken to overcome whatever the for-itself presently lacks and therefore desires. The lack or **desire** gives meaning to the action in that the action is essentially that which is undertaken to overcome the lack, to satisfy the desire.

The for-itself is the particular lacks or **negativities** that determine the situation as a situation. To illustrate that the lacks that determine the situation of the for-itself are lacks that the for-itself places into being in order to give rise to its situation, **Sartre** gives the example of a situation in which a person judges that the moon is not full. In itself the crescent moon is what it is, it does not lack being a full moon. It is understood as a partial appearance of the full moon, as a lack of the full moon, by a for-itself that is able to surpass the being of the crescent moon towards the non-being of the full moon. It is the non-being or lack of the full moon that gives the crescent moon its meaning for **consciousness**. For consciousness the crescent moon exists in the mode of being the non-being of the full moon. The crescent moon is understood as what it is by virtue of what it lacks. See also **existential absence**, **formal absence** and **'man is a useless passion'**.

Laing, Ronald D. (1927–89)   Scottish psychiatrist who developed Sartre's theory of **existential psychoanalysis** and applied it in the clinical setting. **Sartre** knew and respected Laing's work and wrote an introduction to *Reason and Violence* (1964), a book by Laing that summarizes the approach to psychology and personal history adopted by Sartre in *Saint Genet* (1952) and other works. Laing's best-known work, *The Divided Self: An Existential Study in Sanity and Madness* (1960), explores psychosis and schizophrenia from a **phenomenological** perspective.

   According to Laing, traditional psychiatry identifies schizophrenia as a general condition that people suffer from as though it were an illness. It is assumed that because schizophrenics tend to exhibit similar symptoms they *have* schizophrenia in much the same way as a person *has* a cold. Laing argues that this approach does not so much explain a schizophrenic person as explain him away by characterizing his condition as the product of various impersonal processes. For Laing, no one *has* schizophrenia. Schizophrenia is not an entity that a schizophrenic possesses in common with other schizophrenics but a product of his own unique **choice** of himself in response to the peculiarities of his own unique situation. Thus, for Laing, so called 'insanity', for the person concerned, is a normal response to an abnormal situation. Understanding a schizophrenic's behaviour is not achieved through the application of certain clinical labels that refer to pseudo-irreducible drives and desires (see **pseudo-irreducibles**), it is achieved through a thorough exploration of his personal history that aims to identify his **fundamental choice** of himself and the **fundamental project** that he has adopted in response to that fundamental choice. For

Laing, the task of the psychiatrist is not to curb or control a patient's schiz-ophrenic behaviour but to provide safe and non-judgemental circumstances in which his schizophrenic behaviour is allowed full expression in the hope that it will reveal the patient's fundamental choice and fundamental project to the psychiatrist and ultimately to the patient himself. For the patient, identifying his fundamental choice and project can be the end of a process of self-discovery whereby his insanity resolves itself and he moves beyond it. Sartre's theory of **consciousness** implies that insanity, like every other mode of consciousness, is not a fixed state. The possibility remains, therefore, of a **radical conversion** to an alternative and more positive way of being.

Laing remains an influential figure in the move towards a patient- or client-centred approach in psychiatry, clinical psychology and counselling that seeks to place the individual understanding of a person and the peculiarities of his history at the heart of his diagnosis and treatment.

the look   In *Being and Nothingness* (1943) **Sartre** examines *the look*, the significance of being looked at and seen by another person – the **Other**. Sartre argues that when a person is looked at by the Other he ceases to be a free **transcendence** of the world and becomes instead an object in the world of the Other. His free transcendence is transcended by the transcendence of the Other. He becomes a **transcendence-transcended**. It is through his examination of the look and various concrete examples of the occurrence of the look that Sartre unfolds his detailed account of the existence of others and the phenomenon of **being-for-others**. See also **being-in-the-midst-of-the-world** and **conflict**.

Loser Wins   See *The Condemned of Altona*.

love   Sartre's analysis of love focuses on romantic or erotic love. He argues that the ideal of such love, unity with the other, is doomed to failure. **Sartre** has little or nothing to say about other **phenomena** that are also often referred to as love, such as strong affection for friends, children or animals, for example.

Romantic love is essentially other-related and it is as an aspect of **being-for-others** that Sartre explores the phenomenon. Love belongs to what Sartre refers to in *Being and Nothingness* (1943) as our 'concrete relations with others'. He asks, 'Why does the lover want to be loved?' To understand why it is that the lover wants to be loved is to understand what love is. The lover is not satisfied with the mere physical possession of the **Other**. The lover may have contrived to have the Other physically close to him at all times, but if the lover does not possess the **consciousness** of the Other, if the other does not choose to direct her consciousness towards the lover in a particular way, the lover will be dissatisfied. In desiring to possess the consciousness of the Other the lover does not want to enslave the Other, he does not want to possess a robot-thing whose passions flow mechanically in his direction, but a genuine Other who chooses at each moment to be possessed by him. The lover wants to be loved because he wants to possess the **freedom** of the Other, not as an enslaved freedom that would no longer be a freedom, but as a freedom that remains free though it is possessed because it continually *chooses* itself as possessed. It is important to the lover that the **choice** to be possessed be constantly renewed by the Other. The lover will be dissatisfied with a love that continues to be given through loyalty to an oath, for example. Lovers are insecure and demand pledges of love, but as Sartre points out, lovers are nonetheless irritated by pledges because they want love to be determined by nothing but the freedom of the Other. The lover does not even want to deliberately cause the Other to love him because a love that is deliberately caused by him is a love determined by something other than the freedom of the Other. Ideally, the lover wants to be loved by a freedom that is no longer free, not because this freedom has been enslaved or causally determined but because it continually wills its own captivity.

In wanting to possess the Other the lover wants to be nothing less than 'the whole world' for the beloved. He wants to be the meaning and purpose of the Other's world, that around which and for which the Other's entire world is ordered. The lover wants to be an object for the Other, but not the object that he is for those who do not love him, a **being-in-the-midst-of-the-world** alongside other objects, but a sacred object that symbolizes the entire world and in which the freedom of the Other consents to lose itself. The lover wants to be chosen as the limit of the Other's **transcendence**. He wants to be that towards which the Other transcends the entire world, without ever being that which the beloved transcends. Ultimately, the lover wants to cease being a contingent and indeterminate being subject to his own shifting evaluations and the evaluations of those who transcend him, and instead assume for himself the absolute, un-transcendable value he believes he would have for the Other if the Other chose to love him.

According to Sartre, romantic love is doomed because what the lover wants is unachievable. It is impossible for the lover to possess the freedom of the Other while the Other remains free because as soon as the Other loves the lover she experiences him as a subject and herself as an object confronted by his subjectivity. The lover wants to possess the transcendence of the Other as a transcendence while at the same time transcending it, but in taking possession of the transcendence of the Other he will inevitably negate it and reduce it to a **facticity**. Transcendence is always the transcendence of facticity and the lover can only transcend the Other as a facticity and not as a transcendence.

In seeking to take possession of the transcendence of the Other the lover runs the risk of being possessed by the transcendence of the Other and being reduced to a facticity. The lover wants the freedom of the Other to elevate him to an absolute value but he is playing with fire in that the freedom of the Other may suddenly look upon him with contempt or **indifference** and reduce him to an object among other objects.

It is important to stress that the lover is Other for the Other and that everything that has been said of the lover applies to the Other as well. The lover desires the Other to love him and thereby make him an absolute value. But if the Other loves the lover it is only because she wants him to make her an absolute value. **Conflict**, which Sartre tends to view as the essence of all human relationships, is inevitable. For Sartre, to love is to want to be loved, so when one person loves another he does not in fact want, as the Other wants him to, to make the Other an ultimate value. Instead, his love consists of wanting the Other to make him an ultimate value. Sartre notes that 'love is the demand to be loved'. As a pure demand love can never supply what is demanded of it. See also **hate**, **masochism**, **sadism** and **sexual desire**.

Lucifer and the Lord (1951)   A play by **Sartre** set in Medieval Germany. The play begins at the siege of Worms. The men of Worms have decided to kill the priests who are barricaded in the monastery. Heinrich, a priest of Worms, is given a key by his bishop as the bishop dies. The key unlocks a secret tunnel from the town. Heinrich can save the priests if he betrays the town to the besieging army. He is confronted with the **radical choice** of saving two hundred priests or twenty thousand men. Heinrich decides he should save the priests, not least because his bishop has commanded it. He escapes the town through the secret tunnel and meets with Goetz the leader of the besieging army. By the time he meets Goetz, Heinrich is unsure about what he should do and hopes that he can somehow avoid choosing. He is in **bad faith**. Goetz, the central character of the play, is an evil, violent man who has betrayed his half-brother Conrad and caused his death. It emerges that Goetz chooses to be evil in order to exercise his **freedom** and assert his will over the will of **God**. He believes that if he is sufficiently evil he will *force* God to damn him thus revealing a limit to God's power. Goetz offers various arguments to persuade Heinrich to tell him where the secret tunnel is. He tells Heinrich that it would be wrong to spare the lives of the people of Worms. Killing them will prevent them from killing the priests and so save them from eternal damnation and so on. The play is full of such theological arguments and dilemmas.

The play takes an unexpected turn when Heinrich convinces Goetz that there is nothing special about doing evil because everyone is doing it, whereas nobody has ever done only good. Goetz undergoes a **radical conversion** and decides to do only good. He lifts the siege without bloodshed and returns to his own lands. To the consternation of the neighbouring barons Goetz gives his land away to the peasants. Peasants on the neighbouring lands revolt demanding the same and a war begins that costs more lives than a massacre at Worms would have done.

One of the main aims of the play is to argue that good and evil are indistinguishable. Any **action** can produce positive or negative consequences that were not or could not be foreseen. As for intentions, they are no clearer than the consequences of actions. A person can be in bad faith with regard to his intentions. Goetz initially believes that in giving his lands away he is motivated by kindness and a desire for social justice, but he later questions his motives recognizing that his desire to do good stems from a selfish desire to be better than everyone else. He also wonders if perhaps he has given his lands away as a final betrayal of his despised family. At the end of the play Goetz undergoes a second radical conversion. Unable to decide throughout the play whether Lucifer or the Lord guides his actions, he finally decides that neither exists. Declaring that 'God is dead' (see

Nietzsche) he becomes the leader of what remains of the peasant army. He no longer desires to be good or evil but to be a man of action.

Darkly comical, the play generates an atmosphere of fear and hysteria as it traverses a broad range of **existential** and theological issues, raising questions and dilemmas about morality, **love**, **hate**, reason, superstition, salvation, damnation and the silence of God. There are also various Marxist themes running throughout the play with Sartre, like Marx, attributing the greater part of human suffering to religious superstition and social inequality (see **Marxism**). Above all, the play explores the nature of human freedom and motivation in light of the existence or non-existence of God.

— M —

'man is a useless passion'   A phrase coined by **Sartre** in *Being and Nothingness* (1943) describing the **human condition** with particular reference to the impossibility of complete satisfaction. As a **being-for-itself** a person is constituted as a **lack** of **being**. Every person constantly strives to overcome the lack of being that he is, but given that he is and must be a lack of being he can never do so. Every person strives to be a being-for-itself that has become a **being-in-itself**, what Sartre calls a **being-for-itself-in-itself**, a being, like **God**, in which existence and essence are one. A person can never achieve this unity, however, because he is only ever the **negation** of being-in-itself and must be so in order to exist as a person, as a **consciousness**. The lack of being that being-for-itself has to be is revealed by **desire** and the fact that desire *per se* can never be satisfied. A *particular* desire can be satisfied, but the satisfaction, the removal, of any particular desire is always immediately surpassed towards a further desire. Man is a passion that aims at complete fulfilment, but in so far as complete fulfilment and the overcoming of all lack and desire is unachievable, man is a *useless* passion.

Marxism   See *Critique of Dialectical Reason*, *The Family Idiot*, *Lucifer and the Lord*, *Nekrassov*, **Sartre** and *What is Literature?*.

masochism   Sartre explores the phenomenon of masochism as an aspect of **being-for-others**, as a feature of our 'concrete relations with others'. An understanding of Sartre's theory of **sexual desire** is required to fully understand his theory of masochism because the phenomenon of masochism, like **sadism**, emerges when sexual desire fails to achieve its goal of reciprocal **incarnation**.

Sartre argues that to want to be loved is to want to possess the **freedom** of the **Other** while the Other remains free and Other – a free subject (see **love**). It is, however, impossible to possess the freedom of the Other while the Other remains free because as soon as the Other loves me she experiences me as a subject and herself as an object confronted by my subjectivity. My inevitable failure to possess the Other as a free subject and identify with her in that way may lead me to attempt the obliteration of my freedom as an obstacle to my hoped-for unity with the Other. I may attempt identification with the Other by surrendering my freedom to hers and allowing her to possess me as an object. This new attempt to identify with the Other is masochistic. A person who resorts to masochism will attempt to become for the Other a mere object without subjectivity. He will attempt to engage himself wholly in his objective being. He will attempt to deny his **transcendence** with the intention of becoming a pure **facticity** for the transcendence of the Other. The masochist wants to become a **transcendence-transcended** by the Other to the extent that his transcendence is utterly annihilated by the freedom of the Other. As a mere object for the Other he will feel ashamed but he will love his shame as the measure of his objectivity. The more ashamed, naked, helpless and debased the masochist becomes before the Other the more of an object he will feel himself to be.

In desiring to be an object for the Other the masochist desires to be an object for himself. In fact, he wants to be an object for the Other in order to satisfy his desire to be an object for himself. Sartre argues that the masochist does not in fact attempt to fascinate the Other with his objectivity, he attempts to fascinate himself with his objectivity for the Other. Masochism may appear even to the masochist as a final and utterly selfless attempt to fascinate the Other through a total surrender to the Other, but in so far as the masochist aims ultimately to fascinate himself with his objectivity for the Other he is acting selfishly and, indeed, using the Other.

The masochist wants to be constituted as a facticity by the Other so as to experience his own transcendence as nothing. The masochist's project of seeking to be for himself the mere object that he is for the Other is not least a project of seeking to escape the **anxiety** he feels as a free transcendence that is burdened with having to make choices. As an abdication of transcendence masochism is a species of **bad faith**.

Masochism, as Sartre points out, is and must be doomed to failure. To attempt to fascinate himself with his objectivity for the Other the masochist must be conscious of himself as an object for the Other. If he is conscious of himself as an object then he is not that object but rather the transcendence of that object. He can only aim at being the object he is for the Other through a transcendence that always places him at a distance from being the object that he is for the Other. The harder he tries to be his objectivity the more he will assert his subjectivity. Furthermore, his project of fascinating himself with his objectivity for the Other actually uses the Other as an instrument. As Sartre points out, if a masochist pays a woman to whip him she becomes his instrument, he treats her as an object and is in transcendence in relation to her.

Men Without Shadows (1946)   A play by **Sartre** set in World War II France. A group of Resistance fighters have been captured by forces loyal to the Vichy Government. Locked in an upstairs room, handcuffed, they await their fate – to be tortured then killed. The youngest of them, François, shows his fear and frustration by complaining that he did not expect such dire consequences when he joined the Resistance. The others, François' sister, Lucie, and three older men, Sorbier, Canoris and Henri, are more resigned. They fear pain and death but their primary concern is to avoid exposing themselves as cowards. If they scream and beg for mercy their torturers will triumph. If they keep silent they will win a moral victory. They view the situation more as a battle of wills on a personal level than anything to do with the cause for which they are fighting. As they initially have no useful information to give their interrogators, they are more concerned with not betraying themselves and their reputation than with betraying others.

Sorbier is taken out and tortured. His screams are heard in the distance. The leader of the group, Jean, is brought into the room. The enemy do not know who he is. In their view he is simply a man they are detaining temporarily while they check his story. Jean's arrival gives the others information that they must try to withhold. They prefer this as it gives their suffering purpose and will provide a mental distraction when their torture begins. Sorbier is returned to the room aware of his limited courage. Seeing Jean he says he would have betrayed him had he known where he was. Canoris and Henri are tortured. Henri cries out in pain but neither man betrays Jean. Sorbier is tortured again. Unable to stand the pain he tells his torturers that he will give them information if they untie him. Untied he runs to the window and jumps to his death. Lucie is tortured and raped but does not crack. She returns to the room feeling emotionally dead, unable to love Jean as she had at the start of the play. Jean has been growing increasingly guilty that the others are suffering for him. He feels excluded and wants to share their suffering in order to feel he is one of them. He wants François to denounce him so that he can be tortured along with the others. He hopes Lucie will love him again if this happens. He even attempts to torture himself by beating his hand with a log. Lucie is not impressed. She argues that this does not compare with her torture because it is not a violation. A person cannot violate himself. Fearing that François will talk under interrogation, Henri strangles him to death. Lucie does nothing to defend her brother.

Still unaware of Jean's identity the torturers release him and the following morning the three surviving prisoners are sent for. Suspecting that the remaining prisoners will not give in and having no real appetite for torture, the enemy leader, Landrieu, says he will spare their lives if they give in and talk. Winning a personal battle of wills has become more important to him than any information his prisoners have to give. The prisoners feel they have won a moral victory. Unable to crack them with torture, Landrieu is now trying to bribe them. Canoris wants to talk and give false information agreed with Jean before his release. The other two do not even want to give false information if it looks as though they cracked. Henri wants to die to be rid of the guilt of killing François, Lucie wants to die to be rid of the shame of being raped. Canoris convinces Henri that he must live in order that his future actions justify his killing François. Together they persuade Lucie that life is still worth living if she can stop dwelling on her suffering and enjoy the simple pleasures that life offers. They give Landrieu their false story and he is prepared to let them live. Clochet, however, a man who enjoys torture for its own sake, a man who used to sell cream cakes before the war, acts against Landrieu's orders and has the prisoners shot.

Comparable to Sartre's short story *The Wall* (1939), *Men Without Shadows* explores the complex psychology of torturers and tortured, executioners and condemned, and the struggle for **transcendence** that exists between them. It is not enough for the torturer to inflict pain or even death, he gains ascendancy over his victim only if his victim 'cracks' by crying out, pleading for mercy and ultimately disclosing information. If the tortured person endures his suffering and remains silent he has refused to be a victim, he has won the power struggle with his torturer and gained ascendancy over him. Sartre suggests that the fear of losing this power struggle, the fear of being exposed as a coward and having to live with that knowledge, can become greater than the fear of pain and death.

People who are tortured are often tortured for information about others. They may endure torture and remain silent to protect others, or they may endure only for the sake of their own pride. Whatever their motives, their silence benefits others, leaving others feeling uncomfortably indebted. Through the character of Jean, Sartre explores the situation of a person for whom others suffer torture. Jean's lack of suffering excludes him from the group and makes him feel inferior. He experiences such intense guilt over his lack of suffering that he desires to be tortured himself. His own torture would remove his guilt and sense of inferiority and reunite him with those who have suffered for him.

A recurrent theme in the play is the fear people have of dying without a witness and being utterly forgotten. Before she is raped and loses her love for Jean, Lucie consoles herself with the thought that she will live on in his memory. Though dead, she will continue to have a **being-for-others**. The fear the prisoners feel that they will not be missed after they have died gives the play its title. They fear being men without shadows, anonymous corpses that died for nothing with only their killers knowing how or when they died.

mental image   See *The Imaginary*.

Merleau-Ponty, Maurice (1908–61)   French **existentialist** philosopher. Merleau-Ponty attended the École Normale Supérieure in Paris at the same time as **Sartre** and graduated the year after Sartre in 1930. His major philosophical work, *Phenomenology of Perception* (1945) was conceived to some extent as a response to Sartre's **Being and Nothingness** (1943). In

October 1945, along with Sartre and **de Beauvoir**, Merleau-Ponty founded the left-wing political journal, *Les Temps modernes*. In 1949 he became Professor of Child Psychology at the Sorbonne and in 1952 the youngest ever Professor of Philosophy at the Collège de France, a post he held until his untimely death in 1961 at the age of 53.

Merleau-Ponty is often identified as a member of Sartre's 'inner circle', but like de Beauvoir and **Camus**, he was far from being a mere follower of Sartre as some popular accounts have suggested. Sartre simply happened to be the most prominent figure in a group of fiercely independent thinkers who shared and refined their ideas in an atmosphere of often intense mutual criticism. Merleau-Ponty and Sartre, both heavily influenced by the **phenomenology** of **Husserl** and **Heidegger**, were intellectual equals who influenced each other and held many ideas in common.

The fact that Merleau-Ponty and Sartre share a lot of common **phenomenological** ground regarding **embodiment**, perception, **action**, **temporality** and other **phenomena** central to the **human condition** should not be forgotten when considering the significant differences and disagreements existing between them. As is often the case in philosophy, their broad agreement is the basis or starting point for their various specific disagreements. If their viewpoints were *radically* different, lacking any common ground, their incommensurability would render constructive debate impossible. Merleau-Ponty is Sartre's best-known and arguably most astute critic. In criticizing Sartre he strives to refine and develop Sartre's ideas rather than simply dismiss them. In his early philosophy at least, Merleau-Ponty presupposes that he and Sartre are working together on the same philosophical project, that they are employing the same phenomenological methodology to refine descriptions of the same phenomena.

Central to Merleau-Ponty's phenomenology is his opposition to the dualistic way of thinking that, in his view, has characterized and misled Western philosophy for centuries. He argues that the human condition, our way of being in the world, cannot be correctly understood or described until philosophy dispenses with such related dualisms as mind and body, subject and object, inner and outer. Merleau-Ponty increasingly came to realize that the main obstacle to dispensing with these dualisms is linguistic, that the very structure of language itself encourages dualistic ways of thinking. The desire to overcome **dualism** is as central to Sartre's philosophy as it is to Merleau-Ponty's. Nonetheless, according to Merleau-Ponty, Sartre often slides into subject–object dualism mainly as a result of the language he uses. The later, far more linguistically oriented Merleau-Ponty even levelled the charge of dualism against himself, suggesting that his earlier work, *Phenomenology of Perception*, had ultimately failed in its attempt to overcome dualism. Despite the retrospective claims of its author, it is generally held that the work in fact succeeds in extensively undermining the subject–object dichotomy through the detailed account it provides of the lived body or body-subject.

The term 'body-subject' identifies the subject, the person, *as* their body, rather than as an 'inner' that possesses a body as 'outer'. The term also identifies the body as no mere object that can be, for example, moved away from oneself like other objects, but as that which *is* situation, perspective, perception, action, **desire**, intention and a host of other phenomena that comprise the self. 'I am my body', says Merleau-Ponty, echoing Sartre. To be embodied is not to *have* a body, but to *be* a body, and it is inconceivable to both Merleau-Ponty and Sartre that being a subject in the world could be achieved in any other way than by being a body.

Comparable though their views on embodiment are, Merleau-Ponty nonetheless criticizes Sartre for falling into a dualistic way of thinking about embodiment and, more specifically, of underestimating the importance of embodiment in the experience of the **Other** as subject. In his theory of **being-for-others**, Sartre supposes that the Other must exist for me, as I must exist for the Other, as either **transcendent subject** or transcended object. The Other exists for me as a subject only when he transcends my **transcendence** and reduces me to an object. The problem with this picture for Merleau-Ponty is that it ignores the fact that the Other exists for me most frequently as an embodied **consciousness**. That is, I am most often aware of the Other as a subject, not because my experience of my own embodiment indicates a subject who has transcended me, but because I experience a living, acting, embodied subject before me; a subject incarnate. I do not experience him either as an Other or as a body; his Otherness and his embodiment are given together.

Merleau-Ponty's views on embodiment also lead him to criticize Sartre's thesis that **freedom** is limitless and that all evaluations are a matter of abstract, **groundless choice**. Merleau-Ponty argues that the physical limitations of the body in relation to its environment constitute a **natural**

self that, in making certain evaluations inevitable, grounds choices and renders them more than merely arbitrary.

On a different note, Merleau-Ponty is averse to the notion of **authenticity** that is so central to Sartre's thought and that of other existentialists. Identifying authenticity with unattainable individualism, Merleau-Ponty always avoids making use of the concept. He argues that the profound complexities and ambiguities of the human condition make it impossible to distinguish a striving for personal authenticity from a response to social demands and expectations. Arguably, Merleau-Ponty's position here shows a failure to appreciate that the project of authenticity is not always or essentially about striving for an unattainable individualism and freedom from social demands and expectations, but about an individual taking full **responsibility** for his situation and his responses to that situation. As most situations are to some extent human social situations, meeting the demands of most situations requires a degree of social conformity. As Sartre's later writings acknowledge, for a person to take full responsibility for his **being-in-situation**, and hence be authentic, he may well have to determine himself to comply with the demands and expectations that result from his social and historical circumstances.

Merleau-Ponty's criticisms of Sartre are many and varied and it is not possible even to touch on them all here. Some of Merleau-Ponty's criticisms expose serious flaws in Sartre's reasoning, some of them can be refuted and some of them, according to de Beauvoir, are levelled against a Sartre of Merleau-Ponty's own invention. In 1955, de Beauvoir, always Sartre's staunchest ally, wrote an article, 'Merleau-Ponty et le Pseudo-Sartrisme', in which she accuses Merleau-Ponty of misrepresenting many of the central notions of Sartre's philosophy. By this time, political differences had soured personal relations between Merleau-Ponty and Sartre and they were no longer disposed to polite disagreement against a background of mutual empathy. While Sartre remained a staunch Marxist long after World War II, Merleau-Ponty, like Camus, became ever more disillusioned with Communism. Increasingly angry disagreements between Merleau-Ponty and Sartre – comparable to those between Sartre and Camus – led eventually to the acrimonious ending of their long, philosophically creative friendship. Their worsening relationship was a source of inspiration for de Beauvoir's 1954 novel, *The Mandarins*.

Merleau-Ponty's attempts to dispense with dualistic thinking and modes of expression gave his later philosophy an increasingly linguistic orientation. He was far more involved than Sartre in the 'linguistic turn' of post-war Continental philosophy and enjoyed an exchange of ideas with influential proponents of structuralism such as the social anthropologist, Claude Lévi-Strauss, who dedicated his 1962 book, *The Savage Mind*, to Merleau-Ponty's memory. Lévi-Strauss maintains that Merleau-Ponty's last work, *The Visible and the Invisible* (published posthumously, 1964), although unfinished, achieves a synthesis of phenomenology and structuralism, a view increasingly shared by contemporary philosophers as Merleau-Ponty's ideas permeate and his influence grows. One of the major figures of twentieth-century French philosophy, Paul Ricoeur, praises Merleau-Ponty (not Sartre) as 'the greatest of the French phenomenologists'.

metastable   A term used by **Sartre** to refer to the *apparent* stability of modes of **consciousness** such as **bad faith** and **authenticity**. These **phenomena** may appear as stable states of being that a person has achieved once and for all, when in fact they are ongoing projects that must be sustained against the constant threat of collapse. Bad faith and authenticity, like the **for-itself** that realizes them, have precarious, metastable structures. A person can not simply *be* in bad faith, or *be* authentic, he *has to be* in bad faith or authentic, constantly choosing these modes of being. In physics, metastable refers to an apparent state of equilibrium maintained by something that is not inherently stable. It refers to a precarious equilibrium that is not fixed but must be continually self-perpetuated.

Mitsein   German for 'being-with'. **Sartre** follows **Heidegger** in using the term 'Mitsein' to refer to the phenomenon of being-with-others, to the phenomenon of 'we'. In his account of **being-for-others** Sartre argues that **conflict** is the essence of human relationships. Each **being-for-itself** struggles to transcend the **transcendence** of the **Other** and reduce him to a **transcendence-transcended**. Sartre recognizes that this account is incomplete as it makes no reference to situations in which a person is in community with the Other rather than in conflict with him. Sartre considers how it is possible for there to be a 'we' subject in which a plurality of subjectivities apprehend one another as transcendences-transcending rather than as transcendences-transcended. He argues that for the 'we' to occur there must be a common **action**, a collective enterprise or an object of common perception that is the explicit object of **consciousness**. For example, a member of an audience absorbed in watching a play is explicitly conscious of the play rather than the audience around him. In being explicitly conscious of the play, however, he is also implicitly or non-thetically conscious of being conscious of the play and of being a co-spectator of the play (see **non-thetic consciousness**). Being-with can only occur in this implicit, non-thetic way, it cannot be the explicit object of consciousness. If a spectator makes his fellow spectators the explicit object of his consciousness rather than the shared experience of the play he will cease to be a co-spectator with them of the play and they will cease to be his fellow spectators. His being-with them as part of a 'we' will be lost as they become the object of his consciousness and he transcends their transcendence.

mortality   For **Sartre**, mortality is one of the **existential truths** of the **human condition**. To fully recognize that one's life is a finite project – as opposed to deluding oneself that one is somehow immortal – is an aspect of **authenticity**. Unlike **Heidegger**, however, Sartre does not think that death, as the limit of all possibility, is among a person's possibilities. See also **affirmation of mortality**, **being-towards-death**, **everydayness** and **ownmost possibility**.

mortality, affirmation of   For both **Sartre** and **Heidegger**, **authenticity** requires that a person live without **regret**, recognizing and affirming the **existential truths** of the **human condition**. One such existential truth is **freedom**. **Mortality** is another. Affirming mortality involves a person recognizing that his life is finite and the implications that this has for the way he lives his life. The person who affirms mortality does not seek death – it is not a suicidal tendency – but neither does he value timid self-preservation above the affirmation of his freedom. For both Sartre and Heidegger embracing life's finitude is a prompt to **authentic action**. Heidegger goes further than Sartre in arguing that death is a person's **ownmost possibility** – the possibility that is most his own. For Heidegger the human condition is fundamentally **being-towards-death** and authentic existence is fundamentally authentic-being-towards-death. Sartre disagrees with Heidegger on this point. Although Sartre accepts that authentic existence involves recognizing that life is finite, he does not accept that death is a person's ownmost possibility. Indeed, like Wittgenstein, who argues that 'death is not an event in life', Sartre argues that death is not among a person's possibilities at all. As the absolute limit of all of a person's possibilities death is not itself a possibility. See also **everydayness**.

— N —

natural self   **Merleau-Ponty** criticizes **Sartre** for supposing that all evaluations that a person makes are a matter of abstract personal **choice**. Sartre does not allow that there is anything natural to a person that limits his **freedom** by making certain evaluations inevitable and disposing him towards certain choices. He denies the existence of any kind of **human nature**, allowing only that there is a **human condition** to which all people are subject. Merleau-Ponty argues against Sartre that people have a natural self based upon the natural limitations of the **body** and its basic physical relationship with the environment. A person's natural self disposes him to sustain intentions that are not the result of decisions he has made and to interpret his surroundings in ways he does not choose. Sartre holds that if a choice could be influenced in any way by values or beliefs it would be a caused phenomenon rather than a genuine choice. Sartre's critics insist that he fails to recognize that choices can in some sense be caused and yet remain choices. That Sartre does not allow grounds for choosing is, arguably, a serious weakness in his theory of **existential freedom**. To insist that all choices are groundless is to insist that all choices are arbitrary (see **groundless choice**). In insisting that all choices are arbitrary Sartre fails to shed any light upon the phenomenon of choosing and reduces it to a mysterious phenomenon. The natural self provides grounds for choosing; it provides a pre-structure or framework of inescapable interpretations within which comprehensible evaluations and choices can be made that are more than arbitrary.

Nausea (1938)   Sartre's first published novel. Highly polished, due to the exhaustive redrafting of the text over a period of several years, *Nausea* is a stylistic masterpiece that firmly established Sartre's reputation as both a writer and a philosopher. It remains his best-known and most widely read work. The novel explores the **contingency** and **absurdity** of the **human condition** through its alienated central character, Antoine Roquentin.

Roquentin drifts about the town of Bouville (loosely based on Le Havre) anxiously contemplating the loss of all sense of meaning and purpose in his life and the lies and **bad faith** by which bourgeois people – the *salauds* (swine) – seek to give their lives meaning and purpose. **Sartre** details the personal development of a *salaud* in his short story, **The Childhood of a Leader** (1939), written around the same time as **Nausea**. Roquentin is pursued by 'the nausea', an overwhelming and terrifying awareness of the utter contingency and absurdity of existence. Though the novel makes no reference to mind-altering drugs, the nausea echoes Sartre's disturbing experience with the hallucinogenic drug mescaline. Sartre was injected with mescaline at Sainte-Anne Hospital under experimental conditions by his friend, Doctor Daniel Lagache, in January 1935 (see **The Imaginary**).

Roquentin is writing a biography of Adhémar, the Marquis de Rollebon, but abandons the exercise deciding that he is merely trying to distract himself from his own futile existence by attempting to give Rollebon's existence a significance it did not possess. Roquentin avoids friendships but is nonetheless befriended in the library by a man he refers to as the Autodidact. The Autodidact is attempting to educate himself in all knowledge autodidactically by working his way through the library catalogue from A to Z. The Autodidact is a humanist and a socialist, a lonely, unattractive, unloved man who rapturously declares his love for all mankind and seeks to label Roquentin a misanthrope. Roquentin finds him physically and intellectually repulsive and flees a meal with him in disgust as he begins to suffer a serious attack of the nausea. The Autodidact is eventually exposed as a paedophile when he molests a boy in the library. Despite being a loner Roquentin finds himself looking forward to the visit of his former lover, Anny, though he reminds himself that there are no perfect moments. When they meet they discover that they have developed similar thoughts on life. Anny says she has outlived herself. Roquentin can offer her no reasons for living. They part company, perhaps forever, realizing that there is nothing they can do to help one another.

Roquentin recognizes his limitlessly free and utterly superfluous existence in a meaningless and Godless universe and, above all, he recognizes that there is nothing that he was, is or will ever be in the mode of being it. It is widely held that Roquentin is a supremely authentic **existentialist** hero attempting to live his life free from bad faith in accordance with the **existential truths** of the human condition (see **authenticity**). However, it can be argued that Roquentin is not authentic but actually inauthentic and deluded to the point of insanity. He is attempting to *be* his own **nothing-ness** in a last desperate attempt to escape the **indeterminacy** of his being and as such has fallen into the most desperate project of bad faith – the **faith of nihilism**. A genuinely authentic person realizes that although there is nothing that he is in the mode of being it, he must continually make himself be what he is by suspending disbelief in himself and playing a role to the best of his ability. Roquentin is unable to play a role because he has lost faith in his own performance of himself. Unable to make-believe he is anything at all he has come to the false belief that he is nothing at all, a **non-being-in-itself**.

The novel ends on a relatively optimistic note with Roquentin deciding to leave Bouville and write a novel. He does not think that writing a novel will distract him from his existence, as he hoped writing the biography of Rollebon would, but he hopes that once it is written he will be able to look back on writing it and that it will at least give meaning and purpose to his **past**.

Rivalled only by Camus' *The Stranger*, which it inspired (see **Camus**), *Nausea* has achieved cult status as the archetypal existentialist novel. Its central themes of contingency, absurdity, **anxiety** and alienation have become synonymous with **existentialism** in the popular consciousness, even if properly understood existentialism is a far more optimistic and con-structive philosophy than *Nausea* suggests. *Nausea* is a truly philosophical novel in its questioning of the nature of existence and self-identity but it is not a treatise on the philosophy of existentialism. Essentially, it is a witty and disturbingly incisive exploration of extreme **nihilism**.

negation In *Being and Nothingness* (1943), **Sartre** explicitly endorses Hegel's claim that 'the mind is the negative'. Like **Hegel**, Sartre places negation at the centre of his **ontological** theory of **consciousness**, his theory of **being-for-itself**. Negation is being-for-itself in so far as being-for-itself exists as the negation or denial of **being-in-itself**. Being-for-itself is a **borrowed being** in so far as it borrows its being from being-in-itself by being the negation of being-in-itself. Negation is the act of negating being-in-itself, the act by which **non-being** or **nothingness** arises. Negation is or gives rise to denial, **nihilation**, **absence**, **lack**, **negativities**, emptiness of being, privation of being. The being of **reflective consciousness** in so far as it exists as the negation of **reflected-on consciousness**. See also **concrete negation**, **double negation**, **internal negation**, **original negation** and **radical negation**.

negation, concrete   The logically *subsequent* dimension of the **double negation** that is **being-for-itself**. The logically *prior* dimension of the double negation, the **radical negation**, is being-for-itself as the **negation** of the *whole* of **being-in-itself**. As the negation of being-in-itself, however, being-for-itself also negates being-in-itself, not in the form of a radical negation of the whole of being-in-itself but in the form of *particular* concrete negations of being-in-itself known as **negativities**. **Sartre** calls this dimension of the double negation the concrete negation. The concrete negation is so called because it is that by which particular concrete **phenomena** appear – this as distinct from that, this as not that and so on. See also **differentiated being** and **lack**.

negation, double   Being-for-itself is a double negation: a **radical negation** and a **concrete negation**. Being-for-itself is the radical negation of the *whole* of **being-in-itself**, and it is also that which negates being-in-itself in the form of *particular* concrete negations known as **negativities** that differentiate being and give rise to **phenomena**. See also **differentiated being** and **negation**.

negation, internal   Being-for-itself is the internal negation of **being-in-itself**. Describing being-for-itself as an internal negation emphasizes the nature of its logically internal, as opposed to logically external, relationship to being-in-itself. The relation of being-for-itself to being-in-itself is an **internal relation**. See also **external relations** and **negation**.

negation, original   The original and **radical negation** of **being-in-itself** that is **being-for-itself**. See also **negation**.

negation, radical   The logically *prior* dimension of the **double negation** that is **being-for-itself**. **Original negation**. Being-for-itself as the negation of the *whole* of **being-in-itself**. The logically *subsequent* dimension of the double negation is the **concrete negation**. See also **negation**.

negation, surpassing   See **surpassing**.

négatités   See **negativities**.

negative choice   See **choice, negative**.

negative freedom   See **freedom, negative**.

negative will to power   See **Nietzsche** and **will to power**.

negativities (négativités)   Particular negations or privations of **being-in-itself**. **Being-for-itself** is a **double negation**, it is the **radical negation** of the *whole* of being-in-itself and it also negates being-in-itself in the form of *particular* concrete negations of being-in-itself. Being-for-itself, as **concrete negation**, differentiates **undifferentiated being** into **differentiated being**, into distinct **phenomena**, by placing negations into being. The **negation** that is being-for-itself negates being in the form of particular negations of being. These particular negations or privations of being are called negativities or négativités. Negativities arise, for example, when being is questioned. To question is to expect a disclosure of **non-being**. It is possible to discover, for example, that there is *nothing* in the carburettor. Even when a reply is positive, negativities arise. If a person discovers that his dinner is ready, for example, then it is the case that his situation is this way and *not* another way. A negativity is a **lack** of being. This lack does not belong to being-in-itself but to the **for-itself** that negates being. The for-itself always chooses a course of **action** in order to overcome a perceived lack. A necessary condition of action is the recognition of an objective lack or negativity. See also **existential absence**.

Nekrassov, A Farce in Eight Scenes (1956)   A darkly comical play by **Sartre** set in Paris in the early 1950s. Sibilot, a journalist who writes anti-Communist propaganda for a right-wing newspaper, *Soir à Paris*, faces dismissal unless he can come up with a new idea. His luck improves when he finds Georges de Valéra, an internationally renowned swindler, hiding in his house. Georges is on the run from the police and has just made an unsuccessful attempt to drown himself in the River Seine. To help Sibilot and to disguise himself, Georges decides to impersonate the Russian Interior Minister, Nikita Nekrassov, who, according to some news reports, has recently disappeared. Georges fools the editor and directors of *Soir à Paris* that he is Nekrassov and that he has defected to the West. They believe him, largely because it serves their interests to do so. He offers them the exclusive right to publish a series of political revelations, including the names of those important enough to be shot by firing squad when Russia invades France. Sibilot saves his job and is given a pay rise, the circulation of *Soir à Paris* reaches record heights and the purposes of capitalism and anti-Communism are served in a variety of ways.

Though a genius at manipulating others, Georges begins to lose control of the situation when people he has not mentioned in his fabricated stories are accused of plotting with Russia to overthrow France. Government agents who have been acting as Georges' bodyguard soon discover that he is not Nekrassov. Nonetheless, they decide to preserve the illusion that he is Nekrassov in order that he can testify against anyone they wish to accuse of treason. They hold Georges prisoner but he escapes and makes arrange-ments with Véronique, Sibilot's daughter, to sell his story, 'How I became Nekrassov', to the socialist newspaper, *Libérateur*. The publication of the truth threatens to ruin *Soir à Paris*, exposing the editor and directors as either deceitful or hopelessly deceived. To save the paper the editor is fired and replaced by Sibilot who is given the task of inventing the story that Georges de Valéra has sold out to the Communists and Nekrassov has been kidnapped by the Russians. It is not expected that anyone will believe this story but it will be enough to cast doubt on the truth of Georges' story in *Libérateur*.

The play satirizes the French right-wing press and the paranoid fear of Communism that its propaganda helped to generate during the Cold War years. Sartre's message is clearly a Marxist one: The popular press is owned and controlled by capitalists for the purpose of preserving and promoting capitalism. Inciting fear of Communism or any other non-capitalist ideology helps to sell newspapers and to create a sense of collective identity and purpose in face of a common enemy. The masses are persuaded that they are better off and better protected under their system of government than are people who live under alternative systems. It is simply a part of the ideology of the popular press that its primary function is to tell the truth. In reality, its primary function, apart from maximizing circulation, is to preserve the political and economic order that most benefits the kind of wealthy, powerful people who own newspapers. Exaggeration and lies further this end at least as much as telling the truth. Stripped of the ideology it perpetuates, that truth-telling and reasoned argument are sacrosanct, the popular press is revealed as shaping the opinions of the masses through its relentless appeal to their fear, hatred, lust, envy and conceit. The popular press enables the ruling class to shape and define the social and political values of the masses to such an extent that they become incapable of distinguishing truth from lies, reality from appearance.

To some extent *Nekrassov* is also an indirect comment on McCarthyism. Although McCarthy is mentioned only once, Sartre clearly portrays France as suffering from the same atmosphere of national paranoia that in the USA culminated in the McCarthy anti-Communist 'witch-hunts' of 1954. Not surprisingly, the play touched a nerve and was slated by all but the most left-wing French newspapers.

Nietzsche, Friedrich (1844–1900)   German philosopher who became a professor at Basel University at the age of only twenty-four. Nietzsche was a friend of the composer Wagner until they famously fell out. Nietzsche is the author of a series of classic philosophical works including *The Birth of Tragedy* (1872), *Thus Spoke Zarathustra* (1883–85), *Beyond Good and Evil* (1886) and *On the Genealogy of Morals* (1887). Nietzsche's genius was coupled with mental instability. Syphilis contributed to his mental decline and in 1889 he became insane.

Nietzsche agrees with his predecessor Arthur Schopenhauer (1788–1860) that 'God is dead', that the Enlightenment killed the idea of **God** as an explanation for existence and a justification for morality. For Schopenhauer, the death of God implies that people are doomed to pointless suffering and **despair** in a meaningless universe. Nietzsche attempts to push Schopenhauer's **nihilism** to its ultimate conclusion, to demolish faith in religious-based values to such an extent that the way is made clear for a 're-evaluation of all values', including moral values. For

Nietzsche, nihilism carried to its conclusion annihilates itself as a value and becomes anti-nihilism. To overcome nihilism people must overcome the guilt and despair of having killed God. To achieve this people must become gods themselves by taking **responsibility** for themselves and creating their own values.

Nietzsche's radical and penetrating views on religion, morality and the **human condition** have influenced and inspired a wide variety of individuals and movements from Sigmund **Freud** to Joseph Conrad, from the existentialists to the Nazis. Nietzsche's writing is poetic, esoteric, ambiguous, ironical and occasionally self-contradictory. His later writing is coloured by a growing megalomania, a symptom of his declining mental health. His writing offers, or appears to offer, something for everyone, especially when read selectively. The Nazis read Nietzsche selectively and were helped to do so by Nietzsche's sister, Elizabeth, who presented her friend Hitler with a collection of suitably inspiring extracts from her brother's writings. Undoubtedly, certain passages from Nietzsche's vast output chime with the ideology of the Third Reich – his talk of 'blond beasts' for example – but it is incorrect to view him as a Nazi or even as a proto-fascist. Nietzsche despised the anti-Semitism of his sister's husband, Förster, and was consistently critical of German nationalism. There is nothing in his writing that advocates the genocide conducted in Nazi Germany years after his death and presumably he would have identified it as a supreme act of depravity on the part of a culture he so often accused of decadence. Far from being a fascist, Nietzsche is generally hailed as a champion of individualism who advocates freedom from state power, religion and 'herd' morality.

Nietzsche is an **existentialist**, though he has not often been described as one. Certainly, he helped to set the agenda for what later became known as **existentialism**. Several of his most central philosophical concerns were taken up in the twentieth century by the existentialist movement and his writings had a significant influence on **Sartre** and upon one of Sartre's biggest influences, **Heidegger**.

At the start of **Being and Nothingness** (1943) Sartre endorses Nietzsche's rejection of metaphysics and **idealism**; his rejection of 'the illusion of worlds-behind-the-scene'. Sartre agrees with Nietzsche that reality does not lurk behind **appearances** in some other-wordly realm. What appears *is* reality. As there is nothing beyond appearances the primary task of philosophy is to describe **phenomena** as they appear to us without resorting to speculative metaphysical explanations. True to the implications of their respective existentialist and anti-metaphysical positions, Sartre and Nietzsche are both atheists (see **atheism**). Not atheists who simply dismiss God's existence and think no more about it, but atheists who are moved by the profound implications of God's non-existence for human reality and morality. For both of them the non-existence of God implies that all existence, including human existence, is without ultimate meaning or purpose. Neither rests here, however, and in a move that is vital to the development of their respective philosophies they both strive to forge an ultimately anti-nihilistic philosophy from a starkly nihilistic initial position. They each argue in their own way that to reach their full potential people must overcome the **inauthenticity** and cowardice involved in clinging to uncertain beliefs, particularly religious beliefs. Each person must stop mistakenly assuming that some higher authority has decided everything for him and recognize that his personal existence has only the meaning and purpose he chooses to give it.

Nietzsche significantly influenced Sartre's theory of **authenticity** and their views on the subject are remarkably similar. For Sartre, **bad faith** is a **choice** not to choose. It can be described as **negative freedom** that exercises itself in denying and repressing itself. **Freedom** is often exercised in this way in accordance with what Nietzsche refers to as the **ascetic ideal**. Opposed to the ascetic ideal is Nietzsche's notion of the **noble ideal**. The noble ideal involves what Sartre identifies as the **affirmation of freedom**. A noble person positively affirms himself as a free being. He does not concern himself with denying and repressing his freedom but affirms it through decisive **action**, through overcoming and self-overcoming, through the acceptance of self-responsibility and the refusal to **regret** and, above all, through the choice of his own values. For Nietzsche, such freedom is expansive; it glories in its own strength as a positive **will to power**. For Nietzsche, a person cannot not be a will to power, just as, for Sartre, a person cannot not be free. Whereas Nietzsche has the concepts of positive and negative will to power, Sartre has the concepts of the **positive freedom** of the responsible, authentic person and the negative freedom of the inauthentic person who acts in bad faith choosing not to choose. Sartre argues that freedom can value itself as the source of all values. This positive freedom projects itself in accordance with the principles of Nietzsche's noble ideal. It is a positive will to power. A person does not achieve a **radical conversion** to authenticity by rejecting and divorcing his former self through the exercise of bad faith, but by overcoming his former self, his former values, to become the creator of his own values. There is a definite sense in which, for Sartre, radical conversion to authenticity involves a person becoming something akin to Nietzsche's overman (*Ubermensch*), the man who has overcome himself. As the creator of his own values the overman creates himself; he is the artist or author of his own authentic existence. See also **eternal recurrence**, **formula for greatness**, *Saint Genet* and **slave ethic**.

nihilation   Another term for **negation** rather than for **annihilation**.

nihilism   From *nihil*, Latin for 'nothing'. Extreme denial or scepticism about everything to the point of **despair**. **Sartre** is often viewed as a nihilist but in fact his philosophy is ultimately positive and constructive. Indeed, he has an anti-nihilist agenda comparable to that of **Nietzsche**.

Sartre is not a sceptic for scepticism's sake, but an academic sceptic who employs the destructive power of scepticism with a constructive goal. Philosophy builds by this process because it progresses through the destruction of assumptions. Sartre's views on the **human condition**, including his views on the phenomenon of despair, are not the result of despair on his part and neither are they intended to produce despair in others. Nevertheless, certain aspects of Sartre's **existentialism** are described as nihilistic, particularly by critics who are not sympathetic to the **existentialist** view of the human condition. For example, some describe Sartre's **atheism** – his view that the existence of **God** is impossible – as a form of nihilism, not least because in the view of some to deny that God exists is to be in despair.

Sartre is also often considered to be a nihilist for claiming that human reality is absurd. He certainly makes this claim, most famously in his novel **Nausea** (1938), which explores extreme nihilism through its central character, Roquentin. However, it is important to note that Sartre's reflections on **absurdity** are only part of the picture. Sartre's philosophy, like the philosophy of Nietzsche, has a strong current of anti-nihilism in so far as he argues that a person can overcome the absurdity of his existence and the absence of God by imposing meaning on his life through **authentic**

action. Life, for Sartre, is absurd in that it has no meaning in itself, but, he argues, it does have the meaning a person chooses to give it.

Sartre is also sometimes characterized as a nihilist for his apparent moral subjectivism, for his view that ethics is both necessary and impossible. He was, however, never comfortable with this sceptical conclusion and made several attempts, with varying degrees of success, to produce an **existentialist ethics**. Most notably, between 1945 and 1948, he made extensive notes on ethics, many of which were published posthumously as **Notebooks for an Ethics** (1983). Above all, his enduring scepticism regarding the possibility of objective, independently existing, moral facts does not amount to a nihilistic rejection of all values. Sartre believes very much in the possibility of creating values. An authentic person affirms **freedom** itself as a value and treats it as a source of values. In *Notebooks for an Ethics* Sartre speculates that in affirming his own freedom an authentic person would also respect and affirm the freedom of other people. Thus, he indicates a possible link between **authenticity** and ethics, suggesting that ethics is other-related authenticity. See also **faith of nihilism** and **regret**.

nihilism, faith of   A person's belief that he can become or has become identical with his own **nothingness**. A person may attempt to become one with his own nothingness as a desperate response to the realization that he is unable to become anything in the mode of being it. This attempt to be a **non-being-in-itself** is as much an attempt to escape the **indeterminacy** of his being as is the attempt to be a **being-for-itself-in-itself**. In so far as the faith of nihilism seeks to establish nothingness as a substantial being that a person is without having to be it, the faith of nihilism is another form of **bad faith**. Arguably, Roquentin, the central character of Sartre's novel **Nausea** (1938), is in bad faith in so far as he adopts the faith of nihilism and seeks the annihilation of his personal identity in an attempt to become his own nothingness.

No Exit   See **In Camera**.

Nobel Prize for Literature   In October 1964, the same year as the publication of the autobiography of his childhood, **Words**, **Sartre** was offered and declined the Nobel Prize for Literature. He discovered in advance that he was to be awarded the prize and wishing to avoid a scandal wrote a letter to the Secretary of the Swedish Academy politely declining it. This letter had to be redirected and was not received by the Secretary before it was officially announced that Sartre was the nominated laureate. The Swedish Academy had to make a second announcement stating that the nominated laureate had declined the prize. With dignity they insisted that Sartre's refusal did not alter the validity of the nomination. Pursued by the press, Sartre was obliged to give an official statement in which he was careful not to offend the Swedish people. He insisted that it was his policy to decline official distinctions – he had refused the Legion of Honour after World War II – and that 'The writer must refuse to let himself be transformed by institutions, even if these are of the most honourable kind . . .'. As one commentator later put it, Sartre did not want to be embalmed alive and prematurely canonized. Even if it had not been his intention, Sartre enjoyed both the prestige of having been offered the prize and the notoriety of having rejected it. His publishers reaped the profits of this priceless advertisement. Sartre's only regret was that the considerable prize money of 250,000 crowns would have supported various political causes. See also **Gallimard**.

noble ideal   For **Nietzsche**, a person who has adopted the noble ideal values the positive affirmation of his **freedom** above all else and for its own sake. A noble person affirms himself as a free being through decisive action, the acceptance of self-responsibility, the refusal to **regret** and, ultimately, through the choice of his own values. To adopt the noble ideal is to overcome what **Sartre** identifies as **bad faith** through the exercise of **positive will to power**. To live according to the noble ideal is to be authentic. The noble ideal is opposed to Nietzsche's notion of the **ascetic ideal**. See also **affirmation of freedom**, **authentic action**, **authenticity**, **positive choice**, **positive freedom** and **sustained authenticity**.

non-being   The **negation**, or a negation, of **being-in-itself**. **Nothingness**. The **ontological** status of **being-for-itself**. An alternative name for being-for-itself. See also **lack**.

non-being-in-itself   An impossible state of being in which **non-being** or **being-for-itself** achieves identity with itself and becomes its own **nothingness**. A non-being-in-itself would be identical with **being-in-**

itself and as such its being as a non-being would be annihilated. A less common term for **being-for-itself-in-itself**. See also **annihilation, faith of nihilism** and *Nausea*.

non-positional consciousness   See **consciousness, non-thetic**.

non-thetic consciousness   See **consciousness, non-thetic**.

Notebooks for an Ethics (1947–48, published posthumously 1983) At the end of ***Being and Nothingness*** (1943) **Sartre** wrote that he would consider the ethical implications of his theory of **being-for-itself** in a later work. That he seriously intended to produce a fully developed **existentialist ethics** is evidenced by the extensive notes he made on ethics between 1945 and 1948, nearly 600 pages of which were published posthumously as *Notebooks for an Ethics*. It is known that a significant amount of Sartre's material on ethics remains unpublished, although exactly how much is a matter of debate.

Of all Sartre's publications, *Notebooks for an Ethics* is the most fragmentary and unpolished. The writing is not unclear in itself but it does not reflect Sartre's considered opinion. The fact that Sartre never saw fit to publish these notebooks in his lifetime indicates that he was still far from satisfied with what he had written. The material is what its title suggests, working notes. It is Sartre musing, brainstorming, thinking against himself, developing his thoughts. It is not a work in the sense of a completed thesis and therefore should not be viewed or criticized as one. In places, Sartre may not even agree with what he has written down. He may simply be experimenting, setting thoughts down in writing to scrutinize their worth more closely later. There is, then, a danger of reading too much into these notes, of misrepresenting Sartre's position (what position?) and attributing to him views he never really held. Having said this, there is sufficient consistency and recurrence of themes in the notebooks for some general conclusions to be drawn with relative certainty. Some ideas expressed in the notebooks can also be checked against ideas expressed in published works written around the same time, such as Sartre's ***Existentialism and Humanism*** (1946) and de Beauvoir's *Ethics of Ambiguity* (1947). Sartre and **de Beauvoir** collaborated very closely during this period and held many ideas in common.

Sartre scholars generally agree that although the notebooks offer some interesting insights into the possible nature of an ethics consistent with both Sartre's own **ontology** and that of **Heidegger**, they do not succeed in detailing such an ethics. A synthesis between **existentialism** and ethics is not achieved and may be ultimately unachievable. The notebooks do not answer the question of what ethics is for Sartre, they show Sartre in the process of trying to decide that question for himself. The notebooks are a process of enquiry that Sartre hopes will bring him to a position where he can write a book that presents a fully worked out existentialist ethics. Unfortunately, due to other commitments and perhaps the impossibility of the task, he never wrote such a book. As he wrote elsewhere, 'Published after my death, these texts will remain unfinished and obscure, since they formulate ideas which are not completely developed. It will be up to the reader to decide where they might have led.'

What is certainly clear is Sartre's view that an existentialist ethics cannot be based on an abstract, a priori moral principle such as Kant's Categorical Imperative. It is this view that prevents Sartre from aligning his position with that of **Kant**, even though he seems repeatedly tempted towards a broadly Kantian position in other respects. Sartre also rejects, as he does in *Existentialism and Humanism*, an ethics based on the existence of a moral **God**. Like **Nietzsche**, Sartre is an atheist who argues on **ontological** grounds that the existence of God is impossible. He argues that we are abandoned in the world with no God to give us purpose or moral direction (see **abandonment**).

What is also clear is that Sartre sees ethics as an other-related phenomenon, as a feature of **being-for-others**. He argues that no action is unethical until another person judges it to be so. An ethical state of affairs, although Sartre does not say how it is to be achieved, is one in which people respect and affirm each other's **freedom**. His difficulty is to accommodate this claim with his view that the freedom of the **Other** always negates my freedom, that his being-for-itself always transcends mine, thereby reducing me to an object, to a **transcendence-transcended**. Sartre takes the position, again without fully justifying it, that the objectification and alienation of a person by others, although unavoidable on a mundane level, need not result in active oppression as it has done historically. Although people will always experience themselves as objects for others, they need never be *mere* objects for others. A person is capable of recognizing on all occasions that the human object before him is also a person and a free **transcendence**, what **Merleau-Ponty** refers to as an *embodied consciousness*. For Sartre, to recognize and affirm one's own freedom is to be authentic (see **authenticity**), while to affirm the freedom of others is to be ethical.

It appears to follow from this that a person must be authentic to be ethical, he must affirm his own freedom in order to affirm the freedom of others. That is, he must fully recognize freedom in himself in order to achieve full recognition of freedom in others. In short, a person must be authentic to affirm the freedom of others. To be authentic is to recognize and embrace the inescapable **existential truths** of the **human condition**, such as **mortality**, **indeterminacy**, freedom, being-for-others, the being of others and so on. One of these existential truths is the existence of the freedom of others. Therefore, not only must a person be authentic to affirm the existential truth of the freedom of others, to affirm the freedom of others *is* to be authentic. Arguably, ethics is other-related authenticity.

Seemingly, an existentially ethical world would be one where a history driven by human freedom has realized an end to the exploitation and oppression that results when one freedom does not respect and affirm another. For Sartre, how this world is to be achieved is unclear. For Kant, it is to be achieved by every person adhering unerringly to the universal moral principle of the Categorical Imperative. Sartre, however, will not help himself to the Categorical Imperative because he refuses to base his ethics on a priori moral principles. For Sartre, it appears that behaving ethically is a matter of acting authentically in any given, concrete situation involving others, rather than a matter of adhering to the same abstract universal principle in all situations involving others. Sartre's ethical world is surely very similar to Kant's kingdom of ends, a world in which every person treats every other person as a self-determining end-in-himself, rather than as a mere means lacking freedom, as an object acted upon. In advocating something similar to Kant's kingdom of ends, Sartre's ethics are somewhat Kantian. In wanting to make his ethics a matter of authentic responses to concrete situations, responses that depend on the authentic assessment of situations rather than upon adherence to a universal moral principle, Sartre is not a Kantian deontologist but arguably the advocate of a form of virtue ethics. Like the virtue ethics of Aristotle, Sartre's ethics is not about following abstract moral rules, but about achieving one's full potential and flourishing as a free human being alongside other free human beings.

Notebooks for an Ethics also considers the problem of history. As we do not presently have a world where every freedom fully respects and affirms every other freedom then this ethical state of affairs can only be achieved, if it is achievable, via an historical process. Sartre explores Hegel's philosophy of history (see **Hegel**). He accepts Hegel's view that history is a dialectical process, but rejects any suggestion that inevitable deterministic forces drive the historical dialectic. History, Sartre argues, must be driven by human freedom, otherwise human freedom and **responsibility** are illusory. Sartre returns to this key problem years later, considering it in great detail in his *Critique of Dialectical Reason* (1960 and 1985). In that work, as in *Saint Genet* (1952) and *The Family Idiot* (1971–72), he applies categories first developed in his *Notebooks for an Ethics*. Like his *War Diaries*, written 1939–40 but also published posthumously, Sartre's *Notebooks for an Ethics* was a valuable resource for the creation of other works, an ultimately unroadworthy vehicle never fit for publication in Sartre's lifetime, but nonetheless fantastically useful for spare parts.

nothingness   An alternative name for **non-being** that has arisen in translation from French to English. Although the term is common and is even found in the title of the English translation of Sartre's major work, *Being and Nothingness* (1943) some critics argue that it is misleading in that it suggests that non-being is its own nothingness rather than the non-being, the **negation**, of **being-in-itself**.

nothingness-in-itself   See **non-being-in-itself**.

noumenon; noumena (*pl.*)   The thing-in-itself; things-in-them-selves. That which comprises existence as it is in itself apart from awareness or **consciousness** of it. **Kant** contrasts noumena with **phenomena** or **appearances**. Kant's distinction between noumena and phenomena relates closely to Sartre's distinction between **being-in-itself** and phenomena to the extent that **Sartre** can be described as a genuine post-Kantian. Ordinary minds perceive the world from a particular point of view in the form of particular phenomena. A divine mind (Sartre, unlike Kant, rejects the possibility of a divine mind) would conceive the world as it is in itself, non-perceptually and non-empirically, as noumena or as a noumenon. The traditional view of the noumenal world is that it underlies the world of phenomena like a substratum. Arguably, this traditional 'two worlds view' of Kant is rather crude and should be replaced by a more subtle 'two aspects view' that claims that there is only a single realm of being that can be encountered from two distinct standpoints. This 'two aspects view' of Kant is closer to what Sartre proposes when he draws a distinction between the **undifferentiated being** of being-in-itself and the **differentiated being** of phenomena. Sartre explicitly rejects the traditional view of Kantian noumena, arguing that being-in-itself does not lurk behind appearances as a noumenal foundation that underlies phenomena. For Sartre, because it is the **negation** of being-in-itself that gives rise to phenomena, phenomena are founded not upon being-in-itself, but upon **non-being**. Being-in-itself is not the foundation of phenomena, being-in-itself is the foundation of the non-being of **being-for-itself** that phenomenalizes being-in-itself by negating it.

— O —

obscenity   See **sadism**.

ontological   A term referring to the fundamental logical structure of existence, reality, **being**. To explore this fundamental logical structure is to conduct an ontological enquiry, to describe it is to produce an ontological description and so on. Sartre's own ontological exploration yields a description of being and **non-being** – **being-in-itself** and **being-for-itself** – and the logic of the relations existing between them. The ultimate aim of his ontological exploration is to describe how the relationship between being-in-itself and being-for-itself gives rise to the various related **phenomena** of which human existence is comprised – **temporality, consciousness, transcendence, freedom, bad faith** and so on. Ontological descriptions reveal the fundamental logical structure and composition of phenomena. See also **ontological level, ontology** and **phenomenological level**.

ontological level   Reality considered at the level of the logical or **ontological** relations existing between **being** and **non-being**, or what **Sartre** more often refers to as **being-in-itself** and **being-for-itself**. Sartre's description of reality at the ontological level is very generalized and abstract and tends to underpin his more specific and concrete description of reality at the **phenomenological level**. Ontological level and phenomenological level do not signify two distinct levels of reality but different levels of analysis and description. See also **ontology**.

ontology   Philosophical enquiry into the fundamental nature of existence, reality, **being**. Different philosophers subscribe to different ontologies in that they hold different views about what exists at the most fundamental or general level. The ontology of **Descartes**, for example, consists of minds, matter and **God**, while Sartre's ontology consists of being and its **negation, non-being**. Ontology is sometimes described as a branch of metaphysics, but it is really a broader term than metaphysics in that there are metaphysical and non-metaphysical ontologies. Metaphysical ontologies, Plato's theory of forms is a good example, hold that fundamentally reality consists of ideas or essences, whereas non-metaphysical ontologies, Sartre's **existentialism** for example, hold that the existence of being is fundamental. See also **'existence precedes essence'**, **ontological** and **ontological level**.

opacity   An essential characteristic of objects. For **Sartre**, objects are opaque in always having aspects that are not presently appearing – insides and hidden sides. Even a transparent object does not reveal all its possible **appearances** at once because it can only be viewed from one perspective or angle at a time. The actual appearances of an object at any one time indicate an infinite series of **transphenomenal** appearances that are not presently appearing but which could appear. Sartre's main aim in describing objects as opaque is to contrast their opacity with the **translucency** of **consciousness**.

original negation   See **negation, original**.

original synthesis   A term used by **Sartre** to describe the type of relation that exists between **phenomena** that cannot in reality be separated and never were separate. 'Synthesis' implies 'bringing together' but phenomena that are in an original synthesis were never apart in order to be brought together. For example, **transcendence** and **facticity** are in an original synthesis because transcendence is the transcendence of facticity. **Past** and **future** are also in an original synthesis because each one requires the other and the existence of each one implies the other. The past is a **past-future** and the future is a **future-past**. As for **being-for-itself** and **being-in-itself**, there never was a time nor could there ever be a time when being-for-itself was not wholly dependent upon being-in-itself for its **borrowed being**. Being-in-itself, however, can exist without being-for-itself, not as a phenomenon separated from being-for-itself, but if and when there is no being-for-itself. Whenever and wherever being-for-itself exists it must exist as the **negation** of being-in-itself and can exist in no other way, as such it is locked in an original synthesis with being-in-itself. See also **internal relation**.

the Other   Sartre's term for another person, particularly one who looks at me, sees me and judges me. The Other is a subject that a person experiences as such by experiencing himself as an object for the Other. Not least, the term 'the Other' allows for ease of explanation when discussing the various aspects of the phenomenon of **being-for-others** and the complex interplay of objectivity and subjectivity that occurs when this person encounters that person. When reading about the Other it is important to keep in mind that the person encountering the Other and being encountered by the Other is Other for the Other. See also **the look** and **transcendence-transcended**.

other minds (problem of)   In identifying the phenomenon of **being-for-others**, **Sartre** does not claim to have proved the existence of other minds; he does not claim that other minds must exist if a person can experience himself in the mode of being-for-others. To feel shame, for example, a person has only to believe that he is seen and comprehended by another mind. He need not know there is another mind there. If, in order to experience shame, a person need only believe there is another mind there, then shame can arise when that belief is false. The existence of shame cannot remove the problem of other minds because it is possible that the belief in another mind that inspires shame might be false on every occasion.

On the grounds that the (supposed) **being-for-itself** of another person is not on principle an object of knowledge the existence of which can be confirmed by experience, Sartre holds that the problem of other minds is impossible to solve by any means whatsoever. Rather than seek to prove the existence of other minds, Sartre shows that the existence of other minds cannot be realistically doubted given a person's own experience of himself as ashamed, embarrassed or proud before others. He holds that although the existence of other minds cannot be proven, it is continually suggested by intrinsic structures of a person's own being. Ironically, it is only when we seek to prove the existence of other minds that doubts about their existence emerge. Sartre notes that if we do not conjecture about other minds we affirm them. Although the sceptic is correct to insist that the existence of other minds cannot be proven, even the sceptic will find himself continually affirming the existence of other minds pre-reflectively in the way that he behaves and experiences his own being. See also **solipsism**.

ownmost possibility   For **Heidegger**, death is a person's ownmost possibility. **Sartre** disagrees with this on the grounds that death, as the limit of all possibility, is not among a person's possibilities. See also **affirmation of mortality**, **being-towards-death** and **mortality**.

— P —

past   See **past-future** and **temporality**.

past-future   **Sartre** describes the past in **phenomenological** terms as a **future** that is now past. A term that captures the fact that what is now a person's past was once his future. For Sartre, each of the three dimensions of time – past, **present** and future – stands outside of itself in the other two and has being only in terms of the other two. The past of a **being-for-itself** is the past-future of that for-itself; a past-future that, in the past, was the **future-past** of that for-itself. See also *ekstasis* and **temporality**.

phenomena   Objects, relations, events, dispositions, emotions, desires, etc., as they appear and are manifest to **consciousness** (see **appearances**). **Kant**, who influenced **Sartre**, contrasts phenomena or appearances, that which is manifest, with **noumena** (things-in-themselves), that which comprises existence as it is in itself apart from awareness or consciousness of it. **Differentiated being** as distinct from **undifferentiated being**. For Sartre, existence considered at the **phenomenological level**, at the level of differentiated being, is comprised of phenomena. Existence considered at the **ontological level** is not comprised of phenomena as described above, although Sartre does sometimes refer to the 'phenomenon' of **being-for-itself** and so on even when it is clear that he is speaking ontologically. To appreciate exactly what Sartre means by a particular instance of 'phenomenon' or 'phenomena' requires an appreciation of the context in which he is using the term. See also **intentional object**, **intentionality**, **phenomenological**, **phenomenology** and **realism**.

phenomenological   The perspective of **phenomenology** on **consciousness**, the world and the relationship between them. A perspective on reality that focuses on the nature of **phenomena** as they appear to consciousness. From a phenomenological point of view a physical object, for example, is identified not as a thing in itself but as an **intentional object** comprised of a series of **appearances** *to* consciousness. The intentional object is nothing beyond these appearances, save an infinite series of **transphenomenal** appearances that are not presently appearing but which could appear. Phenomenology maintains that that which appears *is* reality, rather an indicator of reality that conceals reality.

phenomenological level   **Consciousness** and the world and all that arises from the relationship between them considered at the level of **phenomena**. Sartre's specific and concrete description of reality at a phenomenological level builds on his very generalized and abstract description of reality at a purely logical or **ontological level**. Phenomenological level and ontological level do not signify two distinct levels of reality but different levels of analysis and description.

phenomenological ontology   Sartre's preferred term for his own philosophy in preference to '**existentialism**'. Sartre's philosophical theory of the fundamental features of the **human condition** arrived at through an application of the methods and approaches of **phenomenology**. Sartre's major work, *Being and Nothingness* (1943), is subtitled *An Essay on Phenomenological Ontology*. In so far as other thinkers, **Heidegger** and **de Beauvoir** for example, employ the methods and approaches of phenomenology, their philosophy can also be described as phenomenological ontology. See also **ontological**, **ontology** and **phenomenological**.

phenomenological reduction   See **Husserl**.

phenomenologist   Any philosopher who subscribes to **phenomenology** and employs its methods when reasoning about the nature of **consciousness**, reality and experience. **Sartre** is a phenomenologist, as are **Husserl**, **Heidegger**, **de Beauvoir** and **Merleau-Ponty**.

phenomenology   A philosophical method or approach developed by **Brentano** and **Husserl** and refined by **Heidegger**, **Sartre**, **de Beauvoir**, **Merleau-Ponty** and others. The twentieth-century **existentialism** of Sartre et al. is so rooted in phenomenology that it is best seen as a branch of phenomenology (see **phenomenological ontology**). Phenomenology involves the examination and description of **phenomena** as they appear to **consciousness** (see **appearances**). Phenomenology sets aside questions concerning the actuality of phenomena in favour of questions concerning the defining characteristics of phenomena as they are experienced. Phenomenology examines and describes experience by examining and describing objects of experience. Phenomenology is interested in how a person experiences phenomena, although it is not particularly interested in the mechanisms of experience. It is not a science of perception. Phenomenology is interested in 'the way of being' of phenomena as they appear to consciousness. A **phenomenologist** investigating an entity is not guided by the question, 'What is *x*?' – that is, by questions regarding the category or categories to which *x* belongs and the causal processes that brought *x* about in a certain time and place – but by the question, 'How is *x*?' That is, 'How is *x* in its way of being as an entity that a person is presently conscious of?' Phenomenologists also ask, 'What are the defining characteristics of a person's consciousness of *x*?' The second question cannot be separated from the first because experience cannot be investigated in isolation from what is experienced. Consciousness has no reality or meaning other than as the consciousness *of* something, and all philosophical questions concerning consciousness ultimately refer to what is experienced. Visual experience, for example, cannot be characterized without describing the way in which what is seen appears. According to phenomenology, consciousness is always directed towards phenomena. It is directedness towards phenomena and nothing beyond that, a view that Sartre sums up in the maxim **'consciousness is consciousness of ___'**. At the heart of phenomenology is the theory of **intentionality**, the view that consciousness always *intends* its object. See also **phenomenological**.

positional consciousness   See **consciousness, positional**.

positional self-consciousness   See **self-consciousness, thetic**.

positive choice   See **choice, positive**.

positive freedom   See **freedom, positive**.

positive will to power   See **Nietzsche** and **will to power**.

practico-inert   See **Critique of Dialectical Reason** and **facticity**.

praxis   Greek for 'action'. See **Critique of Dialectical Reason**.

pre-reflective consciousness   See **consciousness, non-thetic**.

pre-reflexive consciousness   See **consciousness, non-thetic**.

presence   The presence of **being-for-itself** to **being-in-itself**. For **Sartre**, the **present** or *now* is not a discrete moment of time between **past** and **future**, but rather the situation to which being-for-itself is a *presence*, the situation to which being-for-itself is present as a surpassing of that situation. The meaning of the present for Sartre is presence to ___. See **temporality**.

present   **Sartre** argues that there is no such thing as the present as a discrete moment of time between **past** and **future**. Time does not consist of a succession of moments, one of which is the present moment. Time or **temporality** consists of a past that is no longer and a future that is not yet. When the future is reached it does not become the present even for an instant, it immediately becomes a **past-future**. The present is rather the **presence** of **being-for-itself** to **being-in-itself**. *Now* is not a discrete moment of time but the situation to which being-for-itself is a presence, the situation to which being-for-itself is present. The meaning of the present for Sartre is presence to __. Past and future are separated by nothing, by **non-being**. The non-being of the present, and the non-being of being-for-itself in the present, are one and the same. To say that the present is nothing is to say that being-for-itself is nothing in the present. Being-for-itself is a **temporal flight** towards the future and is only ever present (has presence) as a flight or a **surpassing** towards the future.

present-at-hand   A term originally used by **Heidegger** to describe the way of being or mode of existence of instruments (any object is potentially an instrument) that are not in use or cannot be used due to malfunction or lack of skill. Tools and instruments assert their independence from a person and remind him of their existence as objects when they cannot be utilized. That is, when they cease to be instruments that are **ready-to-hand** in the service of his purposes, and become instead obstacles that are present-at-hand. Presence-at-hand corresponds to **facticity** and reveals a person to himself as a **being-in-the-midst-of-the-world**. The meaning of 'present-at-hand' can only be fully grasped by contrasting it with 'ready-to-hand'. See also *practico-Inert* and **system of instrumentality**.

primitive project   See **faith of bad faith**.

The Problem of Method   See *Search for a Method*.

pseudo-irreducibles   **Phenomena** that are treated as fundamental within a non-phenomenological theory or discipline that **phenomenology** is able to further analyse and reduce. The psychoanalysis of **Freud**, for example, attempts to explain people in terms of universal and irreducible drives and desires, but drives and desires are phenomena that can themselves be analysed and described in terms of more fundamental phenomena. **Sexual desire**, for example, can be analysed and described phenomenologically in terms of various aspects of **being-for-itself** and **being-for-others**, in terms of **transcendence** and **transcendence-transcended**, in terms of the **facticity** of the **body**, in terms of **sadism** and **masochism** and so on. **Sartre** argues, as does **Laing**, that to explain a person in terms of pseudo-irreducible drives and desires is to reduce him to those drives and desires, and hence to explain him away.

psychic duality   Psychic duality exists in the case of two separate consciousnesses but not, for **Sartre**, within a single **consciousness**. Consciousness is translucent, it is consciousness through and through in the sense that thoughts exist only in so far as a person is conscious of them. Consciousness exists only in so far as it is consciousness *of* something. **'Consciousness is consciousness of __'** and it cannot have parts where thoughts are concealed from other parts. Sartre rejects Freud's theory of **self-deception** and self-censorship, his theory of repression, on the grounds that it posits the impossible psychic duality of conscious and **unconscious**. Sartre explains as forms of **bad faith** the attitudes and behaviours that **Freud** explains as products of a psychic duality. See also **deceiver-deceived duality**, **Id** and **translucency**.

psychic objects   Hypothetical quasi-objects mistakenly assumed to exist *within* **consciousness**, such as love, hate and other emotions. Psychic objects do not exist as such, they are mere **appearances** resulting from the reflection of **being-for-itself** upon its own previous states and actions. For **reflective consciousness**, particular fleeting phases of the **for-itself** as it is in its immediate relation to the world – reactions, aversions, desires and so on – appear as aspects of present, psychic objects that exist in their own right – love, hate, hope, fear and so on. In turn, these psychic objects appear as aspects of a further psychic object, a present and enduring ego or *I* posited by reflection as the underlying unity of these psychic objects. A psychic object is an **intentional object**. See also **self-consciousness** and *The Transcendence of the Ego*.

psychoanalysis   See **existential psychoanalysis**, **Freud**, **Laing**, **pseudo-irreducibles** and *Sketch for a Theory of the Emotions*.

psychology   **Sartre** is sometimes described as being, and sometimes describes himself as being, a psychologist as well as a philosopher. He writes that as a teenager he even mistook psychology for philosophy, and certainly he sought throughout his career to forge links between these two disciplines and to show how they could shed light on one another. He was never a pure psychologist in the sense of conducting scientific research into human behaviour, but he was certainly interested, particularly in his early philosophical works, in philosophically analysing and criticizing the findings of pure, empirical psychology. Generally, he held that psychology would only make real progress if it were underpinned by the methodology of **phenomenology**, a view he expounds in his introduction to *Sketch for a Theory of the Emotions* (1939). Sartre's career is characterized, perhaps above all else, by an abiding interest in the intricacies of human motivation, behaviour and character – what is called, in broad terms, human psychology. See also **existential psychoanalysis**, **Freud**, **Laing** and *The Imaginary*.

The Psychology of Imagination   See *The Imaginary*.

— **Q** —

quasi-duality   That which appears to be a duality but is not. **Being-in-itself** and **being-for-itself** are often mistakenly identified as a duality, as two distinct entities each having being in its own right with each being externally related to the other. **Sartre** rejects this view, arguing that being-in-itself and being-for-itself are not a duality because they are internally related, with the being of the **for-itself** existing only as the **negation** or denial of the **in-itself** (see **internal relation** and **original synthesis**). As there is here only being and its negation, the for-itself being nothing in itself, there are not two entities. It is only in abstraction and in talking about the relationship between the in-itself and the for-itself that they appear as separate, as a genuine duality like the Cartesian duality or **dualism** of mind and body, but in fact they present merely a quasi-duality. See also **Descartes**.

radical choice   See **choice, radical**.

radical conversion   A person is the product of his choices. The core of his personality is not a fixed nature or essence but his **fundamental choice** of himself. The actions that a person chooses in response to his fundamental choice comprise his **fundamental project**. Often a life is defined by a single fundamental project based on a single fundamental choice. However, **Sartre** holds that it is possible for a person to undergo a radical conversion in which he establishes a new fundamental choice of himself. The type of radical conversion Sartre is most interested in is the radical conversion from **bad faith** to **authenticity**, and by 'radical conversion' he generally means 'radical conversion to authenticity', although he appears to allow that a radical conversion to bad faith is possible, as in the case of Lucien Fleurier, the central character of his short story, **The Childhood of a Leader** (1939). Radical conversion to authenticity involves a person abandoning a fundamental project in which he strives in his own particular way to deny that he is free in favour of a new fundamental project whereby he affirms his **freedom** and takes full **responsibility** for himself and his **being-in-situation**. Radical conversion to authenticity involves a radical shift in a person's attitude away from denying the **existential truths** of the **human condition** towards accepting them. Sartre explores radical conversion through his analysis of the lives of Flaubert in **The Family Idiot** (1971–72) and Genet in **Saint Genet** (1952).

radical negation   See **negation, radical**.

reading   See **What is Literature?** and **Words**.

ready-to-hand   A term originally used by **Heidegger** to describe the way of being or mode of existence of instruments (any object is potentially an instrument) when they become extensions of the embodied **for-itself** as it acts to achieve its goals. When a person encounters the world as ready-to-hand he exists as a **transcendence**, as a **being-in-the-world**, rather than existing as an object, a **being-in-the-midst-of-the-world**. When a person has learnt to use any instrument or tool reasonably well, however complex, the tool is overlooked and forgotten by him while in use and is surpassed towards the achievement of the task for which it is being used. When, for example, a person pokes dirt with a stick in order to discover if it is soft or hard he feels the texture of the dirt there at the end of the stick, at which moment he does not feel the stick in his hand. For a person using a tool, if he knows how to use it and it is functioning, the tool vanishes as an object to become one with the activity of the transcendent for-itself. Whatever a person acts upon resists him and asserts its objectivity, its **facticity**. Whatever a person acts with does not resist him and succumbs to his subjectivity, his transcendence. It becomes the expression of his subjectivity. When a tool fails, however, or a person fails to use it correctly, it ceases to be an instrument and presents itself as an obstacle. It reasserts its resistant objectivity, its facticity. It ceases to be ready-to-hand and reverts to what Heidegger refers to as **present-at-hand**. See also *praxis* and **system of instrumentality**.

realism   The theory that there is an external world occupying public space that is comprised of **phenomena** that exist independently of the mind. At times, **Sartre** is a realist, claiming that phenomena exist as they appear to us independently of us. However, he offers no arguments that secure this claim. At most he appeals to common sense, insisting that the world must exist as it appears to us in all its diversity apart from anyone's awareness of it. At other times, Sartre is not a realist but a transcendental idealist in the style of **Kant**. He argues that **appearances** are dependent on the mind and must be appearances to __. To endorse this view is not to hold that appearances are simply ideas in the mind of the perceiver (**solipsism**), but rather to hold that appearances appear out there, to **consciousness**, when consciousness arrives on the scene.

Sartre's philosophy swings between realism and transcendental idealism, exhibiting a serious inconsistency that is seemingly impossible to resolve. His realism is arguably the more intelligible of his two positions because it makes perfect sense to suppose the world is out there quite apart from any consciousness of it; that it is not just formed out of **undifferentiated being** when consciousness is present. Any description of reality cannot help assuming that phenomena are there as they appear to us, with various relations holding between them and undergoing their own motions and processes quite apart from us. This view, however, is not without difficulties. Whatever common sense suggests, it is impossible to know that objects do not collapse into undifferentiated being when all consciousness departs the scene because by definition we cannot be where we are not to know what happens there. The wealth of evidence suggesting that the world endures in our absence will not satisfy the sceptic who is right to insist that we have no way of knowing that the world is as it appears to us when it is not appearing to us. It may be, as Sartre argues in his transcendental idealist mode, completely undifferentiated apart from us, requiring the presence of consciousness for phenomena to arise. Transcendental idealism is certainly more deeply rooted in Sartre's thought than realism. It is inseparable from his fundamental **ontology**, unavoidably implied by his view of the relationship between **being-in-itself** and **being-for-itself** that lies at the heart of his system. Sartre quite clearly holds that being-in-itself is undifferentiated and that phenomena arise entirely through the **negation** of being-in-itself that is being-for-itself. See also **Descartes**, **idealism** and **noumenon**.

reflected-on consciousness　　See **consciousness, reflected-on**.

Reflections on the Jewish Question　　See ***Anti-Semite and Jew***.

the reflective　　See **self-consciousness, thetic**.

reflective consciousness　　See **self-consciousness, thetic**.

reflective for-itself　　See **self-consciousness, thetic**.

reflective self-consciousness　　See **self-consciousness, thetic**.

reflexive consciousness　　See **self-consciousness, thetic**.

reflexive self-consciousness　　See **self-consciousness, thetic**.

regret　　Like **Nietzsche**, **Sartre** recognizes that a person who regrets is inauthentic; he is, in Sartre's terms, in **bad faith**. A person who regrets wishes he had acted differently in the **past**, he wishes his past were different. As a person *is* his past, the sum total of all the choices he has made, to regret his past is to wish that he were not the person he is. **Authenticity**, as the positive **affirmation of freedom**, requires that a person take full **responsibility** for all his choices, those he has made and those he will make. In so doing a person takes full responsibility for himself and the situation in which he finds himself. It can be argued that a person who regrets takes responsibility for his past, in so far as to regret past deeds is to acknowledge them. Regret, however, is a wholly negative and irre-sponsible acknowledgment. It acknowledges only to renounce and disavow. A person who regrets does not say, 'Yes, I did that deed and it is part of what I am', he says, 'I wish I hadn't done that deed and I would have it that it was not a part of what I am'. As is commonly understood, to regret is to dwell uselessly on the past wishing the past were different. To cease to regret is to change the meaning of the past by choosing and affirming the past, it is for a person to act in such a way that he always defines past deeds positively as he flees the past towards the **future**. Sartre recognizes that a person's ongoing actions define the meaning of his past. A man who resigns from his job, for example, can regret it or by his actions define his resignation as a positive step.

For Nietzsche, to be authentic is to dispense with regret, it is 'to redeem the past and to transform every "it was" into "thus I willed it"'. For Nietzsche, the truly authentic person, the overman or man who has overcome himself, wants everything in his life to be just as it is, so much so that he is prepared to live his life all over again in every detail an infinite number of times. This is Nietzsche's **formula for greatness**: the desire for **eternal recurrence**.

Similarly, for Sartre, it is authentic to embrace one's past and affirm it as part of the situation, the **facticity**, in terms of which one must choose one's **transcendence** towards the future. On the other hand, it is bad faith to regret the past, as regret is a disavowal, a refusal to take responsibility. To regret is to complain about what one is. It is to bemoan one's **being-in-situation** rather than take responsibility for it, confront it, choose it and act on the basis of it. Whatever a person in bad faith identifies as a regrettable experience to be disavowed, the authentic author of his own life, whose aim is to affirm his entire life, will identify as a learning experience that helped to make him stronger and wiser. He regrets nothing because every experience has contributed to making him what he is.

If authenticity involves living without regret, then it can be argued that authenticity is impossible because it is impossible to live without regret (see **sustained authenticity**). Regret, it seems, is an unavoidable feature of the **human condition** because anyone with the capacity to imagine alternatives cannot help wishing, at least occasionally, that they had made a different **choice**. In response to this objection it can be argued that it does not show authenticity is impossible, simply that it is very difficult to achieve. If a person can come to regret less then arguably he has the potential to master himself completely and regret nothing. Perhaps the task of complete self-mastery and self-overcoming is too difficult to achieve in one lifetime, particularly for people raised in a culture of regret and recrimination. Yet it remains a **noble ideal** worth striving for because it is surely always better to take charge of one's life and one's situation than it is to be a **buffeted consciousness**. It is better, not least, because a person who constantly strives to confront his situation and overcome it, a person who thereby constantly strives to confront and overcome himself, gains self-respect. A cowardly person, on the other hand, who dwells on regret, refusing to confront his situation and his being in that situation, knows only his own weakness and sense of defeat. Anyone might slip into regret at any moment. What Sartre wants to stress is that everyone is capable of overcoming regret by exercising their freedom positively and thereby taking responsibility for their past. See also *Age of Reason*, *The Flies*, *Iron in the Soul*, *Saint Genet* and *War Diaries*.

The Reprieve (1945)   The second volume of Sartre's trilogy of novels, **Roads to Freedom**. Set in Europe in 1938, *The Reprieve* covers the eight days from September 23 to 30 leading up to the controversial Munich Agreement that gained Europe a temporary reprieve from war at the cost of appeasing Hitler and abandoning Czechoslovakia to Nazi tyranny. The principal characters of **The Age of Reason**, Mathieu, Jacques, Marcelle, Daniel and Ivich reappear in *The Reprieve*, taking their place among a host of widely dispersed subsidiary characters including political leaders, workers, soldiers, prostitutes; anyone at all who is effected by the gathering clouds of war.

Mathieu, although largely apolitical, determines to fight in the war when it comes and awaits conscription. He believes war will usher in a new, more vital and committed phase of his life, it will make him a man of action and consign his irresponsible and profligate youth to the **past**. His wealthy elder brother Jacques, who in *The Age of Reason* challenges Mathieu's decision to obtain money for an abortion for his mistress Marcelle, now challenges Mathieu's resigned and uncomplaining attitude towards conscription and the approaching war. Jacques has certain sympathies with fascism. He is in favour of the appeasement of Hitler and hopes, though he does not really believe it, that the Munich Conference will bring lasting peace.

Marcelle is now married to Daniel who has grown thoroughly bored with her company. Relaxing at the seaside with Marcelle, while reassuring her without much conviction that there will be no war, Daniel gazes at a bare-backed youth on the beach and is overcome by the homosexual desires he is so ashamed of. He tries to ignore his desires and shrug them off. He wonders if the shock of war with its 'visions of tainted, wrecked and bleeding bodies' will snap him out of his desires and finally put an end to them, but he realizes that his desires will endure the horrors of war and that war will probably afford him opportunities to indulge himself. He imagines himself in a lull in the fighting, sitting and eyeing the bare back of a young soldier. Daniel is as bored with himself as he is with Marcelle, but he realizes that even war cannot change a person so radically that he becomes an entirely new person.

Towards the end of the novel Mathieu is ready to leave Paris for Nancy to commence his military service. Having spent the night with a woman he met the day before Mathieu returns to his apartment to collect his suitcase. He discovers an unexpected visitor, Ivich, a female student who, in *The Age of Reason*, he is infatuated with and pursues without success. He is not particularly surprised to see her or moved by her presence. He still cares for her but his old infatuation has gone. He gives her his apartment and belongings and leaves. As his train pulls out of Paris he feels a thrill of joy. He is glad to leave behind him his apartment, Paris, Ivich, glad that the life he has known is over. He looks forward to a future that will bring 'war, fear, death perhaps, and freedom'.

Whereas *The Age of Reason* is a masterpiece of miniaturization that takes place in central Paris over just two days, *The Reprieve* deliberately and radically dispenses with continuity of time, place and action to produce a panoramic, multifaceted view of a Europe teetering on the brink of total war. *The Age of Reason* could be adapted into a play, *The Reprieve* could only be adapted into a movie. **Sartre** was influenced by the work of film directors such as Eisenstein and Pudovkin. *The Reprieve* reflects this influence as it exploits to the full the cinematic possibilities of the novel form. Like a movie, a novel has the capacity to shift location in an instant and to weave a meaningful stream of consciousness from a medley of many people's words and thoughts. *The Reprieve* has an overtly cinematic quality, relentlessly cutting from one scene to another, sometimes in mid-sentence. The novel's fragmented structure can be confusing at first, but the writing is expertly managed and soon serves to produce a coherent and almost omnipresent overview that forges profound connections between separate events. The very structure of the novel indicates that only the novelist, filmmaker or historian can have this overview, and then only after events have taken place. Great political events such as wars, invasions and reprieves are identified as a single unified phenomenon only with the benefit of hindsight, at the time there is nothing beyond the series of individual lives, decisions, triumphs and tragedies. With the exception of Hitler, with his fanatical visions of world domination, the statesmen and political leaders that feature in *The Reprieve* are placed on a par with all the novel's other characters in that they too, and rather disturbingly, are seen to be without an overview or a clear sense of the nature and direction of events. Their decisions shape world history, but like the decisions of the 'ordinary' characters in the novel, their decisions are personal responses to the **facticity** of their immediate, concrete situation – a hot room, a meeting that has gone on too long, a feeling of frailty, a personal desire to avoid the blame of taking Europe to war.

The unhappy peace secured by British Prime Minister Neville Chamberlain and others under the Munich Agreement lasted just eleven months until Hitler invaded Poland and war was declared.

The Respectable Prostitute (1946)   A play by **Sartre** set in the deep south of the USA. The background to the play is an unprovoked attack by four white men on two black men that took place on a train the previous day. During the attack one of the black men was shot dead. The white men have lied that they acted to stop the black men from raping a white girl. Accused of rape, the surviving black man has become a fugitive. The play begins with him calling at the door of the central character, Lizzie, asking her to hide him and testify to his innocence. Lizzie refuses and slams the door in his face. Lizzie witnessed the attack and is the white girl who is supposed to have been raped. She arrived by train from New York the previous day with the intention of making a living as a prostitute. Fred, her first client, a man she has spent the night with, enters from the bathroom unaware of who was at the door. Fred has enjoyed his night with Lizzie but his motive in picking her up was not primarily sexual. He is the cousin of Tom, the murderer, and is part of a plot to persuade Lizzie to testify against the black man.

The police arrive, friends of Fred, and threaten to charge Lizzie with prostitution unless she signs a statement accusing the black man of rape. She refuses. Senator Clarke arrives, Fred's father, and adopts a more subtle approach to persuade Lizzie to sign. He implores her to spare the life of Tom's poor mother who will die of shock if her son is convicted. He implores her to be a good American and to save a young, white, Harvard-educated man of respectable family; a man who is an employer, a leader and a 'rampart' against Communism. He asks her what Uncle Sam would do if he had to choose between such a man and a useless Negro who did nothing but sing and buy fancy clothes. He tells her the whole town will be grateful and that a whole town can't be wrong if it thinks someone has done the right thing. Bewildered, flattered and moved to patriotism by his emotive words Lizzie signs the statement.

Eventually, a black man is lynched by a white mob, though not the black man they have been searching for. Regretting having signed the statement Lizzie threatens to shoot Fred who by now has declared his desire for her. Fred defends himself with arguments similar to those used by his father, the senator, to defend Tom. He claims that as the only male heir of an old and powerful American family he has a right to live. Lizzie surrenders the gun. He promises to buy her a fine house and visit her regularly. She acquiesces and becomes his mistress, his respectable prostitute.

The play highlights the violence and injustice of racism in the Southern USA prior to the emergence of the Civil Rights Movement. It shows how this racism is rooted in an ideology of white supremacy that appeals to patriotism and a distorted version of history, and how it is promoted by corruption and nepotism at the highest levels of authority. Politically radicalized by the events of World War II, Sartre sought to expose what he saw as a great hypocrisy. The USA had helped to defeat Nazism abroad in the name of liberty and democracy, yet it tolerated racial prejudice, inequality and violence on its own streets.

Lizzie represents the ordinary person caught up in this or any other unfavourable political situation. She is well-meaning with an initially clear sense of justice but she is too easily influenced by the rhetoric of those with power and wealth. She fails to stand up for justice and eventually yields to the demands and expectations of those she has sought to resist. She falls into **bad faith**, aspiring to relinquish **responsibility** for herself in order to become a plaything of the ruling class. In Sartre's view, her acquiescence makes her a collaborator, as responsible in her own banal way for the racial injustices that surround her as those who actually commit the crimes. Sartre's message is revolutionary: injustice will continue until ordinary people like Lizzie find the intelligence and courage to positively affirm their **freedom** by resisting corrupt authority.

responsibility   **Being-for-itself** is not a fixed, determined entity. There is nothing that it is or can be in the mode of being it. Being-for-itself must continually create itself in response to its situation through the choices that it makes. Being-for-itself cannot not choose itself in response to its situation because not to choose is in fact a **choice** not to choose. According to **Sartre**, the only limit to a person's **freedom** is that he is not free to cease being free. As his responses to his **being-in-situation** are always chosen he is responsible for them. He is burdened with the responsibility of his freedom. A person is not always responsible for his situation, for his **facticity**, but in so far as he must choose his responses to his situation, and in so doing choose himself in his situation, he is obliged to assume responsibility for his situation. For example, a disabled person may well not be responsible for bringing about his disability, but he is nonetheless responsible for his disability in the sense that he is free to choose his response to it and decide upon its meaning. If he decides that it is the ruination of his life then that is his choice, his responsibility. This is what Sartre means when he argues, controversially, that a person chooses to be a cripple.

Bad faith, as a choice not to choose, is an attempt to evade or relinquish responsibility. Sartre's **flirt**, for example, attempts to avoid taking responsibility for her actions and her being-in-situation, whereas Sartre's **homosexual**, for example, attempts to avoid taking responsibility for his past deeds. **Sincerity** is another form of bad faith in which a person attempts to avoid taking responsibility. A sincere person, a person who makes a confession for example, declares, 'I am what I am', in order to abandon what he is to the **past**. He is the **transcendence** of the facticity of his past, and as such is responsible for his past, but he aims at separating his facticity and his transcendence, his past and his **future**, so as to become a pure transcendence in a virgin future where he has escaped what he was and is no longer responsible for it.

Authenticity, as the antithesis of bad faith, involves a person taking full responsibility for himself, his past and his being-in-situation without blame, excuse or **regret**. Rather than seeking to deny the reality of his situation through the exercise of **negative choice** – choosing not to choose – the authentic person faces up to the demands of his situation through the exercise of **positive choice**. The authentic person acts positively and decisively to meet the demands of his situation without complaint; without wishing he was not responsible for meeting the demands of his situation. Indeed, he embraces and celebrates being responsible in so far as responsibility implies freedom. Freedom is not freedom from responsibility, freedom is having to make choices and therefore having to take responsibility. The person in bad faith, the inauthentic person, seeks to avoid recognizing that one of the fundamental **existential truths** of his being is that he is free and responsible, whereas the authentic person not only recognizes that he is free and responsible, he strives to come to terms with it and to treat it as an ultimate value and a source of values.

Sartre's theory of freedom and responsibility has been criticized for being too uncompromising. His critics argue that there are limitations to freedom; that people do not always choose their responses to their situation and are therefore not always responsible for their actions. **Merleau-Ponty**, for example, argues that there is a **natural self** based upon the natural limitations of the **body** that renders certain evaluations inevitable and disposes a person towards certain choices. In failing to acknowledge that a person's interactions with the world and other people are pre-structured by a natural self, Sartre also overlooks various behavioural and dispositional phenomena that signify limitations to choice and responsibility. Among phenomena that are cited by Sartre's critics are sense of humour, sexual preference and mental disturbance. Examining these phenomena reveals that not every conscious response is freely chosen. Although education and experience may change a person's sense of humour over time, if he finds a joke funny at the time he hears it he is not choosing to find it funny. Although sane people are responsible for actions that stem from their sexual preferences they are not responsible for their sexual preferences. They do not choose them and cannot choose to change them. Psychiatrists recognize that the genuinely mentally disturbed have obsessive, compulsive tendencies over which they have little or no control. Sartre's theory of freedom does not allow for the diminished responsibility that is the accepted hallmark of insanity.

Sartre is right that responsibility cannot be avoided or freedom limited by choosing not to choose. He is also right that helplessness in many situations is a sham. He appears, however, to be wrong that people are always responsible for what they do and the evaluations they make. The uncompromising nature of Sartre's theory of freedom and responsibility is to some extent a result of the historical period in which it was produced. Sartre, his thoughts increasingly influenced by political considerations, sought to counter the rising tide of fascism that culminated in World War II by arguing in favour of individual freedom and inalienable personal responsibility. See also **Truth and Existence**.

Roads to Freedom (1945–49)   A trilogy of novels by **Sartre** set before and during World War II. The trilogy includes **The Age of Reason** (1945), **The Reprieve** (1945) and **Iron in the Soul** (1949). Sartre wrote two chapters of a fourth volume before abandoning the project.

The Room (1939)   A short story by **Sartre** contained in a collection of short stories entitled **The Wall**, *The Wall* being the lead story in the collection. The robust and practical Charles Darbédat troubles and tires his sick wife with his growing concerns about their daughter, Eve. He wants Eve to commit Pierre, her obsessive, deluded, paranoid husband, to a sanatorium for the insane and to make a fresh start in life, but Eve refuses to do so. She loves Pierre and cannot bear to be parted from him. She prefers his company to that of 'normal people' like her father who are shallow, insensitive and lack imagination. She spends most of her time in the room that Pierre never leaves, a room that is always darkened against the daylight and smells heavily of incense. Much to the annoyance of her father, who believes that 'one should never enter the delirium of a madman', Eve allows herself to be drawn into Pierre's private, irrational world and to be captivated by his fantasies, rituals and fears. She seeks to understand the purpose of his strange rituals, helping him to perform them, and though she is sane, she manages to share temporarily in his madness by sharing in the fear he feels when his imaginary flying statues arrive and buzz about the room. Eve has a deeper and more genuine fear that Pierre's condition is growing worse, that finally he will lose his mind completely and sink into a permanent stupor. She intends to kill him before that happens.

M. Darbédat and his friend Dr Franchot want to label Pierre insane so as to reduce him to a stereotype and dismiss him as a person. M. Darbédat is suspicious, disapproving and ashamed of Pierre's condition, he believes it is something his daughter ought to rid herself of in order to return to the bright, respectable, predictable, secure world of well-balanced, practical people – the family of mankind. Eve is intensely aware that Pierre is still a person despite his condition, that for him his delusions are real and meaningful. She can partially comprehend their power and significance when she plays his games and uses her imagination to enter into his make-believe world. Indeed, to her, Pierre is more of a person than 'normal people'. He has a rich and complex inner life and a certain awareness of the mystery of being, whereas the people she sees from the window talking and laughing so thoughtlessly as they hurry about their business seem to her to be two-dimensional, having no real inner life or sense of mystery at all.

Apart from exploring different attitudes to insanity and to some extent the phenomenon of insanity itself, *The Room* explores the familiar Sartrean themes of **authenticity** and **bad faith**. Through his insanity Pierre has achieved a kind of authenticity, he is genuine with a view of reality and an approach to life that is all his own. 'Normal people', on the other hand, lack his unique vision, they share in a collective view of reality, they have faith – bad faith – in the predictability of the world, the certainty of their perceptions and the soundness of their narrow ideas. The story exhibits Sartre's usual contempt for bourgeois attitudes (primarily, in this story, bourgeois attitudes to insanity) and for ordinary, normal people who go about their daily lives exercising bad faith in an attempt to avoid giving the **contingency** and **absurdity** of their existence any consideration. Pierre and Eve are alienated from ordinary, normal people. Pierre by his insanity, Eve by her choice to be with Pierre and share his peculiar world. Like Roquentin in Sartre's novel, **Nausea** (1938), Eve chooses to be an outsider looking in on society. 'Normal people think I belong with them. But I couldn't stay an hour among them. I need to live out there, on the other side of the wall.'

The Room bears certain similarities to Sartre's play, ***The Condemned of Altona*** (1959). Both works feature a reclusive, inspired madman who confines himself to darkened quarters where his irrational obsessions create a private, fantasy world that captivates a lover.

— **S** —

sadism   **Sartre** explores the phenomenon of sadism as an aspect of **being-for-others**, as a feature of our 'concrete relations with others'. An understanding of Sartre's theory of **sexual desire** is required to fully understand his theory of sadism as the phenomenon of sadism, like **masochism**, emerges when sexual desire fails to achieve its goal of reciprocal **incarnation**.

A person whose sexual desire is not sadistic wants to exist as flesh for himself and for the **Other**, he also wants the Other to exist as flesh for herself and for him. He wants to achieve what Sartre calls a 'double reciprocal incarnation' of the flesh. The sadist does not want to achieve a double reciprocal incarnation, or is incapable of doing so. He may have a horror of his own incarnation and consider it a humiliating state. The sadist refuses to be incarnated while at the same time seeking to possess the incarnation of the Other. He denies his own **facticity** in his efforts to transcend the Other and possess the facticity of the Other. As the sadist refuses to incarnate the Other through his own incarnation, he must incarnate the Other by using them as a tool. To make a tool of the Other is to make an object of the Other, and it is as an 'instrument-object' that the sadist wants the Other to realize her incarnation.

In his description of sadism Sartre contrasts the graceful with the ungraceful or obscene. A graceful **body** that has poise and moves with ease and precision is an instrument that manifests a person's **freedom**. A person who is naked conceals the facticity and obscenity of their flesh if their movements are sufficiently graceful. An ungraceful or obscene body, on the other hand, one that lacks poise and is awkward and laboured in its movements, is an instrument that manifests a person's facticity. An ungraceful, naked body is, so to speak, more naked and obscene than a graceful naked body for not being clothed in grace. It is the obscene body, the instrument-object that manifests facticity, rather than the graceful body that manifests freedom, that the sadist desires to incarnate. Sadism aims to destroy grace as it is a manifestation of the Other's freedom. The more ungraceful the sadist can make the body of the Other through the pain he inflicts and the humiliating postures he forces the Other to adopt the more he will feel that he has enslaved the Other's freedom.

Pain is a facticity that invades **consciousness**. It is through the pain that the sadist inflicts on the Other that he forces the Other to identify herself with the facticity of her flesh. The sadist uses violence to force the Other into an 'incarnation through pain'. In pain the Other is incarnated for herself and for the sadist. The sadist enjoys the possession of the Other's flesh that he achieves through violence while also enjoying his own 'non-incarnation'. In his state of non-incarnation the sadist is a free **transcendence**, he is all **action**, he feels powerful as he skilfully brings instruments of torture to bear upon the body of the Other in order to capture the freedom of the Other in pained flesh. The consciousness of the Other is ensnared in pain and as the sadist is the cause of this pain he feels he has ensnared the freedom of the Other. Sadism, however, like masochism, **love** and sexual desire, like all attempts to gain possession of the freedom of the Other, is doomed to failure.

The sadist wants to incarnate the flesh of the Other by using the Other as an instrument, but to apprehend the body as an instrument is very different from apprehending it as flesh. Instruments refer to other instruments, to a **system of instrumentality**, they are utilizable, they have potential, they indicate the **future**. Flesh revealed as flesh is an 'unutilizable facticity' without potential, it is simply there in its **contingency** referring to nothing beyond itself. The sadist can utilize the flesh of the Other as an instrument to reveal flesh, but when the flesh *is* revealed in all its unutilizable facticity suddenly no instrument remains for the sadist to possess through utilization. The sadist strives for possession by utilization, but his very utilization of the flesh of the Other eventually incarnates flesh that cannot be utilized and, therefore, does not allow possession by utilization. The sadist realizes his failure to possess the Other at the very moment he achieves complete mastery over the Other because in mastering the Other and reducing her to pained, contingent flesh, to a non-instrument, there is nothing left for him to utilize.

The sadist could utilize the flesh of the Other to satisfy himself sexually, to achieve orgasm through intercourse and so on, but as this would involve the incarnation of his own flesh by the flesh of the Other it would not be sadism as defined. As noted, the non-incarnation of the flesh of the sadist is central to the phenomenon of sadism. In giving way to the desire for the incarnation of his own flesh he would cease to be sadistic. It is always possible that the project of sadism will be undermined by the emergence of desire within the sadist for the incarnation of his own flesh. 'Sadism is the failure of desire, and desire is the failure of sadism.'

The project of sadism also fails because the freedom of the Other that the sadist strives to possess remains out of reach. The sadist's actions aim at recovering his being-for-others, but the more he acts upon the Other, torturing and inflicting pain, the more the Other slips away from him into her consciousness of being assaulted. The Other is not a being he has possessed but a being lost to him in her preoccupation with her own suffering.

The sadist discovers the failure of his sadism most acutely when the other looks at him and thereby transcends his transcendence. As a **transcendence-transcended** he experiences himself as an object for the subjectivity of the Other. **The look** of the Other alienates his freedom and reduces him to a **being-in-the-midst-of-the-world**. The 'mere' gaze of the Other triumphs over all his sadistic violence and cruelty.

Saint Genet, Actor and Martyr (1952)   A book by **Sartre** about his personal friend, the French novelist, dramatist and poet, Jean Genet (1910–1986), author of *The Maids* (1947) and other works. As with Sartre's other books about writers – **Baudelaire** (1946) and **The Family Idiot** (1971–72) – *Saint Genet* is not so much a biography of Genet, detailing the main events of his life in chronological order, as an exhaustive psychological study. The book started as a preface to Genet's works but grew into a 600-page epic as Sartre became fascinated with Genet's character. The book is above all a masterful exercise in **existential psychoanalysis** in which Sartre systematically deconstructs Genet's personality through an analysis of Genet's writings and through conversations Genet had with Sartre and his associates.

Sartre once told journalists that **Camus** was not a genius but that Genet was. In *Saint Genet* Sartre undertakes to explain the origins of that genius – Genet's rare insight into the **human condition** – by examining the crucial events and choices that shaped him. He explores his metamorphoses in response to various crises, from saint to thief to aesthete to writer.

Abandoned by his mother at birth, Genet was placed in the care of peasants. Small, quiet, intelligent, respectful, a good boy, grown-ups conferred upon him the virtue of innocence. He accepted this label and aspired to live up to it, aspired to be saintly. He admired the saints for their asceticism and their intimacy with **God**. God replaced Genet's absent mother and made him feel his existence was necessary rather than accidental. 'In becoming an object of concern for an infinite being, Genet will acquire the being which he lacks. He will be a saint since he is not a son.' Meanwhile, Genet stole from his foster parents and neighbours. He saw no inconsistency between his saintliness and his thefts because he did not reflect on or judge his actions. He had no shame because in his innocence he was unaware of existing for others, of his **being-for-others**. Genet was well cared for materially and did not steal to survive. He stole in order to have a 'possessive relationship with things' that was ordinarily denied him. As a charity case, an adopted child rather than a son and heir, he had no right to the things he was given. Others were free not to give him what he was not free to refuse. Everything was a gift for which he had to be grateful. Nothing was really his own. Even his earnings were not really his own because the work itself was a charitable gift. He stole to possess things for which he did not have to say 'thank you'. Ironically, only stolen things truly felt as though they belonged to him, they were genuine appropriations and he enjoyed his power of ownership over them. In relation to these stolen objects he was a free **transcendence** rather than a **transcendence-transcended** by the charity of others. Genet was born to 'poverty and bastardy'. In response he became both a thief and a saint with stolen goods substituting for property and God substituting for his mother. The saintly thief gave no thought to the contradiction until he was found out.

Genet was about ten when he was caught stealing. He considered it the decisive event of his life, the occasion of his first and most profound metamorphosis, a moment of awakening to his being-for-others. In being caught he acquired self-identity, he became a **being-in-the-midst-of-the-world**, an object judged guilty by adults and labelled a thief. Worse, he was a thief who hid behind a facade of innocence and was ungrateful for the charity he received. Genet felt he had learnt what he was *objectively*. A monster, an evil thing, a thief from birth to death. Branded a thief, shunned, outcast, constantly suspected, Genet decided to refuse the shame and **regret** of not being what others told him he ought to be, and *chose*, as an act of self-assertion and defiance, to be what others told him he was. 'I decided to be what crime made of me' he later wrote. He might have attempted to dispense with what he was through **confession** and endlessly making amends, but instead he embraced the thief-object that he was for others and chose being a thief as his destiny. He positively affirmed his **freedom** by creating himself as the thief that others would have him be. In taking **responsibility** for his **being-in-situation** without regret Genet made a **radical conversion** to **authenticity**.

For **Nietzsche**, to be authentic is to dispense with regret, it is 'to redeem the past and to transform every "it was" into "thus I willed it"'. This is Nietzsche's **noble ideal** and Genet, as Sartre portrays him, is a noble character in the Nietzschean sense, an **existentialist** hero (a saint even) who comes very close to achieving the **existentialist ideal** of **sustained authenticity**. Genet's **fundamental choice** of himself was to take responsibility for himself, to assert his freedom as his ultimate value and to be unrepentant. He unashamedly took possession of being a bastard, a thief, a convict, a homosexual and further redeemed his past by eventually transforming his experiences and his extraordinary vision of life into literature.

Saint Genet is an ambitious undertaking even by Sartre's standards that employs the entire conceptual apparatus of his **existentialism** to give an exhaustive account of the development of a unique character. Sartre spares no effort and misses no opportunity to convince his reader that a person is not simply the product of his circumstances, his personal and social **facticity**, but the perpetual transcendence of his circumstances. *Saint Genet* details the triumph of an individual freedom over the perennial forces of oppression: convention, morality, guilt, other people.

Sartre, Jean-Paul (1905–80) French **existentialist** philosopher, novelist, dramatist, biographer, journalist, critic and political activist. Jean-Paul Sartre was born in Paris on June 21, 1905. His infancy was marked by the death of his father, Jean-Baptiste, on September 17, 1906. As Sartre writes in **Words** (1964), the autobiography of his childhood, his character developed free from the oppression of a paternal will that might have crushed him. He lived with his doting mother, the former Anne-Marie Schweitzer, at the house of her father, Charles Schweitzer, until Anne-Marie re-married in 1917. Charles was the founder and director of a language school and the uncle of the medical missionary, Albert Schweitzer. As is also documented in *Words*, Charles played the most important role in Sartre's early intellectual development. By his own account he was a small, cross-eyed, bookish child with an extremely precocious manner that made it difficult for him to gain acceptance from other children. Secure in the love and attentions of his family, his childhood was not an unhappy one. Nonetheless, in *Words*, the ageing Sartre declares, perhaps ironically, 'I loathe my childhood and all that remains of it.'

From 1915 to 1917 Sartre attended the Lycée Henri IV in Paris before transferring to a lycée in La Rochelle when his mother married Joseph Mancy. Unsettled and badly behaved at La Rochelle he was transferred back to the Lycée Henri IV as a boarder in the hope that his behaviour would improve. Sartre became best friends with Paul Nizan who inspired in him a desire for social justice that remained with him all his life. In 1922 the two friends were transferred to the select Lycée Louis-le-Grand and Sartre subsequently gained entrance to the prestigious École Normale Supérieure. He began studying philosophy, taking some of his classes at the Sorbonne. During his time at the École Normale Supérieure he met Simone **de Beauvoir**, who remained a close friend for the rest of his life. Sartre initially failed his final exams but passed them at the second attempt by taking the advice of his close friend Raymond Aron and adapting his approach to the traditional requirements of the examiners.

As a graduate he taught philosophy at the Lycée François Ier in Le Havre until 1936. The Le Havre years have been characterized as a period of dull, provincial exile for Sartre. Publishers rejected some of his early manuscripts and it appeared that he would not achieve the fame he had always confidently expected. Nonetheless, the Le Havre years were important to his personal and philosophical development. He was an excellent but unconventional teacher, very popular with his students but distrusted by the school authorities. It was in Le Havre that he began writing and repeatedly revising a work on **contingency** that finally emerged several years later as the novel ***Nausea*** (1938). Bouville, the town in which *Nausea* is set, is loosely based on Le Havre and somewhat reflects its character. Sartre's association with Le Havre was certainly maintained by choice and he even returned there in 1934 after spending several months at the French Institute in Berlin.

At a now legendary meeting in Paris in the spring of 1933, Raymond Aron, who was studying philosophy in Berlin, introduced Sartre and de Beauvoir to the **phenomenology** of **Husserl**. Sartre was fascinated, and so began his lifelong interest in phenomenology. He hatched a plan with Aron to exchange positions. Aron would cover for him in Le Havre while he took a sabbatical in Berlin that would begin in the autumn of 1933. In Berlin Sartre immersed himself in the study of Husserl and to a lesser extent **Heidegger**, whose complex vocabulary he says he found difficult to penetrate. In his intellectual ivory tower Sartre appears to have been largely unaware of the rise of Nazism taking place around him, or at least to have given no serious consideration to its possible consequences. By 1937 he had published his first major work, *The Transcendence of the Ego*. His *Sketch for a Theory of the Emotions* and his **phenomenological** investigation into the imagination, *The Imaginary*, followed soon after. In 1938 he finally published *Nausea*, his first novel. A highly polished, stylistic masterpiece, it explores the classic existentialist themes of contingency, **absurdity** and alienation, and in some respects reflects his disturbing experience with the hallucinogenic drug mescaline three years earlier. (In January 1935 Sartre was injected with mescaline at Sainte-Anne Hospital under experimental conditions by his friend, Doctor Daniel Lagache. See *The Imaginary*.) *Nausea* established Sartre's reputation and remains his most widely read work.

In 1939 Sartre was conscripted into the French military and assigned to the meteorological section in charge of weather balloons. As he writes in his *War Diaries, Notebooks from a Phoney War 1939–1940*, his duties were not particularly arduous and he was free to read and write for many hours a day. He is reputed to have written a million words in eight months. He was captured by the Germans in June 1940 and detained first in a prison camp at Baccarat on the Meurthe River in France and then at Stalag XII D, Mount Kemmel near Trier (Trèves), Germany. He enjoyed the collective life of the camp and spent his time reading, writing plays and teaching the philosophy of Heidegger. Sartre identified his months of captivity as a watershed period in his life. He wrote in a letter to Simone de Beauvoir that prior to this time he had done nothing but 'juggle harmless old ideas in front of a bunch of kids'.

Dramatic events had finally made him politically aware. He recognized his place in history and committed himself to a future of political engagement in support of left-wing causes. Rather reluctantly, but feeling he could only actively resist the German occupation of France if he returned to Paris, he obtained his release in March 1941 with the aid of a fake medical certificate that declared him physically unfit for military service.

He became involved in the Resistance movement, founding a resistance group, **Socialism and Freedom**, that sought a third political way between the resistance of the capitalist Gaullists on the right and the Communists on the left. Squeezed between these two much larger organizations Sartre's group eventually folded. In 1943 he completed his greatest work, **Being and Nothingness**, arguably the most important book of the existentialist school of thought. 1943 also saw the start of his doomed friendship with the novelist Albert **Camus** whom he helped to found the Resistance newspaper, *Combat*. After the war he founded the literary and political review, **Les Temps modernes** and continued to publish at a prodigious rate. Articles and essays, plays such as **In Camera** (1944) and **Dirty Hands** (1948), the **Roads to Freedom** trilogy (1945–49) and biographies of Baudelaire (see **Baudelaire**) and Genet (see **Saint Genet**). Sartre used the medium of biography to explore ideas such as **fundamental choice** and **radical conversion**, thereby advancing his theory of **existential psychoanalysis**.

By 1948 his **atheism**, his anti-authoritarianism and his constant questioning of accepted values led the Catholic Church to place his complete works on the Vatican index of prohibited books. In 1960, after three years of amphetamine-fuelled work, he published the first volume of the vast **Critique of Dialectical Reason** in which he attempted to amalgamate **existentialism** and **Marxism**. Volume two, which remained unfinished, was not published until 1985, five years after his death. Sartre's interest in Marxism had grown steadily since World War II and in 1954, the year after Stalin's death, he made the first of many trips to the Soviet Union. Although he continued to promote Marxist ideas for most of his life and to give broad support to the Soviet ideal, he became increasingly disillusioned with the existing Soviet system and condemned the Soviet invasions of Hungary and Czechoslovakia. In the early 1960s he became fascinated with the Marxist revolution in Cuba and visited Fidel Castro, but once again disillusionment set in until he finally withdrew his support for the dictatorship.

Sartre was an outspoken critic of the French colonial policy in Algeria and campaigned for Algerian independence. In both 1961 and 1962 the OAS, a terrorist organization opposed to Algerian independence, bombed his Paris apartment. Sartre's was the most famous signature on the 'Manifesto of the 121', which called for 'insubordination' by French troops in Algeria. Many considered the document treasonable and Sartre would have faced trial and possible imprisonment had President de Gaulle not had the political savvy to avoid an explosive confrontation with Sartre, a living legend in France, with his famous declaration, 'You do not imprison Voltaire.'

In 1964 Sartre politely turned down the **Nobel Prize for Literature** on the grounds that writers should refuse to be transformed by institutions. In 1965 his close friend of several years, Arlette **Elkaïm**, became his adopted daughter. He became increasingly involved in the movement against the Vietnam War and in 1967 headed a tribunal set up by the British philosopher, Bertrand Russell, to investigate US war crimes in Indochina. He supported the student riots and French General Strike of 1968 and against this background of political unrest continued writing his last significant work, *The Family Idiot*, an extensive biography of the novelist Flaubert, published 1971–72. Sartre continued to court controversy into his old age, visiting the terrorist Andreas Baader in Stammheim Prison, Germany in 1974. In 1977 he claimed he was no longer a Marxist but his political activity continued until his death.

By 1973 his body, long abused with tobacco, alcohol, amphetamines and overwork was prematurely exhausted. Blind in his right eye since the age of four, hypertension caused the sight in his left eye to fail also, destroying his ability to write. Protected by his inner circle of friends he struggled against his declining health for seven years until he died in Paris of oedema of the lungs on April 15, 1980. Over fifty thousand people lined the streets at his funeral.

Simone de Beauvoir tells how Sartre had the gift of almost total fluency. He could write for hours, hardly pausing, completed sheets of paper falling from his desk. This fact is evidenced by his immense output in the areas of philosophy, biography, literature and drama. Amphetamines fuelled a certain amount of this activity and arguably some of his later works are somewhat rambling and would have benefited from further editing. His ideas continue to be enormously influential particularly on Continental philosophy. Set against the entire history of Western philosophy Sartre is still a very recent figure and his ideas are still being extensively digested and explored. Philosophers are in the process of developing Sartre's insights in various directions. His thought has been slower to influence the British analytical tradition but in recent times British philosophy has begun to take him seriously and to find great value in his ideas. Sartre is the archetypal twentieth-century French intellectual – brilliant, prolific, passionate, political, subversive and controversial. He not only sought to philosophize about the **human condition** but to urge people towards greater honesty and **responsibility** in face of life's demands. Through his writings and through the personal example he set, he continues to inspire people the world over to resist the oppression of establishment values and to take full and committed possession of their inalienable **freedom**.

scarcity   See *Critique of Dialectical Reason*.

Search for a Method (1960)   Alternative title *The Problem of Method*. An essay by **Sartre** on the relationship between **existentialism** and **Marxism** that is part of a much larger work, the ***Critique of Dialectical Reason***. *Search for a Method* was translated into English some time before the rest of the *Critique* and is still available as a separate publication. *Search for a Method* is actually a postscript to the *Critique* considering the 'regressive–progressive' method of reasoning by which existentialist-Marxism may seek to understand both individual people and history (see ***The Family Idiot*** for an illustration of this method). Sartre, however, placed *Search for a Method* at the start of the *Critique* so that it would not appear that 'the mountain had brought forth a mouse'. *Search for a Method* stands as a work in its own right and is often read as a first step towards penetrating the complexities of the *Critique*.

self-consciousness   **Sartre** holds that there are two modes of self-consciousness: Non-thetic consciousness (of) consciousness and thetic consciousness of consciousness.* Strictly speaking, the former is not self-

---

* When referring to non-thetic consciousness (of) consciousness the 'of' is placed in brackets to indicate that non-thetic consciousness is not, as an unqualified 'of' might suggest, a further act of consciousness. As thetic consciousness of consciousness is a further act of consciousness the 'of' is used without qualification.

consciousness because it does not involve **consciousness** contemplating itself as an **intentional object**. The latter is self-consciousness as ordinarily understood: consciousness reflecting on itself and taking itself as the intentional object of its contemplation. Non-thetic consciousness (of) consciousness is implicit, non-positional, pre-reflective consciousness. It is a necessary condition of positional consciousness of intentional objects. Without non-thetic, pre-reflective consciousness (of) consciousness, consciousness would not be conscious because to be conscious is to be conscious of being so. Non-thetic consciousness (of) consciousness is not a separate act of consciousness that is brought to bear on positional consciousness of intentional objects. It is an internal and essential feature of positional consciousness without which positional consciousness could not be. Non-thetic consciousness (of) consciousness exists by virtue of the **translucency** of consciousness. As nothing but consciousness of intentional objects, consciousness is consciousness through and through; it is without **opacity**. Non-thetic consciousness (of) consciousness belongs, therefore, to the very being of consciousness as that which is utterly translucent. Consciousness that is not non-thetically and pre-reflectively conscious of itself is impossible because consciousness is consciousness (of) being conscious of objects.

Thetic consciousness of consciousness is self-consciousness as ordinarily understood. It is positional, explicit and reflective self-consciousness. It is self-reflection. Consciousness, as positional consciousness of intentional objects, is also capable of positional consciousness of itself as an intentional object. This positional consciousness of consciousness is thetic self-consciousness or reflective consciousness.

Reflective consciousness is non-thetically conscious (of) itself. Non-thetic consciousness (of) consciousness is an internal and essential feature of all acts of consciousness. It follows, therefore, that non-thetic consciousness (of) consciousness must also be an internal and essential feature of reflective consciousness. Without non-thetic consciousness (of) reflective consciousness, reflective consciousness cannot occur. Non-thetic consciousness (of) reflective consciousness is a necessary condition of reflective consciousness without which reflective consciousness would not be conscious.

Reflective consciousness is not separate from **reflected-on consciousness**, but neither is it identical with it. In fact, it is necessary that reflective consciousness both be and not be reflected-on consciousness at the same time. Reflective consciousness exists as a relation to or a **negation** of reflected-on consciousness. Reflection is not one consciousness reflecting on another consciousness within an individual person, as though the person consisted of two externally related consciousnesses. Rather, reflection is consciousness conscious of itself. This relation of consciousness to itself requires an absence of identity as much as it requires an absence of independence. Consciousness or **being-for-itself** is never identical with itself. It is always what it is not and not what it is. It exists always at a distance from itself and as such is capable of being an appearance for itself and witnessing itself.

Being-for-itself is the negation of **being-in-itself**. Reflection is the negation of being-for-itself by itself. The origin of this further negation is a further attempt on the part of the **for-itself** to cease being what it is not and not what it is and become what it is. By reflecting upon itself the for-itself attempts to establish itself as an object, as a consciousness in itself that witnesses itself as such, as a **being-for-itself-in-itself**. This project is doomed to failure because the for-itself cannot witness itself unless it is at a distance from itself. Reflection aims to render the for-itself identical with itself, but reflection requires that the for-itself be other than itself. Sartre argues that reflection is precisely the failed effort of the for-itself to be its own foundation.

Consciousness is essentially temporal (see **temporality**). It follows, therefore, that the reflection of consciousness upon itself has temporal dimensions. Reflected-on consciousness is always **past** for reflective consciousness because reflective consciousness flees reflected-on consciousness towards the **future** in order to attempt to fix it in the **present**. Reflected-on consciousness appears as present to reflective consciousness. It appears as a consciousness present in itself all at once; a **temporal flight** recovered and condensed into an instant. To reflective consciousness, reflected-on consciousness appears as a being-for-itself-in-itself. This is a mere appearance because reflective consciousness is consciousness exterior to itself. Consciousness must be exterior to itself in order to reflect upon itself as an apparent for-itself-in-itself. Not least, the appearance of reflected-on consciousness as a for-itself-in-itself has to be perpetually renewed by reflective consciousness. A genuine for-itself-in-itself (which is impossible) would maintain itself and would not have to be perpetually renewed in this way.

The appearance of reflected-on consciousness as a for-itself-in-itself for reflective consciousness is the basis of the appearance of the self or 'I'. Through reflection, the particular reactions, aversions, desires, etc., of consciousness as it is in its immediate relation to the world appear as aspects of **psychic objects** such as **love**, **hate**, hope, fear and so on. In turn, these psychic objects appear as aspects of a present and enduring 'I' posited by reflection as the supposed underlying unity of these psychic objects.

self-consciousness, positional   See **self-consciousness, thetic**.

self-consciousness, reflective   See **self-consciousness, thetic**.

self-consciousness, reflexive   See **self-consciousness, thetic**.

self-consciousness, thetic   Explicit **self-consciousness** as opposed to non-thetic consciousness (of) consciousness which is not, strictly speaking, self-consciousness. (See **self-consciousness** for a full explanation of the difference between non-thetic consciousness (of) consciousness and self-consciousness.) Self-reflection in which consciousness reflects on itself as an **intentional object**. Also called positional self-consciousness, reflective consciousness, reflective for-itself, reflective self-consciousness, reflexive consciousness, reflexive self-consciousness and the reflective.

self-deception   **Sartre** argues that self-deception is impossible in the straightforward sense of 'deceiving oneself' or 'lying to oneself'. He argues that deception requires a **psychic duality** of deceiver and deceived. It is possible for me to deceive another person because another person is not conscious of my **consciousness**. Within the unity of a single consciousness, however, there is no **deceiver-deceived duality** because consciousness is wholly conscious of itself as consciousness of the world. Consciousness has the quality of **translucency**, it is consciousness through and through and as such has no parts or divisions. If a person undertakes to lie to himself he must invariably catch himself in the act because in order to attempt to lie to himself he must be conscious of doing so. It is impossible to lie to oneself. In short, self-deception is impossible.

Bad faith has often been incorrectly defined as self-deception. Bad faith often looks like self-deception, but it is not. Far from being self-deception, bad faith, at least in Sartre's philosophy, replaces self-deception as the explanation for attitudes and behaviours that appear to be, but cannot be, products of a deceiver–deceived duality. Bad faith, or at least certain aspects of it, involves **self-distraction** rather than self-deception. See also **Freud**.

self-distraction   **Bad faith** looks like **self-deception**, but in the strict sense of the term self-deception is impossible. A closer analysis of bad faith reveals that it is more akin to self-distraction or self-evasion than self-deception. Sartre's **flirt**, for example, clearly knows the meaning of her situation and what it demands in terms of **positive choice**. As self-deception is impossible, if she knows the meaning of her situation, then she cannot simply lie to herself that her situation is other than it is. Yet it is possible for her to distract herself from her knowledge of the meaning of her situation or, at least, it is possible for her to be the ongoing project of seeking to distract herself. In so far as she knows her situation it cannot be said that she has succeeded in evading it, rather she strives to evade it and this striving is itself a distraction.

A person is able to distract himself from the meaning of his situation, from his responsibilities in that situation, even from what his body is doing or not doing in that situation, by fleeing himself towards the **future**. He aims to be a being beyond his present situation, a pure **transcendence** that no longer has to choose itself in response to its **facticity** and as such be the transcendence of its facticity. He chooses not to choose, he chooses to aim at being a being that does not have to choose. This **negative choice** of himself preoccupies him; he allows it to serve as a distraction from his knowledge of his situation and what it demands. See also *Truth and Existence*.

self-reflection   See **self-consciousness, thetic**.

sexual desire   **Sartre** explores the phenomenon of sexual desire as an aspect of **being-for-others**, as a feature of our 'concrete relations with others'. He argues that sexual desire is not simply sexual instinct. A person could not experience sexual desire (or anything else) if he did not have a **body**, and sexual desire very much involves the body, but sexual desire is not generated by the body, or more specifically the sex organs, as a demand for sex, orgasm or procreation. Viewed objectively, sexual desire appears as an appetite like hunger that seeks satisfaction from a particular object. From the internal perspective of **being-for-itself**, however, sexual desire differs radically from hunger. Hunger is a physiological urge that the **for-itself** becomes conscious of. Hunger is *for* **consciousness**, in so far as to be hungry is to be conscious of being hungry, but unlike sexual desire, hunger is not a state or condition of consciousness. Unlike hunger, sexual desire is a radical modification of consciousness that 'troubles' it and defines it to its core. Sexual desire is consciousness itself 'hungry' for a certain relationship with the body of the **Other** that will bring about a certain relationship with its own body.

Sexual desire is an attempt to make the Other exist as flesh for me and for herself. In Sartre's terms, sexual desire is an attempt to realize the '**incarnation**' of the body of the Other as flesh. But, the critic will say, isn't the Other already incarnated, given that the Other is made of flesh? Certainly, the Other's body is made of flesh but it is not primarily as an object that the Other exists for herself or for others. The Other's flesh is usually concealed, not only by her clothes but by her movements. Even a person who is naked can conceal their flesh as mere flesh with movements that are sufficiently graceful. The Other is not flesh but a being in **action** who transcends her body towards her possibilities. Sexual desire aims to divest the Other's body of its actions, its **transcendence** and its possibilities, so as to reveal the inertia and passivity of the Other's body to them and to the one who desires them. This divesting and revealing is achieved through the sexual caress which, through the pleasure it gives the Other, causes the Other 'to be born as flesh for me and for herself'. Sartre notes that it is possible for a person to caress the Other with his eyes alone. To look at the Other with desire is to caress her and incarnate her as flesh. The person who caresses does so to reveal the Other as flesh, but he does not want his caressing to take hold of her or act upon her. Instead, he wants his caressing to be a passive placing of his body against the Other's body. He wants the very gentleness and passivity of his caresses to reveal his own passive flesh to the Other and to himself. He desires to caress the Other's body in such a way that in caressing the Other's body he is caressed by the Other's body. The person who caresses seeks to incarnate the Other as flesh so as to incarnate himself as flesh, and to incarnate himself as flesh so as to incarnate the Other as flesh. He makes the Other enjoy his flesh through her flesh so as to compel her to be her flesh and so on. This is what Sartre calls 'double reciprocal incarnation'. Ultimately, sexual desire is the desire for double reciprocal incarnation. To achieve double reciprocal incarnation would be to possess the Other's transcendent **freedom** as an incarnated consciousness by possessing the flesh that the Other's transcendent freedom has determined itself to be. Like romantic **love**, with which it is closely associated, sexual desire aims at the unachievable possession of the Other's transcendence as a transcendence rather than as a **transcendence-transcended**.

According to Sartre, the ultimate goal of sexual desire, double reciprocal incarnation, is impossible to achieve. A person cannot at the same time incarnate the Other's body and be incarnated by the Other's body. If the Other's body incarnates his body he will become lost in the enjoyment of his own incarnation. His own incarnation will become the object of his consciousness and he will forget or neglect the incarnation of the Other. Sexual desire is the desire for a mutual caress, but caressing, for all its striving after the mutual caress, remains touching and being touched. As the saying goes, 'There is always one who kisses and one who is kissed.' Sartre argues that it is, not least, pleasure that brings about the failure of the ideal of sexual desire. The more a person feels sexual pleasure in the incarnation of his own body by the Other, the less he will focus on his desire for the Other. In focusing on his own sexual pleasure he will lose sight of the Other as Other and no longer strive to possess her as an incarnated consciousness.

The failure of sexual desire to achieve its ultimate goal of reciprocal incarnation almost inevitably leads to the emergence of some level of sadomasochism. Sartre describes **sadism** and **masochism** as reefs upon which sexual desire may founder. Indeed, sexual desire founders so often and readily upon these reefs that 'normal' sexuality is, he argues, 'sadistic-masochistic'. With regard to sadism, as soon as a person neglects his own incarnation and focuses on the incarnation of the Other, as soon as he surpasses the **facticity** of his own body towards the possibility of acting on the Other, of *taking* the Other, he has already oriented himself in the direction of sadism. With regard to masochism, as soon as a person neglects the incarnation of the Other and focuses on his own incarnation, as soon as he wants to be constituted as a facticity for the transcendence of the Other, to be acted on by the Other and *taken* by the Other, he has already oriented himself in the direction of masochism.

sincerity   Ordinarily, sincerity is equated with honesty. As such, it is held to be a form of **good faith** and the antithesis of **bad faith**. **Sartre** rejects this view, advancing the initially surprising theory that sincerity is a form of bad faith. A person is never what he is but always what he is not and not what he is. He perpetually flees identity with himself in the **past** towards identity with himself in an unobtainable **future**. A sincere person who claims that he is a fixed entity or a given quantity, a person who says 'I am what I am', denies his **transcendence** and seeks to convince himself and others that he is a **facticity**. In denying the fundamental truth of his condition – that he is not a facticity but only ever the transcendence of his facticity – he is in bad faith. In fooling himself that he is a fixed entity a person avoids the **anxiety** of recognizing that he is a free being condemned to having to perpetually choose what he is without ever being able to become it. What has been described so far is a relatively simple form of sincerity that has a relatively simple aim. Sartre, however, also describes a more sophisticated form of sincerity that has a somewhat more complex aim.

This more sophisticated form of sincerity still involves a person declaring 'I am what I am', but here his aim is not to be what he is, but rather to distance himself completely from what he is through the very act by which he declares what he is. In declaring himself to be a thing he aims to become that which declares he is a thing rather than the thing he declares himself to be. He posits himself as a thing in order to immediately escape being that thing; in order to become that which merely contemplates the thing he has ceased to be. Unlike a person who adopts the simpler form of sincerity, he does not aim to be his facticity by denying his transcendence, rather he aims to be a pure transcendence divorced from his facticity. He is in bad faith because bad faith always involves a person attempting to invert or separate his facticity and his transcendence. According to Sartre, a person who makes a confession is in bad faith because by confessing he aims to divorce himself from his facticity and establish himself as a pure transcendence. The person who confesses that he is evil, for example, renders his evil into an object for his contemplation that exists only in so far as he contemplates it and ceases to exist when he ceases to contemplate it. Believing himself to be a pure transcendence he believes he is free to move on from his evil and to abandon it to the past as a disarmed evil that is neither his possession nor his **responsibility**.

situatedness   A term referring to the essential **being-in-situation** of **being-for-itself**. Being-for-itself is a being-in-situation. That is, being-for-itself must be situated in order to be as it exists only as the **negation** of the situation. For being-for-itself, to be and to be situated are one and the same, a point that can be emphasized by comparing Sartre's terminology with one of his biggest influences, **Heidegger**. What **Sartre** describes as 'being-for-itself', Heidegger describes as '**Dasein**'. 'Dasein' is German for 'being-there'. As its name implies, the very being of Dasein is to *be-there*; its being is to be situated.

The situation of the **for-itself** is the **facticity** of the for-itself that the for-itself perpetually transcends towards the **future**. The immediate and inescapable situation or facticity of the for-itself is the **body**. The for-itself perpetually transcends the body towards future situations while also perpetually re-apprehending the body as the very possibility, the very ground, of its **transcendence** (see **embodiment**).

There are no situations apart from the for-itself. Every situation, therefore, is a situation for the for-itself. The situation of the for-itself is *its* situation, a situation existing for the for-itself from its point of view. Existing as the negation of its situation the for-itself is not part of its situation. It negates and transcends its situation in order to realize it as its situation. Every situation is understood not in terms of what it is but in terms of what it lacks, and what every situation lacks is precisely the for-itself for which it is a situation. The for-itself is the basis of the particular lacks, negations or **negativities** that determine the situation as a situation, that render it a situation with possibilities to be realized in future rather than a fullness of being without possibilities (see **lack**).

The for-itself cannot not choose. Its choices must always be made in response to its situation, another way of saying that its free transcendence must be the transcendence of its facticity. The situation of the for-itself is the facticity of the for-itself, the unavoidable exercise of **choice** by the for-itself in response to its situation is the transcendence of the for-itself.

Bad faith involves various strategies whereby the for-itself seeks to deny its situatedness and evade **responsibility** for it, whereas **authenticity** involves the for-itself affirming its situatedness and taking full responsibility for it without **regret** through the exercise of **positive choice**.

Situations, Volumes 1–10   (Vol. 1: 1947, Vol. 2: 1948, Vol. 3: 1949, Vols 4, 5 & 6: 1964, Vol. 7: 1965, Vols 8 & 9, *Between Existentialism and Marxism*: 1974, Vol. 10, *Life / Situations*: 1976.) Collections of essays, articles, obituaries and other miscellaneous pieces by **Sartre** on a wide variety of subjects including philosophy, politics, literature, film and travel, many of which first appeared in the journal *Les Temps modernes*.

Sketch for a Theory of the Emotions (1939)   Alternative title, *The Emotions: Outline of a Theory*. A short and relatively early philosophical work by **Sartre**, the only surviving part of a much larger, abandoned work called *The Psyche*. Though short, the work is important, not only because it offers an excellent insight into Sartre's views on the nature of emotions, but also because, like **The Imaginary** (1940), it develops certain concepts and categories that come to play a central role in Sartre's major philosophical work, **Being and Nothingness** (1943). (*Sketch for a Theory of the Emotions* was drafted in 1937, the year after *The Imaginary*, but published the year before.)

    Sketch for a Theory of the Emotions takes the same approach to emotions as *The Imaginary* takes to mental images. That is, it conducts a **phenomenological** investigation of emotions through the application of the theory of **intentionality** inherited from **Husserl**. In his superb but often overlooked introduction, Sartre compares **phenomenology** with **psychology**, arguing that phenomenology is superior to psychology because it grasps essences whereas psychology only lists facts that appear as accidental. Psychologists can only say that there is emotion, that it involves certain behaviours in certain situations, they cannot explain why there is emotion, what it signifies or why it is an essential aspect of human **consciousness**; a necessary feature of human reality. Psychologists investigate people in situations, but phenomenology investigates what it is for people to be situated. Emotion is an inalienable feature of human **situatedness**, human reality, it belongs essentially to our way of being in the world and is not the accidental addition to human reality that psychology makes it appear. Sartre offers psychology the insights of phenomenology in the hope that psychology will derive a method from phenomenology that will enable it to do more than simply accumulate observational data that it hopes to interpret in future through the accumulation of yet more data. Pure psychology underpinned by phenomenological psychology will be able to comprehend the essential significance of psychological phenomena by identifying them as aspects of a coherent whole.

In moving towards an account of his own phenomenological theory of emotions, Sartre begins by critically examining the classic theories of emotion put forward by William James, Janet and Dembo respectively. James endorses the peripheric theory of emotions, arguing that emotion is consciousness of physiological manifestations. A person feels sad, for example, because they weep, rather than vice versa. If emotion was simply awareness of physiological manifestations, however, then different emotions could not be associated with the same physiological manifestations in the way that they are. Weeping accompanies relief as well as sadness and, as Sartre notes, the fact that the physiological manifestations of joy and anger differ only in intensity does not mean that anger is a greater intensity of joy. The central weakness of the peripheric theory for Sartre is that it overlooks the fact that an emotion is first and foremost consciousness of feeling that emotion and not simply consciousness of weeping or laughing; it has meaning, it is a certain way or relating to the world.

Janet's theory is an improvement on James' as it recognizes that emotion is not simply an awareness of physiological disturbance but a behaviour. Janet defines emotion as 'a behaviour of defeat' that serves to reduce tension. For example, a girl breaks down in tears rather than discuss her case with her doctor. Sartre agrees with Janet that emotion is a behaviour of defeat, but criticizes him for not appreciating that defeated behaviour can only be such if consciousness has conferred that meaning upon it through its awareness of the possibility of an alternative, superior, undefeated behaviour. For Janet, the girl simply begins to cry as an automatic reaction to the situation in which she finds herself. For Sartre, the girl's action is and must be deliberate. She cries in order to avoid talking to the doctor, although in **bad faith** she refuses to recognize that this is her motive or indeed that she has any motive.

Dembo, whose theory is closest to Sartre's own, holds that emotion is an inferior response to a situation that may occur when a superior response has failed. For example, a person becomes angry and kicks the machine he has failed to fix. Sartre agrees with Dembo that emotion is an inferior response to a situation that occurs when a superior response has failed, but argues that Dembo fails to acknowledge the significance of the role played by consciousness in the change of response. One form of behaviour cannot replace another unless consciousness presents the new behaviour to itself as a possible, if inferior, alternative to the present behaviour.

To summarize: All three classic theories, for Sartre, are inadequate because they fail to recognize or sufficiently acknowledge the essential role that consciousness and intention play in the emotions.

Sartre moves on to critically examine the psychoanalytic theory of emotion put forward by **Freud** and his followers. As in *Being and Nothingness*, Sartre argues that the psychoanalytic distinction between consciousness and the unconscious, the domain of primitive drives and desires, is nonsensical in various ways. In *Being and Nothingness* he argues that the ego would actually have to be conscious of the memories and desires it was repressing in order to act as a discerning censor. In *Sketch for a Theory of the Emotions* he questions the very possibility of a relationship between consciousness and an unconscious. For psychoanalysis, emotion is a phenomenon of consciousness, but *essentially* it is 'the symbolic realization of a desire repressed by the censor'. The desire, being repressed, plays no part in its symbolic realization as an emotion. The emotion, then, despite the claims of psychoanalysis, is only what it appears to consciousness to be, anger, fear and so on. Psychoanalysis considers emotion to be a signifier of whatever lurks in the unconscious, but as Sartre points out, the signifier is 'entirely cut off' from what is signified. Psychoanalysis, argues Sartre, treats consciousness as a passive phenomenon, receiving and being the signification of meanings from outside without even knowing what they mean. But consciousness is not a passive phenomenon, it is entirely active, it makes itself, it is nothing but consciousness of being conscious of the world, and as such, whatever meanings consciousness signifies are its own meanings, meanings *for* consciousness, not meanings that are received from 'behind' or 'beneath' consciousness that have no meaning for consciousness. The great error of psychoanalysis, according to Sartre, is that it interrogates consciousness from outside, treating it as a passive collection of signs, indicators and traces that have their meaning and significance elsewhere. In fundamentally misrepresenting the nature of consciousness psychoanalysis overlooks the fact that the significance of emotion lies within consciousness, that consciousness is itself 'the *signification* and what is *signified*'. Phenomenology, unlike psychoanalysis, undertakes to interrogate consciousness itself – as a relation to the world and to itself – for the meaning of emotion.

In outlining his own view of emotion, Sartre argues that although people can always consciously reflect on their emotions, emotion is not originally or primarily a phenomenon of reflection, a state of mind. Emotional consciousness, argues Sartre, is first and foremost consciousness *of* the world. Emotions are intentional, they are a way of 'apprehending the world'. For every emotion there is the object of that emotion, every emotion is directedness towards its object and exists as a relationship with its object. 'The emotional subject and the object of the emotion are united in an indissoluble synthesis.' To be frightened is to be afraid *of* something, to be angry is to be angry *with* something, to be joyful is to be joyful *about* something and so on.

Sartre considers the kind of relationship to the world that emotion is and what is common to all the diverse occasions when emotion occurs. The world presents itself as a **system of instrumentality** that people utilize to achieve their goals. There is always a degree of difficulty involved in utilizing any system, always the possibility of obstacles and pitfalls arising that hinder progress. Difficulty manifests itself as a quality of the world itself. Sartre describes objects as *exigent*, they are exacting and demanding, their potentialities can only be realized by overcoming certain difficulties. (Sartre's notion of *difficulty* here is akin to his notion of **facticity**.) Emotion occurs when the world becomes too difficult for a person to cope with. Finding all ways of acting in the instrumental world barred by difficulty, a person spontaneously and non-reflectively wills the transformation of the world from a world governed by causal processes to a world governed by magic where causal processes no longer apply. Emotion is a spontaneous attitude to a situation that aims to magically transform that situation in such a way that it suddenly no longer presents an insurmountable difficulty or threat to the consciousness of the person concerned. A person faced with great danger, for example, may faint as a means of removing that danger from his conscious grasp, even though fainting does not normally serve to remove a danger in any real, practical sense. Similarly, a person may angrily curse, hit or throw a tool that is proving difficult or impossible to utilize, as though the world had magically become a place where the difficulty presented by a tool could be removed by these 'means'.

In Sartre's view, all emotions are functional. Anger is evidently functional but, prima facie, joy does not seem to fit this description. Unlike an angry or frightened person, surely a joyful person does not need to magically transform his situation; surely he wants his situation as it is with its object or source of joy secured? Sartre distinguishes emotional joy from the joyful feeling that results from adapting to the world and achieving temporary equilibrium with it. Emotional joy, he argues, occurs precisely because the object or source of joy is not yet secured and if it is obtained will only be obtained by degrees and never as an 'instantaneous totality'. Sartre considers a man who is told that he has won a large sum of money. He sings and dances with joy in anticipation of something the pleasure of which will only come to him over time through countless details. His joyful anticipation expresses impatience. A joyful person is very much like an impatient person who cannot keep still or concentrate. Sartre also considers a man who dances with joy because a woman has said she loves him. In dancing, the man turns his mind away from the woman herself and from the difficulties of sustaining and possessing her **love**. He takes a rest from difficulty and uncertainty and in dancing mimes his magical possession of her as an instantaneous totality. According to Sartre, joy, no less than sadness, anger, fear or any other emotion, is a magical behaviour that functions to miraculously transform a situation when that situation becomes too difficult for a person to deal with as a system of instrumentality.

slave ethic   Nietzsche's view of the slave ethic compares with Sartre's view of **bad faith**. **Nietzsche** argues that a person who has submitted to his slavery considers the world as meaningful only from the point of view of his master. That is, only from the point of view of other people for whom he is a **transcendence-transcended**. The slave views himself as an object in his master's world. Not unlike Sartre's **flirt**, an example of a person in bad faith, the slave assumes a position of passivity. If he defies his master he does so only subjectively with resentful thoughts and feelings rather than in any positive, active way. The slave who adopts the slave ethic comes to view his repressed, brooding, cowardly attitude as admirable and ethical. According to Nietzsche, the slave ethic is at the heart of Christian morality. See also **ascetic ideal**, **negative choice**, **negative freedom** and **negative will to power**.

Socialism and Freedom   A Resistance group opposed to the German occupation of France founded by **Sartre** in 1941. Socialism and

Freedom sought a third political way between the resistance of the capitalist Gaullists on the right and the Communists on the left. Squeezed between these two much larger organizations Sartre's group eventually folded.

solipsism   Latin: *sōlus* alone + *ipse* self. The view that one's own mind is all that exists. Most commonly solipsism is the view that there is no external world and no **other minds**, although sometimes in the area of philosophy that deals with the problem of the existence of other minds it is used to refer specifically to the view that there are no other minds. Arguably, Sartre's view that **consciousness** is intentional (see **intentionality**) and nothing but a relation to the world avoids doubts about the existence of the external world – the threat of solipsism – inherent in Cartesian **dualism** and indirect realism. **Sartre** refers to the threat of solipsism as 'the reef of solipsism', meaning to suggest that solipsism is a dangerous reef upon which many a philosophy of mind, particularly that of **Descartes**, has foundered.

surpassing   Being-for-itself is the **negation** of **being-in-itself**. In order to exist as the negation of being-in-itself being-for-itself must perpetually escape, flee, transcend and surpass being-in-itself. Being-for-itself exists as a surpassing of being; its very being is to be a surpassing. To emphasize this point **Sartre** often describes the **for-itself** as a surpassing negation. Through **choice** and **action** the for-itself perpetually surpasses its **body** as an object towards the realization of its projects and the fulfilment of its possibilities, although as it does so it also perpetually re-apprehends its body as the very possibility, the very ground, of its surpassing (see **embodiment**). The for-itself surpasses being-in-itself towards the possibilities that are its own **future**. To emphasize the point that the for-itself refuses being in the **present** and perpetually surpasses the present towards the future, Sartre often describes the for-itself as a temporal surpassing, a **temporal flight** or a **temporal transcendence**. These terms have more or less the same meaning and can often be used interchangeably. Certainly, to refer to the surpassing of the for-itself or to the for-itself as a surpassing, is the same as referring to the **transcendence** of the for-itself or to the for-itself as a transcendence and so on. See also **temporality**.

surpassing negation   See **surpassing**.

suspension of disbelief   See **bad faith, the faith of bad faith** and **the waiter**.

sustained authenticity   See **authenticity, sustained**.

system of instrumentality   Any system of instruments employed by a person to achieve a particular end. Instruments form a passive array of unconnected objects until they are disclosed and united into a coherent and interactive instrumental system or instrumental complex by a person acting towards a goal that requires them as a means. Any system of instrumentality refers back to the person in **action** for whom it is a system of instrumentality. Ultimately, the system is orientated towards the **body** of the person in action, most often towards the hands of the person in action. The hands in action are the system's point of reference, they orientate the system and give it meaning. At the same time the system gives meaning to the activity of the hands because without the system the hands could not act to achieve the ends that the system makes possible. It is important to note, as **Sartre** does, that from his own point of view a person's hands are not part of a system of instrumentality. A person does not act upon his hands in order to act upon the world; the action of his hands is the person himself acting in the world. He is his hands. Of course, one hand can act upon the other hand as it can act upon any object in the world, but the hand that acts upon the other hand remains the person himself acting in the world. See also *Critique of Dialectical Reason*, **present-at-hand** and **ready-to-hand**.

temporal flight   The perpetual flight of **being-for-itself** away from its **past** towards its **future**. Being-for-itself is this flight, an indeterminate being that is perpetually no longer what it was and not yet what it will be. See also **temporal surpassing, temporal transcendence** and **temporality**.

temporal surpassing   The perpetual temporal motion of **being-for-itself** beyond itself away from its **past** towards its **future**. Being-for-itself is this surpassing, an indeterminate being that is perpetually beyond what it was but not yet what it will be. See also **surpassing, temporal flight, temporal transcendence** and **temporality**.

temporal transcendence   The **transcendence** of **being-for-itself** away from its **past** towards its **future**. See also **surpassing, temporal flight, temporal surpassing** and **temporality**.

temporality   Time or temporality appears in the world through the **negation** of **being-in-itself** that is **being-for-itself**. As the negation of being-in-itself, being-for-itself is a perpetual flight from being. But also, as that which would *be* its own negation, the **for-itself** is a flight towards being. In short, the for-itself flees being towards being. This paradox can be explained in specifically temporal terms: The for-itself flees being in the **present** towards being in the **future**. If the for-itself did not flee being in the present – did not perpetually make the present **past** – it would coincide with itself in the present. If it coincided with itself in the present it would become a being in itself, and as such would be annihilated as the non-being that it has to be. Hence, the for-itself projects itself towards being in the future. The for-itself, however, can no more coincide with itself in the future than it can coincide with itself in the present. The for-itself cannot coincide with what is not yet, and when the future becomes the present, the for-itself, as a perpetual flight from being in the present, will already have flown this new present, will already have made of this new present a **past-future**. There is in fact no such thing as the present. Indeed, there are no such things as the past and the future either. The past is no longer and the future is not yet. The correct way to view time is not in terms of three distinct and substantial elements, but in terms of three unified dimensions, each of which, being nothing in itself, is outside of itself in the other two and has meaning only in terms of the other two. **Sartre** refers to this temporal structure as *ekstatic* and to each of the three dimensions of time as an ***ekstasis***. The future is referred to as a **future-past**, while the past is referred to as a past-future. As for the present, it is the immediate **presence** of the for-itself to being, rather than a present moment that can be considered as being *now*.

The indeterminate and paradoxical nature of being-for-itself is best understood in terms of temporality. To say, as Sartre does, that the for-itself is not what it is, is to say that the for-itself is constituted as a **temporal flight** from a past that it is. To say, as Sartre does also, that the for-itself is what it is not, is to say that the for-itself is constituted as a temporal flight towards a future that it is not.

Temporality is a fundamental **ontological** feature of being-for-itself. Without being-for-itself there would be no temporality because temporality is not a feature of being-in-itself, which has no features other than simply being what it is. Being-in-itself is not temporalized. It is only for the for-itself that flees being towards the future that being is temporalized. It is only for the for-itself that being, apparent as **differentiated being**, is apprehended as not yet being what it will be and as no longer being what it was. Past and future belong to the for-itself in its relation to the world. They are not features of the world as it is in itself apart from the presence of the for-itself. The world apart from the presence of the for-itself presumably contains processes, but these processes only have a past and a future for a for-itself that understands that something is not yet what it will be, but will be in future. To claim that there is no time apart from the for-itself is not necessarily to claim that nothing happens apart from the for-itself. Rather, it is to claim that apart from the for-itself the world is without the phenomena of no-longer and not-yet. See also **Dasein**, **Heidegger** and **transcendence**.

Les Temps modernes *(Modern Times)*   A broadly left-wing literary and political journal founded in October 1945 by **Sartre**, **de Beauvoir**, **Merleau-Ponty**, Raymond Aron and others and published by **Gallimard**. With Sartre as its first senior editor the journal adopted engagement and resistance as its guiding principles and immediately assumed a central place in French intellectual life. For over sixty years the journal has provided a respected forum for debate between leading intellectuals about many national and international political issues and crises. With its hundreds of ordinary editions, and special editions devoted to topical questions, *Les Temps modernes* provides a unique record of the cultural and political climate of France since World War II. The journal has also been a forum for several very public disagreements, most famously the row between Sartre and **Camus** that ended their friendship. See also ***Situations***.

thetic consciousness   See **consciousness, thetic**.

thetic self-consciousness   see **self-consciousness, thetic**.

thing-in-itself   See **noumenon**.

time   See **temporality**.

transcendence   The condition of being outside or beyond. Contrasts with **immanence**, the condition of existing, operating or remaining within. For **Sartre**, transcendence is the essential characteristic or activity of **being-for-itself**. The **for-itself** is a transcendence, it is that which transcends. The for-itself is not in the world as objects are but as a transcendence or **transcendent subject**. It is that which transcends the world, including the **body**, in order to be aware of the world and to act upon it. The for-itself is the **negation** of **being-in-itself**. In negating being the for-itself transcends or surpasses being. As that which is a **surpassing** of being it is perpetually beyond being and at a distance from being, yet as nothing but the negation of being it continues to depend entirely on being for its **borrowed being**. The for-itself continually strives to escape being without ever being able to finally and fully escape it. It is an escaping that cannot escape. This can be seen most clearly in the relationship between the for-itself and the body. The for-itself perpetually transcends the body but is perpetually reapprehended by the body as the very possibility, the very ground of its transcendence. The body represents the immediate and inescapable situation or **facticity** of the for-itself that the for-itself continually transcends towards future situations. The for-itself is that which continually transcends the body without ever being able to render the body finally and completely transcended (see **disembodied consciousness**, **embodiment** and **situatedness**).

The for-itself is a **temporal transcendence**. The for-itself perpetually transcends the **past** towards the **future**. Indeed, it is this transcendence that gives rise to past and future and to **temporality** as such. The transcendent **temporal flight** of the for-itself away from the past towards the future realizes the past as that which has been transcended. The past is a **past-future** and the future that the transcendence of the for-itself aims at is a **future-past** that will immediately become a past-future as and when the for-itself transcends it.

It is by virtue of its transcendence that the for-itself is free (see **existential freedom**). The for-itself perpetually transcends the facticity of the **present** towards a future that is open and indeterminate. The for-itself is a **futurizing intention** that transcends the present by choosing – by having to choose – its responses to its facticity. The for-itself is the transcendence of facticity and requires there to be facticity in order to be the transcendence of it. **Bad faith** involves a person denying that he is the transcendence of his facticity. In bad faith he seeks either to be a pure transcendence or he seeks to be a pure facticity without transcendence. Both projects aim at avoiding the **anxiety** and **responsibility** of being that which must continually choose itself as a free, transcendent flight towards the future.

Central to Sartre's theory of **being-for-others** is the notion that the transcendence (the transcendent freedom) of the for-itself can be transcended by the transcendence of the **Other**. When this occurs the for-itself becomes a **transcendence-transcended**.

The Transcendence of the Ego, A Sketch for a Phenomenological Description (1937)   One of Sartre's earliest published works, it first appeared as an article in *Recherches philosophiques* VI, 1936–37. Extremely significant in the development of Sartre's own philosophy, *The Transcendence of the Ego* was inspired by Sartre's detailed study of the German **phenomenologist**, **Husserl**, during a nine-month sabbatical in Berlin beginning in the Autumn of 1933. For the rest of his career **Sartre** adhered to Husserl's **phenomenological** programme of exploring and describing the various types of **phenomena** – the various types of **intentional object**

– intended by **consciousness**. Nonetheless, *The Transcendence of the Ego* is a sustained and closely argued critique of a central feature of Husserl's philosophy of mind: his theory of transcendental subjectivism; his thesis that the *I* or ego is transcendental.

Husserl holds that there is a transcendental *I think* that is, in Sartre's words, 'the inseparable companion of each of our "consciousnesses"'. This transcendental ego unifies each moment of consciousness, each idea and representation, into a single consciousness and in so doing makes consciousness possible. Sartre argues that Husserl's notion of the transcendental ego is to some extent inspired by a misunderstanding of **Kant**. As Sartre notes, Kant certainly argues that, 'the I think *must be able* to accompany all our representations'. This, however, does not mean, as Husserl takes it to mean, that an *I think* is in fact the inseparable companion of all states of consciousness that serves to synthesize all experience. In recognizing that I *must be able* to regard my experience as mine, Kant is not asserting that an *I think* must be present on all occasions in order for consciousness to be possible. Kant, according to Sartre, 'says nothing concerning the actual existence of the *I think*', and even recognizes that 'there are moments of consciousness without the *I*'. Transcendental consciousness, for Kant, is only the set of logical conditions required for the existence of an empirical consciousness and not the absolute, irreducible fact that Husserl takes it to be with his notion of the transcendental ego.*

Sartre notes that Husserl's theory of the transcendental ego contradicts his theory of **intentionality**. If, as the theory of intentionality asserts, **consciousness is consciousness of** ___, if consciousness is nothing beyond a directedness towards the world, nothing but a 'revealing intuition', there cannot be an aspect of consciousness, in the form of a transcendental ego, that is not a directedness towards the world. Husserl argues along the lines

---

* Husserl recognizes that for there to be consciousness there must be consciousness of being conscious. In his view it is the transcendental ego that serves this purpose. He posits the transcendental ego as that which is conscious of all particular moments or acts of consciousness, as that which unifies them and renders them the conscious moments of a single consciousness. Sartre agrees with Husserl that for there to be consciousness there must be consciousness of being conscious, but for him this is not achieved by a transcendental ego but by what he refers to as, **non-positional**, **non-thetic** or **pre-reflective** consciousness (of) consciousness. Sartre's notion of non-positional consciousness, first conceived of in *The Transcendence of the Ego*, becomes a central element of the theory of consciousness later propounded in his major work, *Being and Nothingness*.

that the transcendental ego is an intentional directedness towards perceptions, thoughts, ideas and images. To argue in this way, however, is to regard consciousness as having *contents*, as being a realm of *representations* not unlike a picture gallery, precisely the view that the theory of intentionality was formulated to overcome (see **illusion of immanence**).

Husserl's view of consciousness as a realm of representations is further reinforced by the *epochē* or suspension, his procedure of 'bracketing off' existence and setting aside all questions concerning reality in order to focus on questions concerning the defining characteristics of phenomena as they appear to consciousness. In Sartre's view, Husserl's introduction of the *epochē* causes his phenomenological programme to fail in its primary objective of getting back to the **appearances** themselves. He ceases to focus on appearances themselves and instead focuses on contents of consciousness. Intentional objects become a product of the activity of the ego upon contents of consciousness, representations within consciousness, rather than upon appearances themselves. For Sartre, the Husserlian procedure of the *epochē* not only gives rise to the false notion of contents of consciousness, it renders **phenomenology** impossible. Consciousness is so inextricably involved in the world that there can be no form of phenomenological enquiry whatsoever that deals with a consciousness cut off from the world. As there can be no transcendental ego and consciousness is nothing but an intentional directedness towards the world, to 'bracket off' the world is to be left with no consciousness at all. In the language of **being** and **negation** that Sartre later adopted in his major work, *Being and Nothingness* (1943), being cannot be 'bracketed off' if consciousness is nothing beyond the negation of being, a negation that absolutely requires being in order to be the negation of it.

What then is the *I* or ego for Sartre if it is not a transcendental being in the Husserlian sense? Sartre argues that the ego is not in consciousness at all. Consciousness, he insists, has absolutely no contents. Rather, the ego, 'is outside, *in the world*. It is a being in the world, like the ego of another.' The ego is an intentional object for consciousness that appears to consciousness when consciousness reflects upon itself. The ego is an appearance for **reflective consciousness** realized entirely through reflection. It is the essential **temporality** of consciousness or **being-for-itself** that makes this self-reflection possible. The consciousness reflected on is always **past** for reflective consciousness because reflective consciousness flees the consciousness reflected on towards the **future** in order to attempt to fix it in the **present**. The consciousness reflected on appears to reflective consciousness as a present intentional object – a **psychic object** – enduring through time (some degree of temporal duration is a fundamental characteristic of all intentional objects, including psychic objects). Through reflection, particular, fleeting phases of consciousness as it is in its immediate relation to the world – reactions, aversions, desires, etc. – appear as aspects of present psychic objects – hate, fear, hope, love, etc. In turn, these psychic objects appear as aspects of a further psychic object, a present and enduring *I* or ego posited by reflection as the underlying unity of these psychic objects.

The Transcendence of the Ego is a crucial step in Sartre's philosophical development. Through his critique of Husserlian phenomenology Sartre lays the foundations for a theory of consciousness that becomes the cornerstone of his existential phenomenology, his **existentialism**.

transcendence-in-itself   **Being-for-itself** is a **transcendence**. It is not a transcendence-in-itself, a **being-for-itself-in-itself**, but always the transcendence of its **facticity**. The **for-itself** would like to be a transcendence-in-itself, a being that is what it is rather than an indeterminate being that has to constantly strive to be what it is through its choices without ever finally being able to become what it is. Sartre's **flirt**, one of his examples of a character in **bad faith**, relinquishes **responsibility** for herself, for her actions and her situation, by considering herself to be a transcendence-in-itself, by treating her transcendence as though it were a facticity.

transcendences-transcending   See **Mitsein**.

transcendence-transcended   For himself, a person is not an object alongside other objects. He is not in being. Rather, he is a **transcendence**; he is that which freely transcends being towards the **future**. Following **Heidegger**, **Sartre** refers to this transcendent aspect of a person's being as his **being-in-the-world**. A person, however, has another mode of being that Sartre, again following Heidegger, refers to as **being-in-the-midst-of-the-world**. Being-in-the-midst-of-the-world refers to a person's presence in the world as an object among other objects seen from the point of view of another person (the **Other**). Here, a person's free transcendence is transcended by the transcendence of the Other. He ceases to be a **transcendent subject** and becomes, at least temporarily, what Sartre refers to as a transcendence-transcended. He is still his possibilities, but these possibilities are now a given fact for the Other. They belong also to the Other and are subject to the Other's judgement. This mode of being corresponds to a person's **being-for-others** and is realized when he experiences himself as seen by the Other or when he regards himself from the point of view of the Other. To experience himself as an object for the Other is to experience the Other as a subject. It is this direct and unmediated experience of himself as an object for the Other's subjectivity that reveals the Other to him as Other. He experiences the Other through the immediate, internal negation of his own transcendent subjectivity by the transcendent subjectivity of the Other. For Sartre, to experience the Other is for a person to exist his own being as a transcendence-transcended.

In **Being and Nothingness** (1943) Sartre illustrates the phenomenon of transcendence-transcended with the example of a spy at a keyhole. So long as he is not caught in the act the spy is a transcendence in full possession of the meaning of his act. When he is caught, however, he becomes an object for the Other. His transcendence is transcended by the Other and he is no longer free to determine the meaning of his act. The meaning of his act belongs to the Other who sees him and is free to judge him as he wishes. His **freedom** is 'enslaved' by the freedom of the Other.

It is not the case that when a person's transcendence has been transcended by the transcendence of the Other and his freedom 'enslaved' that he remains a transcendence permanently transcended. The situation is inherently unstable and a person can become Other for the Other by recovering his transcendence, thereby reducing the Other to an object and so on. Sartre characterizes interpersonal relations as a ceaseless power struggle for transcendence and tends to argue that **conflict** is the essence of all human relationships. See also **In Camera**, **the look**, **masochism**, **Mitsein**, **sadism** and **will to power**.

transcendent subject   **Being-for-itself** can exist as a transcendent subject/subjectivity or as a transcended object. As a transcendent subject, what **Heidegger** calls a **being-in-the-world**, being-for-itself freely transcends **being-in-itself** towards its **future** possibilities. The **for-itself** can, however, be reduced to a transcended object, what Heidegger calls a

being-in-the-midst-of-the-world, by the transcendent subjectivity of the **Other**. As a transcended object, as a **transcendence-transcended**, the for-itself exists in the mode of **being-for-others**. It is an object for the Other and is subject to the Other's judgement. As a transcendent subject, as a transcendence-transcending, the for-itself exists for itself and is free to subject the world, including the Other, to its judgements. See also **transcendence**.

transcendent subjectivity   See **transcendent subject**.

transcendental idealism   See **Kant** and **realism**.

transcendental subjectivism   See **Husserl** and *The Transcendence of the Ego*.

translucency   An essential characteristic of **consciousness**. For **Sartre**, consciousness is translucent. To be conscious of a thought is to be conscious of it through and through because a thought exists only in so far as a person is conscious of it. Sartre contrasts the translucency of consciousness with the **opacity** of objects. Unlike the opaque objects of which it is conscious, consciousness is translucent in having no hidden aspects. The translucency of consciousness renders **self-deception**, in the sense of lying to oneself, impossible. In being translucent, in being consciousness through and through, consciousness is conscious of itself as conscious. That is, the translucency of consciousness allows for **non-thetic consciousness** (of) consciousness. If it were not conscious of itself as conscious, consciousness would not be conscious, it would not be. See also **self-consciousness**.

transphenomenal   **Sartre** describes as transphenomenal the infinite series of aspects or possible **appearances** of an object that are not presently appearing (to someone) but which by turns could appear. Sartre's major influence, **Husserl**, refers to these possible appearances as **horizons**. As possible rather than actual appearances the being of these transphenomenal aspects is transcendent. Their being transcends that which appears and is indicated by that which appears. For Sartre, the transphenomenal replaces the notional 'object-in-itself' that is supposed to underpin that which appears. A **mental image**, as opposed to an object of perception, is characterized by having no transphenomenal aspects. It has only the appearances that consciousness gives it while it does so. There is nothing hidden. See also **phenomenological**.

The Trojan Women (1965)   Sartre's adaptation of the tragic play by Euripides. The play is set outside the walls of the city of Troy. The Greeks have finally defeated the Trojans after a siege lasting ten years. Reduced to mere spoils of war, the Trojan women and children await their fate at the hands of the Greeks. Some are killed, such as the child Astyanax, heir to the Trojan throne. Most are to be taken back to Greece as slaves. The women, particularly Hecuba the Queen of Troy, bemoan their fate and that of their dead menfolk, cursing the Greeks and the gods. Hecuba's daughter Cassandra prophesies the death and destruction that will befall the Greeks on their journey home. She offers the Trojan women the consolation that ultimately the Trojan War will be as much a disaster for the Greeks as it has been for the Trojans. Andromeda, the mother of Astyanax and the wife of Hector, Hecuba's slaughtered son, curses Hecuba, blaming her for the war. She reasons that had Hecuba not given birth to Paris he could not have caused the war by taking Helen, the wife of the Greek king Menelaus, away to Troy. Menelaus reclaims Helen intending to take her back to Greece and execute her for adultery, but it is doubtful that he will be able to resist her charms. It appears that Helen, the ultimate cause of the war, will escape justice. The play ends with the god Poseidon cursing mortals for making war and bringing suffering on themselves. Men blame the gods for war but war is the **responsibility** of men. War kills all in the end and brings only hollow victories.

Sartre adapted *The Trojan Women* in order to comment on European colonialism in particular and to condemn war and imperialism generally. (Like most left-wing, French intellectuals Sartre had supported Algeria's bitter struggle for independence. He viewed the French occupation of Algeria that finally ended in 1962 as unjustifiable, comparing it to the German occupation of France during World War II.) The play seeks to emphasize the waste, futility, injustice and depravity of war and to call into question the distinction between victor and vanquished. In bringing death and destruction to both sides war is a means by which mankind defeats himself, a point that has particular resonance in the Nuclear Age.

During World War II Sartre wrote **The Flies** (1943), a play based on the ancient Greek legend of Orestes. As with *The Trojan Women*, he utilized an ancient tragedy to comment on a current political situation.

Troubled Sleep   See *Iron in the Soul*.

Truth and Existence (1948, published posthumously 1989)   A philosophical work by **Sartre** written as a response to *The Essence of Truth* (1943) by Martin **Heidegger**. *Truth and Existence* is not, as its title suggests, an epistemological treatise on truth in the traditional sense. There is, for example, no close analysis of evidence, proof or verification. Neither is it a work concerned primarily with morality as is suggested by Elkaïm-Sartre's preface, notes and arrangement. The central theme of *Truth and Existence* is, in fact, *ignorance* of the truth; ignorance of reality and the way things are. Sartre explores the strategies people employ to avoid the truth and remain ignorant of their real situation, he examines their motives for adopting these strategies and he seeks to draw conclusions about the relationship between ignorance and knowledge. Generally, he is concerned with the *wilful* ignorance that aims at the avoidance of **responsibility** and is at the heart of **bad faith**.

For Sartre, to be ignorant is to deliberately *ignore* some aspect of reality, it is to wilfully refuse to unveil being by adopting a project of evasion and **self-distraction**. In Sartre's major work, **Being and Nothingness** (1943), different forms of bad faith are explored through the examples of **the flirt**, **the waiter, the homosexual** and **the champion of sincerity**. Similarly, in *Truth and Existence* the form of bad faith Sartre is concerned with is explored through the example of a woman with tuberculosis.

A woman who has all the symptoms of tuberculosis nevertheless refuses to acknowledge that she has tuberculosis. She views each of her symptoms in isolation refusing to acknowledge their meaning. 'She refuses to choose herself as tubercular.' She distracts herself from the **choice** her **being-in-situation** demands by absorbing herself in other pursuits that do not allow her time to visit the doctor. Her symptoms place her at the threshold of an unveiling of being, of new knowledge, of knowing the truth, but she chooses ignorance because she does not want the responsibility of *dealing* with tuberculosis, the effort of seeking a cure, etc., that this new knowledge would entail. In various respects – her refusal to confront her situation, her self-distraction, her evasion of responsibility – Sartre's tubercular woman bears close comparison to his flirt in *Being and Nothingness*.

Making a crucial point as far as the directly epistemological interests of *Truth and Existence* are concerned, Sartre notes that ignorance is a mode of knowledge. A person affirms that being is knowable by his very choice to ignore it. Ignorance is motivated by a fearful or anxious awareness of the ever-present possibility of knowledge, of stark reality. Sartre's concern with truth in *Truth and Existence* is primarily a concern with being and reality. To know the truth is to know the way things are, to see life as it is, to unveil being, to affirm the **existential truths** of the **human condition**. To know the truth does not require great intelligence but rather honesty and courage in face of reality as opposed to a wilful ignorance of reality motivated by fear and **anxiety**. Interestingly, Sartre does not equate knowing the truth with knowing lots of facts. Indeed, for him, a preoccu- pation with abstract knowledge whereby a person loses himself in a reassuring, predictable, scientific view of the world is another form of wilful ignorance and hence bad faith. (This form of bad faith is exhibited by the Autodidact in **Nausea** [1938] and Jacques in **Roads to Freedom** [1945–49].) To dispense with wilful ignorance and irresponsibility and instead to courageously affirm the existential truths of the human condition is to reject bad faith in favour of **authenticity**.

Bad faith and responsibility are central themes in *Being and Nothingness*, written five years earlier. *Truth and Existence* expands on these themes in the style and language of *Being and Nothingness*, and in so far as it fills in some of the lacunas left by *Being and Nothingness* it is an important com- plementary text to that much larger work. Given its relevance to those areas of Sartre's thought that are arguably most philosophically interesting and certainly continue to command the most interest, it is unfortunate that *Truth and Existence* was not published when it was written. The consensus among Sartre scholars is that although the text required only moderate polishing to render it fit for publication it was not published because it harked back to themes Sartre decided to leave behind as he forged an **existentialism** that was more historically and politically aware.

— U —

the unconscious   See **Freud, Id, psychic duality** and *Sketch for a Theory of the Emotions*.

undifferentiated being   See **being, undifferentiated**.

unlimited freedom   See **freedom, unlimited**.

upsurge   Sartre's term for the emergence of **being-for-itself** from **being-in-itself**. As the **negation** of being-in-itself, being-for-itself is dependent upon being-in-itself for its **borrowed being**. **Sartre** rejects the hypothesis that being-in-itself undertook to give rise to being-for-itself in order to be known. He does so on the grounds that being-in-itself is what it is and as such is incapable of having projects whereby it aims at being other than it is. Only being-for-itself, which must perpetually be other than itself, is capable of having projects. Sartre insists, furthermore, that any attempt to account for the upsurge of being-for-itself produces only hypotheses than cannot be validated or invalidated, concluding that the upsurge of being-for-itself is an unfathomable mystery. His conclusion does not have to be readily accepted. As being-for-itself expresses the way of being of every conscious human organism, and does not express the way of being of organisms lower down the evolutionary scale, it might be possible to develop an evolutionary theory of the emergence of **consciousness** that explains the evolutionary development of consciousness and identifies the point at which fully developed consciousness was reached.

useless passion   See **'man is a useless passion'**.

— V —

vertigo ('vertigo of possibility')   See **anxiety**.

the waiter   In *Being and Nothingness* (1943) **Sartre** explores the various aspects of **bad faith** through a series of examples of people in bad faith. One of his examples of a person in bad faith – or in this case apparently in bad faith – is that of the waiter. Sartre conjures up a vivid picture of the waiter in action. The waiter comports himself in a deliberate and calculated manner, walking with a robotic stiffness and restraining his movements as though he were a machine; a thing rather than a person. He steps a little too quickly towards his customers, he is a little too eager and solicitous. Sartre concludes that the waiter is playing at being a waiter. The traditional view of Sartre's waiter is that he is in bad faith for striving, through his performance, to deny his **transcendence** and become his **facticity**. He overacts his role as a waiter in order to convince himself and others that he is a waiter-thing. As a waiter-thing he would escape his **freedom** and indeterminacy and the **anxiety** they cause him. From the point of view of others, a person is a **transcendence-transcended**. The waiter aims to become a transcendence-transcended *for himself*. He strives to be at one with his own representation of himself, but the very fact that he has to represent to himself what he is means that he cannot be it.

Certainly, striving to be a thing so as to escape the burden of freedom is an identifiable form of bad faith. However, against the traditional view of Sartre's waiter it can be argued that although the waiter does indeed strive to be a waiter-thing, he is not in bad faith because the purpose of his striving is not to escape his freedom. Arguably, his motives are entirely different from those of a person in bad faith. Arguably, he is no more in bad faith for trying to be a waiter than an actor is in bad faith for trying to be Hamlet. A closer reading of Sartre's description of the waiter reveals that, just like a stage actor, there is a definite sense in which the waiter is aware of what he is doing. His 'tongue is in his cheek', meaning, he acts with insincere or ironical intent. He is consciously – though not self-consciously – doing an impression of a waiter. It is a good impression that he has so refined that it is second nature to him. To claim that acting like a waiter is second nature to him is not to claim that he believes he has become a waiter. Rather, it is to claim that he has become his performance; become it in the sense that when he is absorbed in his performance he does not reflect upon the fact that he is performing. When Sartre says that the waiter 'plays with his condition in order to realize it', he does not mean that he plays with his condition in order to become it. Rather, he means that his condition is only ever realized as a playing with his condition. The waiter knows full well that he can never be identical with his condition because in order to 'be' his condition he must play at being it.

Far from being in bad faith, it can be argued that the waiter is achieving **authenticity**. If he were in bad faith he would be seeking to deny his **being-in-situation**. He would perhaps do his job reluctantly, all the while thinking, 'I am not really a waiter'. Instead, he strives to realize to the full his being-in-situation through his absorption in his performance. As a performer he does not believe he is a waiter, anymore than an actor believes he is Hamlet, but his performance so absorbs him that he does not disbelieve he is a waiter. The waiter's attitude is one of belief in his per-formance; belief in the form of a suspension of disbelief. The waiter's belief or faith in his performance exemplifies what Sartre calls the **faith of bad faith** or the primitive project of bad faith. So, after all, the waiter is in bad faith, but only in the sense of having faith in himself or self-belief. See also **Kean**.

The Wall (1939)   A short story by **Sartre** set during the Spanish Civil War. The lead story in a collection of short stories that also includes **Intimacy**, **The Room**, **Erostratus** and **The Childhood of a Leader**. A captured prisoner, Pablo Ibbieta, is condemned without trial along with many others to be shot at dawn. He spends the night locked in a cold, draughty cellar with two fellow prisoners, Tom and Juan, two guards and a Belgian doctor who is there to observe the prisoners' behaviour as they wait to die. Told from Ibbieta's point of view, the story explores the thoughts, feelings and actions of men who believe they have only a few hours to live.

Juan, who is only a young man, cries and looks for reassurances from the doctor – will it hurt, will it take long? As the night progresses he sinks into deep self-pity and in the morning has to be carried to his execution. Ibbieta unsympathetically identifies Juan's self-pity as a distraction from reality, as fever is a kind of distraction from illness. Tom has more composure but nonetheless urinates in his trousers involuntarily. He becomes philosophical and talks to Ibbieta of his inability to contemplate oblivion. He wonders if there is an afterlife. Again Ibbieta is unsympathetic. He sees Tom's talk as another kind of distraction from reality. Ibbieta feels no attachment to Juan or Tom and as the night passes he ceases to feel any attachment to anything, his **past** or those he has loved. Emotions become painful, disgusting, they are for those who believe they have a **future**. He does not want to think or feel anything. He wants to 'stay hard', to die a clean **death** without any display of fear or emotion. He struggles to maintain control of his **body** that sweats profusely despite the cold. He feels so damp that he wonders if, like Tom, he has wet himself. He is calm but it is a 'horrible calm' in which he feels utterly detached from his own body. He is concerned to give the doctor as little as possible to observe. He looks upon the doctor as a representative of the living. The doctor has faith in science, plans, hopes; the world still makes sense to him. The world has ceased to make sense to Ibbieta. Objects appear withdrawn and lacking in density, they have no other significance but to indicate his approaching death. A deep **nihilism** sets in. Ibbieta sees his whole life as meaningless, valueless and absurd now that he is about to die; so many unfinished, pointless projects premised on the illusion of immortality. 'I had spent my time counterfeiting eternity.' He identifies the uncondemned, with their aspirations and political opinions, as equally absurd. As they will eventually die too, their lives, like all lives, are no more meaningful than his.

The Wall explores such familiar **existentialist** themes as **despair**, death, **absurdity**, meaninglessness and nihilism. Above all, it explores the **existential truth** that life has no meaning other than the relative meaning given to it by our projects. Believing that his time has run out, Ibbieta can have no projects, other than dying with dignity, and as a result all objects and all human endeavour appear to him absurd.

The wall in the title of the story is the unyielding wall against which prisoners stand to be shot, the wall they push against with their backs and would like to get inside to escape the bullets. The wall is also a symbol of death in so far as it presents an absolute limit. For Sartre, death is an unyielding wall offering no compromise that every person must come up against sooner or later. However, as he argues elsewhere, disagreeing with **Heidegger**, people do not experience their finitude as such. Unless they have been condemned to death like Ibbieta, they do not experience themselves as progressing towards an encounter with death, as a **being-towards-death**. Indeed, Sartre argues that a person who in ordinary circumstances views his death as nearer than yesterday is mistaken. He will, of course, live for a certain number of days, but he is mistaken if he thinks that with each day that passes he is using up a sort of quota. He could die now or years from now. It is inevitable he will die eventually, but the time of his death is not predetermined. When he is dead others will total up his years, but this total was not fixed in advance while he was alive and his life was not a process of fulfilling it. Only a condemned person has a quota of days or hours, but even a condemned person can be reprieved or killed unexpectedly before reaching the firing squad. Sartre's key point is that the closeness of death changes with circumstances.

Ibbieta is close to death circumstantially and views his life accordingly, but at the end of the story his circumstances unexpectedly change. Having courageously and authentically accepted his mortality and mastered his fear of death (see **authenticity**), he stubbornly refuses to betray a comrade in exchange for his life. Amused by his captors and the absurdity of their worldly concerns he gives them what he believes is false information simply to perpetuate their farcical behaviour. The information turns out to be correct and his life is spared, or, existentially speaking, his death is indefinitely postponed.

War Diaries, Notebooks from a Phoney War 1939–40 (published posthumously at Sartre's request, 1983)   **Sartre** was mobilized along with thousands of other reservists on September 1, 1939, the day Germany invaded Poland. He was assigned to a meteorological unit in charge of weather balloons and sent to Alsace, Northern France, near the German border. For eight months French and German troops faced each other from their entrenched positions along a frontier of several hundred kilometres. The Germans were busy elsewhere and except for the occasional exchange of artillery all was quiet. This stand-off came to be known as the 'phoney war'. The phoney war provided the inspiration and above all the opportunity for the vast outpouring of words that is Sartre's *War Diaries*. Sartre had few duties: he sent up weather balloons, watched them with binoculars and passed on largely useless information to HQ about wind conditions. For the rest of the time he was free to read and, above all, write. In his letters to **de Beauvoir** Sartre often expresses surprise that he has more time to write as a soldier than he had as a civilian. He filled fourteen thick notebooks, nine of which have been lost or stolen. In her Editor's foreword to the five published notebooks his adopted daughter, Arlette **Elkaïm-Sartre**, writes,

'Perhaps they have been destroyed, or else the people in whose hands they lie are not prepared to let the fact be known.' Notoriously blasé about the security of his manuscripts – he felt he could always write more and better – Sartre would doubtless be amused that his notebooks are destroyed or slumber in private collections, even if scholars rightly consider this a huge intellectual loss. Fortunately, the five published notebooks constitute over 350 pages of text and give more than just a flavour of Sartre's immense war diary.

Sartre writes in his diary about his day-to-day existence, his military duties, his considerable reading list. He analyses his comrades who seem largely to irritate him, particularly Pierre, his over-controlling corporal. He analyses his friends and lovers back in Paris and the emotional complexities of his relations with them. Most significantly, he analyses himself and through this psychoanalytic introspection creates a new Sartre. The individualistic, pre-war Sartre, the author of **Nausea** (1938), is dispensed with, replaced by a more responsible, socially aware, politically committed Sartre. This Sartre is conscious of his place in history and the enormity of the events he is caught up in. He recognizes that it is his **responsibility** and moral duty as a writer to reflect on those events and evaluate them. The diary liberates Sartre, not only from a daily life that would otherwise have been unbearably tedious, but also from the stylistic concerns of more formal writing. The loose, free-flowing prose encouraged by a diary allows Sartre to spontaneously develop thoughts on a range of ideas that become central to his **existentialism**. He writes enthusiastically to de Beauvoir saying that keeping a notebook produces the many ideas he has at the moment. The *War Diaries* is the fertile ground for the growth of his thoughts on **freedom**, **bad faith** and **being-for-others**, ideas that will soon be at the heart of his most important philosophical work, **Being and Nothingness** (1943).

War Diaries also contains his most valuable insights into the phenomenon of **authenticity**. He repeatedly considers what authenticity is as he strives, in his life and in his writing (for him the two are inseparable), to overcome bad faith and achieve authenticity. He comments that, 'it's much easier to live decently and authentically in wartime than in peacetime'. To be authentic a soldier must accept his **being-in-situation** without regret and play to the full the role of a soldier, rather than whinge inauthentically, as his comrade Paul does, that he is not really a soldier but a civilian in military disguise.

While writing his diary Sartre was also drafting what later became his novel, *The Age of Reason* (1945). He considers his plans for the novel in his diary; discussing his characters as though they are among the Parisian friends they are certainly based on.

It is estimated that with his vast diary, his novel and his myriad letters to de Beauvoir, his mother and others, Sartre wrote a million words during the months of the phoney war. It is not surprising that he found it useful to wear a sign around his neck that on one side read, 'You may bug me' and on the other, 'You may not bug me'.

What is Literature? (1948)   A work of literary theory by **Sartre** that analyses from a philosophical and political perspective the nature and purpose of writing and reading and the relationship between writer and reader. The four chapters that comprise the work – 'What is writing?' 'Why write?' 'For Whom Does One Write?' and 'Situation of the writer in 1947' – first appeared as a series of essays in the journal, **Les Temps modernes**. *What is Literature?* is rightly identified by Sartre scholars as a political manifesto – literature, for Sartre, is a form of social / political action, 'action by disclosure' – but it should also be seen as Sartre's most significant contribution to the philosophy of aesthetics. Adopting a broadly **phenomenological** orientation, *What is Literature?* offers various insights into some of the fundamental questions of aesthetics: 'What is art?', 'How do visual art, music, poetry and prose compare and contrast?', 'What is the relationship between a work of art and its audience?' and so on.

The art form Sartre is primarily concerned with in *What is Literature?* is prose, which he argues is radically distinct from poetry. A poet, he argues, is interested in words themselves. A poem is an end in itself, language being the object of poetry rather than its instrument. Prose, on the other hand, is essentially 'utilitarian', it '*makes use* of words'. For the prose writer words are, or should be, transparent instruments unnoticed in themselves, the surpassed means by which the writer conveys his message and hits his target. The distinction Sartre draws between poetry and prose is dubious and has been widely criticized. Certainly, a good poet pays extremely close attention to the words he chooses and the subtle relationships he sets up between them, but this is not to say that he is only interested in the words themselves. However carefully a poet selects and arranges his words, these words would not produce an emotional and symbolic effect unless they were significative; unless they pointed beyond themselves to the world. Not least, a reader can only access a poem if he already has a reasonably refined understanding of ordinary significative language, an understanding of certain associations and references. The poet is dependent on this under-standing. His poetry may develop and refine this understanding in his reader, but his poetry does not and cannot create this understanding by itself. This argument against Sartre is, in fact, somewhat Sartrean. Elsewhere in *What is Literature?*, when writing about prose, Sartre argues that reading is the 'dialectical correlative' of writing and that 'there is no art except for and by others'. It is difficult to see why this principle should not apply to poetry as much as it does to prose.

Critics argue that Sartre's dubious distinction between poetry and prose hides a value judgement. He favours language that is utilitarian, language that most clearly and conveniently expresses what needs to be said in a certain time and place, at a certain point in history, rather than language, like poetry, that is preoccupied with aesthetic considerations. It is important, he argues, for a writer to write well and with style, but the beauty of his writing should be 'a gentle and imperceptible force', a hidden quality that serves the message of his writing rather than being its goal.

What, in Sartre's view, constitutes literature and sets it apart from other forms of writing, such as poetry or mere story-telling for the purpose of entertainment, is the *intention* of the writer, his *commitment* to tackling current issues and raising relevant questions. Key questions for the committed writer are: 'What do I want to write about?' and 'For whom am I writing?' Literature reveals and challenges aspects of the contempo-rary world. The committed writer does not, for example, write about political corruption in the Roman Empire unless it is to make a point about political corruption in his own time. Writing literature heightens the social, political, historical and philosophical awareness of the writer, while reading literature raises these same forms of awareness in the reader. For Sartre, the relationship between writer and reader is of central importance. He argues that without the generosity of the reader the writer as writer cannot exist. His books do not exist as works of art that convey certain ideas unless the reader freely consents to make his books, his ideas, real by reading them. Unread, a book is nothing but marks on paper, it contains no ideas in itself. 'Reading is creation.'

The effect of literature on the reader should be liberating. Literature is nothing if it is not a liberating force. 'However dark may be the colours in which one paints the world, one paints it only so that free men may feel their freedom as they face it.' For the reader to establish a genuine relationship with the writer's work is for the reader to redefine his relationship with his own situation. Perhaps he becomes aware of his alienation or his oppressed condition, perhaps he is inspired to question and actively reject the status quo that he has hitherto accepted without complaint. Increasingly Marxist in his outlook (see **Marxism**), the post-war Sartre of *What is Literature?* is clearly inspired by Marx's view that the purpose of philosophy is not simply to interpret the world but to change it. For Sartre, literature is certainly not an apology for the way things are or a means of flattering the powers that be. Such writing is opposed to **freedom** and deeply inauthentic. Literature is an irritant rather than a sedative, it is capable of bringing an individual, a group, a whole social class, out of a state of alienation into an awareness of their capacity for **positive freedom**. In liberating the reader through his successful efforts to create challenging and provocative works of art, the writer is in turn liberated by the reader and fully realizes his own freedom. The reader brings to final fruition the writer's efforts to respond positively and authentically to his **being-in-situation** (see **authenticity**). Sartre, in common with other politically engaged French intellectuals who aspired to shape post-war Western culture, sees writing literature very much as a form of secondary social and political action. The writer aspires to act upon the world by seeking to raise the awareness of his reader, by seeking to inspire him to question, to challenge and ultimately to change his situation, hence to change the world. The writer succeeds in acting, succeeds in escaping his own alienation, at least temporarily, when his reader acts. For Sartre, literature is a response to history and a desire to shape history that succeeds in doing so through its readership.

According to some critics, in arguing that literature can help people *achieve* their freedom, Sartre is suggesting that they do not in fact possess the fundamental, inalienable freedom that he claims they have in earlier works such as ***Being and Nothingness*** (1943). Arguably, the later Sartre of *What is Literature?* acknowledges that the inalienable psychological freedom he describes in *Being and Nothingness* counts for little if a person is oppressed by his economic, social and political circumstances and his freedom negated by those who exploit him. In *What is Literature?* Sartre begins to move towards a Marxist view, more fully formed in his ***Critique*** *of Dialectical Reason* (1960 and 1985), that people can only be made free in any real practical sense through social and political revolution.

The view of literature that Sartre puts forward in *What is Literature?* is generally very sympathetic to Marxist theory. Nonetheless, he maintains that a writer, in his quest to liberate himself and others, should not be a slave to political ideology to the extent that he becomes nothing more than a mouthpiece of party dogma. Sartre felt that some of his intellectual contemporaries had become dogmatic in their support of the Communist Party. Sartre often supported the Communist Party but was never a member. He maintained a love–hate relationship with it into his old age that was fully reciprocated.

will to power A central concept in the philosophy of **Nietzsche** that relates to and sheds light on central concepts in the philosophy of **Sartre**. Sartre and Nietzsche agree that every person is a conscious, free being with a will of his own. Nietzsche stresses that the ultimate goal and motivation of all acts of will is the increase of power. That is, an increase in the control, domination and influence exercised by an individual will over itself, the world and other wills. This is not so much a desire as the basis of all **desire**. Nietzsche's view compares with Sartre's view that **being-for-itself** is a **transcendence** that cannot not will transcendence over the world and the transcendence of others, thereby reducing them to a **transcendence-transcended**.

Will to power can be either positive or negative. Positive will to power is power as most commonly understood: power that is expansive or even explosive. For Nietzsche, however, the opposite is also will to power – negative will to power. A being that refuses to expand still has will to power. An army making a tactical retreat refuses expansion but it has not thereby lost its will to power. Similarly, a person who conserves his strength behind raised defences exercises will to power in inviting his enemy to expend his strength against those defences. According to Nietzsche, a person cannot not be a will to power, just as, according to Sartre, a person cannot not be free. Whereas Nietzsche has the concepts of positive and negative will to power, Sartre has the concepts of the **positive freedom** of the responsible, authentic person and the **negative freedom** of the in-authentic person who acts in **bad faith** choosing not to choose. See also **affirmation of freedom**, **ascetic ideal**, **authenticity**, **eternal recurrence**, **negative choice**, **noble ideal** and **positive choice**.

Words (1964)   Sartre's powerful autobiography of his childhood. His most critically acclaimed later work published the year he was offered and declined the **Nobel Prize for Literature**. Rich in philosophical and psychological insight, stylish, witty, unsentimental, brilliantly observed and disturbingly honest, *Words* portrays in minute detail the mind and world of a remarkably precocious, self-absorbed and gifted child who read classical literature as an infant and at the age of seven decided his *raison d'être* and destiny would be to achieve the immortality of a great writer.

Sartre's father, Jean-Baptiste died when he was less than fifteen months old. In *Words* **Sartre** considers the absence of a father's oppressive will upon the development of his character. Unlike most boys, he did not have to carry the weight of his father's expectations on his back and was free to enter into a more intimate and equal relationship with his mother, Anne-Marie. The two were close, more like brother and sister. Sartre makes clear his deep and abiding affection for her, even if, like most boys with their mothers, he took her completely for granted. The room they shared at the house of her father, Charles Schweitzer, was known as 'the children's room'. Though her parents dutifully took her back when she lost her husband, they never quite forgave her for marrying a man who had the indecency to die young: 'families naturally prefer widows to unmarried mothers, but only just'. Treated like a child and a servant, a dual role she accepted without complaint, Anne-Marie was shown far less respect and consideration than young Poulou (Sartre's pet name), who was doted on, at least by his grandfather. Sartre's grandmother, Louise, was withdrawn and cynical and largely unimpressed by Poulou's pretensions.

Sartre explores with great insight and humour the complex relationship he had with his grandfather. Sartre clearly resents Charles' attitude towards his mother and there is no indication of any real affection for this stiff, respectable, conceited, overbearing member of the Protestant bourgeoisie who was educated but narrow-minded, who loved books but despised writers, who claimed to love the poor but could not tolerate them under his roof. Cuttingly, Sartre tells how Charles, advancing in years, seized upon the child as a gift from heaven, as an indicator of the sublime and as a solace to his fear of **death**. As the wider family noted, young Poulou turned the old man's head. As Sartre readily acknowledges, Charles was the biggest single influence on his early intellectual development. Charles took charge of his grandson's academic and moral education, allowing him almost unlimited access to his extensive if conservative library. This library became Sartre's childhood playground. 'I began my life as I shall no doubt end it: among books.' Desperate to decipher the mysteries of his grandfather's dusty volumes he soon taught himself to read and immediately began exploring words as other children explore woodlands, finding ideas more real than objects. With few real friends due to his insufferable precociousness and presumed fragile health, his playmates became great dead writers. He confused them totally with their works. Corneille had a leather back and smelt of glue while **Flaubert** was small and cloth-bound.

The two parts of *Words* are 'Reading' and 'Writing' and the young Sartre soon made the step from the former to the latter. More in keeping with the pursuits of an 'ordinary' child he read comic book adventure stories alongside his reading of the classics and these influenced his earliest efforts with the pen. His early 'novels' were trashy, globetrotting tales of heroes and villains with contrived plots that he poured out without re-reading them. His mother loved them and copied them out, although most are now lost. Charles disapproved and would not look at them except to correct the spelling. Sartre says he was not fascinated by what he wrote once the ink had dried but by the act of writing itself that allowed him both to create heroes and to create himself, the writer, as a hero. He was struck by the respect writers received (from all but his grandfather), the gratitude they inspired and the immortality and omnipresence they achieved.

The ageing Sartre, looking back, claims it was his desire for heroic immortality as a writer, set against his rejection of spiritual immortality and salvation, that motivated him, rather than any particular talent or genius. For Sartre, genius is as genius does and he says he deliberately set out from childhood to create his reputation as a 'genius' through sustained hard work and dogged self-belief. Though he does not use the term in *Words*, his choice to be a writer was his **fundamental choice** of himself. It gave him the illusion of substance and removed from him his disturbing childhood feelings of pointlessness and superfluity. (He gives the same feelings to Lucien Fleurier, the central character of his short story, *Childhood of a Leader* [1939], though Lucien 'overcomes' these feelings in a very different way.) His family treated him as a necessity, but from his own point of view, until he defined himself as a writer, he had been travelling on a train without a ticket; travelling through life without justification for his absurd existence.

In *Words* the ageing writer finally writes himself out of the grand illusion that has sustained him all his life. Though he is compelled to write because not writing burns him, he has come to realize that writing cannot remove his **contingency** and superfluity and make him one with himself (see **being-for-itself-in-itself**). He is still, like everyone else, a ticketless traveller on a journey to nowhere. Despite his monumental efforts, he remains unnecessary and mortal, his immortal status as a writer existing only for future generations of mortals. He says that even in his disillusion he fears the cooling of the sun that will one day annihilate all people and with them his legacy.

Words is as much a book about death and growing old as it is a book about childhood and growing up. It is, in a sense, a book about Sartre's entire life, an exercise in **existential psychoanalysis** that shows the child as the father of the man and the man as the child of his works. It brilliantly applies the philosophical ideas of the mature Sartre to an analysis of the young Sartre in order to reveal the **existential** origins of those ideas in his childhood.

writing   See *The Family Idiot*, **Nobel Prize for Literature**, *War Diaries*, *What is Literature?* and *Words*.

— Z —

Zonina, Lena (1922–85)   Russian Jewish writer and dissident. A highly intelligent and cultured woman of exceptional beauty. Sartre's inter-preter, guide and informant on many of his trips to the Soviet Union. Zonina and **Sartre** became romantically attached in the summer of 1962 and it is rumoured that he made a proposal of marriage to her the following year. Sartre dedicated his 1964 autobiography, ***Words***, 'To Madame Z', a work she later translated into Russian. Zonina died in Moscow on February 2, 1985 shortly after publishing her first book, *Thinkers of Our Time: Reflec-tions on French Writers of the 1960s and 1970s*.

Bibliography

The *Sartre Dictionary* indicates the year works were first published in their original language. This bibliography indicates, wherever possible, the year of publication of an English translation.

Works by Sartre

The Age of Reason, trans. David Caute (Harmondsworth: Penguin, 2001).

Anti-Semite and Jew, trans. George J. Becker (New York: Schocken, 1995).

Baudelaire, trans. Martin Turnell (New York: New Directions, 1967).

Being and Nothingness: An Essay on Phenomenological Ontology, trans. Hazel E. Barnes (London and New York: Routledge, 2003).

The Childhood of a Leader, in Sartre, *The Wall*, trans. Lloyd Alexander (New York: New Directions, 1988).

Condemned of Altona, trans. Sylvia and George Leeson, in *Penguin Plays: Altona, Men Without Shadows, The Flies* (Harmondsworth: Penguin, 1973).

Crime Passionnel (Dirty Hands), trans. Kitty Black (London: Methuen, 1995).

Critique of Dialectical Reason Vol. 1, Theory of Practical Ensembles, trans. Alan Sheridan-Smith (London: Verso, 2004).

Critique of Dialectical Reason Vo1. 2, The Intelligibility of History, trans. Alan Sheridan-Smith (London: Verso, 2004).

Erostratus, in Sartre, *The Wall*, trans. Lloyd Alexander (New York: New Directions, 1988).

Existentialism and Humanism, trans. Philip Mairet (London: Methuen, 1993).

The Family Idiot, Vols 1–5, trans. Carol Cosman (Chicago: University of Chicago Press, 1981).

The Flies, trans. Stuart Gilbert, in *Penguin Plays: Altona, Men Without Shadows, The Flies* (Harmondsworth: Penguin, 1973).

The Imaginary: A Phenomenological Psychology of the Imagination, trans. Jonathan Webber (London and New York: Routledge, 2004).

Imagination: A Psychological Critique trans. Forrest Williams (Ann Arbor: University of Michigan Press, 1979).

In Camera and Other Plays (Harmondsworth: Penguin, 1990).

Intimacy, in Sartre, *The Wall*, trans. Lloyd Alexander (New York: New Directions, 1988).

Iron In the Soul, trans. David Caute (Harmondsworth: Penguin, 2004).

Kean, trans. Kitty Black, in *Three Plays: Kean, Nekrassov, The Trojan Women* (Harmondsworth: Penguin, 1994).

Lucifer and the Lord, trans. Kitty Black, in *In Camera and Other Plays* (Harmondsworth: Penguin, 1990).

Men Without Shadows, trans. Kitty Black, in *Penguin Plays: Altona, Men Without Shadows, The Flies* (Harmondsworth: Penguin, 1973).

Nausea, trans. Robert Baldick (Harmondsworth: Penguin, 2000).

Nekrassov, trans. Sylvia and George Leeson, in *Three Plays: Kean, Nekrassov, The Trojan Women* (Harmondsworth: Penguin, 1994).

Notebooks for an Ethics, trans. David Pellauer (Chicago: University of Chicago Press, 1992).

The Reprieve, trans. Eric Sutton (Harmondsworth, Penguin 2005).

The Respectable Prostitute, trans. Kitty Black, in *In Camera and Other Plays* (Harmondsworth: Penguin, 1990).

The Room, in Sartre, *The Wall*, trans. Lloyd Alexander (New York: New Directions, 1988).

Saint Genet, trans. Bernard Frechtman (New York: Pantheon, 1983).

Search for A Method, trans. Hazel E. Barnes (New York: Vintage, 1968).

Sketch for a Theory of the Emotions, trans. Philip Mairet (London: Methuen, 1985).

Situations, Vols 1–7 (Paris: Gallimard 1947, 1948, 1949, 1964, 1965). Vols 8–9, *Between Existentialism and Marxism*, trans. John Mathews (New York: Pantheon, 1974). Vol. 10, *Life/Situations*, trans. Paul Auster and Lydia Davis (New York: Pantheon, 1977).

The Transcendence of the Ego, A Sketch for a Phenomenological Description, trans. Andrew Brown (London and New York: Routledge, 2004).

Trojan Women, trans. Ronald Duncan, in *Three Plays: Kean, Nekrassov, The Trojan Women* (Harmondsworth: Penguin, 1994).

Truth and Existence, trans. Adrian van den Hoven (Chicago: University of Chicago Press, 1995).

The Wall, in Sartre, *The Wall*, trans. Lloyd Alexander (New York: New Directions, 1988).

War Diaries: Notebooks from a Phoney War, 1939–1940, trans. Quintin Hoare (London: Verso, 2000).

What is Literature?, trans. Bernard Frechtman (London and New York: Routledge, 2002).

Words, trans. Irene Clephane (Harmondsworth: Penguin, 2000).

Selected Works about Sartre

Barnes, Hazel E., *Sartre* (London: Quartet Books, 1974).

Barnes, Hazel E., *Sartre and Flaubert* (Chicago: University of Chicago Press, 1981).

Bernasconi, Robert, *How to Read Sartre* (London: Granta, 2006).

Cohen-Solal, Annie, *Jean-Paul Sartre: A Life*, trans. Anna Cancogni (New York: The New Press, 2005).

Cox, Gary, *Sartre: A Guide for the Perplexed* (London and New York: Continuum, 2006).

Danto, Arthur C., *Sartre* (London: Harper Collins/Fontana, 1991).

de Beauvoir, Simone, *Adieux: A Farewell to Sartre*, trans. Patrick O'Brian (New York: Pantheon, 1985).

Detmer, David, *Freedom as a Value: A Critique of the Ethical Theory of Jean-Paul Sartre* (La Salle, IL: Open Court, 1986).

Fell, Joseph P., *Heidegger and Sartre: An Essay on Being and Place* (New York: Columbia University Press, 1983).

Greene, Norman N., *Jean-Paul Sartre: The Existentialist Ethic* (Oxford: Greenwood Press, 1980).

Grene, Marjorie, *Sartre* (Lanham, MD: University Press of America, 1983).

Hoeller, Keith (ed.), *Sartre and Psychology* (Atlantic Highlands, NJ: Humanities Press International, 1993).

Howells, Christina (ed.), *The Cambridge Companion to Sartre* (Cambridge: Cambridge University Press, 2005).

Kamber, Richard, *On Sartre* (Belmont, CA: Wadsworth, 2000).

Leak, Andrew, *Sartre* (London and Chicago: Reaktion, 2006).

Levy, Neil, *Sartre* (Oxford: Oneworld, 2002).

Manser, Anthony, *Sartre: A Philosophic Study* (Oxford: Greenwood Press, 1981).

McBride, William L. (ed.), *Sartre and Existentialism: Philosophy, Politics, Ethics, the Psyche, Literature and Aesthetics, Volumes 1–8* (London: Garland / Taylor and Francis, 1997).

McCulloch, Gregory, *Using Sartre: An Analytical Introduction to Early Sartrean Themes* (London and New York: Routledge, 1994).

Murdoch, Iris, *Sartre: Romantic Rationalist* (London: Vintage, 1999).

Myerson, George, *Sartre: A Beginner's Guide* (London: Hodder and Stoughton, 2001).

Natanson, Maurice, *A Critique of Jean-Paul Sartre's Ontology* (Lincoln, NE: University of Nebraska Press, 1951).

Priest, Stephen (ed.), *Jean-Paul Sartre: Basic Writings* (London and New York: Routledge, 2001).

Santoni, Ronald E., *Bad Faith, Good Faith and Authenticity in Sartre's Early Philosophy* (Philadelphia, PA: Temple University Press, 1995).

Strathern, Paul, *The Essential Sartre* (London: Virgin Books, 2002).

Wider, Kathleen V., *The Bodily Nature of Consciousness: Sartre and Contemporary Philosophy of Mind* (New York: Cornell University Press, 1997).

Other Works Referred To

Baudelaire, *Flowers of Evil*, trans. James McGowan (Oxford: Oxford University Press, 1998).

Bergson, Henri, *Time and Free Will* (Boston, MA: Adamant, 2000).

Brentano, Franz, *Psychology from an Empirical Standpoint*, trans. A. Rancurello, D. Terrell and Linda McAlister (London and New York: Routledge, 2004).

Camus, Albert, *Lyrical and Critical Essays*, trans. Ellen Conroy Kennedy (London: Vintage, 1970).

Camus Albert, *The Myth of Sisyphus*, trans. Justin O'Brien (Harmondsworth: Penguin, 2006).

Camus, Albert, *The Outsider (The Stranger)*, trans. Joseph Laredo (Harmondsworth: Penguin, 2000).

Camus, Albert, *The Rebel*, trans. Anthony Bower (Harmondsworth: Penguin, 2006).

de Beauvoir, Simone, *The Ethics of Ambiguity*, trans. Bernard Frechtman (New York: Citadel Press, 2000).

de Beauvoir, Simone, *Letters to Sartre*, trans. Quintin Hoare (London: Vintage, 1992).

de Beauvoir, Simone, *The Mandarins*, trans. Leonard M. Friedman (London and New York: Norton, 1999).

de Beauvoir, Simone, 'Merleau-Ponty et le pseudo-sartrisme', *Les Temps modernes* 10, 1955.

de Beauvoir, Simone, *The Second Sex* (London: Vintage, 1997).

Descartes, René, *Meditations and Other Metaphysical Writings*, trans. Desmond M. Clarke (Harmondsworth: Penguin, 1998).

Engels, Friedrich, *Anti-Dühring*, in *Karl Marx and Friedrich Engels Collected Works* (International: New York, 1987).

Flaubert, Gustave, *Madame Bovary*, trans. Geoffrey Wall (Harmondsworth: Penguin, 2003).

Genet, Jean, *The Maids / Deathwatch* (Emeryville, CA: Avalon, 1989).

Hegel, George Wilhelm Friedrich, *The Phenomenology of Spirit*, trans. J.B. Bailey (New York: Dover, 2003).

Hegel, George Wilhelm Friedrich, *Science of Logic*, trans. A.V. Miller (New York: Humanity Books, Prometheus, 1998).

Heidegger, Martin, *Being And Time*, trans. John Macquarrie and Edward Robinson (Oxford: Blackwell, 1993).

Heidegger, Martin, *The Essence of Truth* (London and New York, Continuum, 2004).

Husserl, Edmund, *Cartesian Meditations: An Introduction To Phenomenology*, trans. Dorion Cairns (The Hague: Martinus Nijhoff, 1977).

Kant, Immanuel, *Critique of Pure Reason*, trans. Norman Kemp Smith (London: Macmillan, 2003).

Kierkegaard, Søren, *Either-Or: A Fragment of Life*, trans. Alastair Hannay (Harmondsworth: Penguin, 1992).

Kierkegaard, Søren, *Fear and Trembling*, trans. Alastair Hannay (Harmondsworth: Penguin, 1985).

Kierkegaard, Søren, *The Sickness unto Death, A Christian Psychological Exposition for Edification and Awakening*, trans. Alastair Hannay (Harmondsworth: Penguin, 1989).

Lagache, Daniel, *Les Hallucinations Verbales et Travaux Cliniques* (Paris: Presses Universitaires des France, 1977).

Laing, Ronald. D., *The Divided Self: An Existential Study in Sanity and Madness* (Harmondsworth: Penguin, 1990).

Laing, Ronald D., *Reason and Violence*, introduction by Jean-Paul Sartre (London: Random House, 1983).

Lévi-Strauss, Claude, *The Savage Mind* (Oxford: Oxford University Press, 1988).

Levinas, Emmanuel, *The Theory of Intuition in Husserl's Phenomenology*, trans. Andre Orianne (Evanston, IL: Northwestern University Press, 1995).

Merleau-Ponty, Maurice, *Phenomenology of Perception*, trans. Colin Smith (London and New York: Routledge, 2002).

Merleau-Ponty, Maurice, *The Visible and the Invisible* (Evanston, IL: Northwestern University Press, 1969).

Nietzsche, Friedrich, *Beyond Good And Evil: Prelude To A Philosophy of the Future*, trans. R.J. Hollingdale (Harmondsworth: Penguin, 2003).

Nietzsche, Friedrich, *The Birth of Tragedy: Out of the Spirit of Music*, trans. Shaun Whiteside (Harmondsworth: Penguin, 1993).

Nietzsche, Friedrich, *On The Genealogy of Morals*, trans. Francis Golffing (Oxford University Press, 1998).

Nietzsche, Friedrich, *Thus Spoke Zarathustra*, trans. Graham Parkes (Oxford: Oxford University Press, 2005).

Schopenhauer, Arthur, *World as Will and Representation* Vols 1 & 2, trans. E.F.J. Payne (New York: Dover, 1967).